Larry Gorman

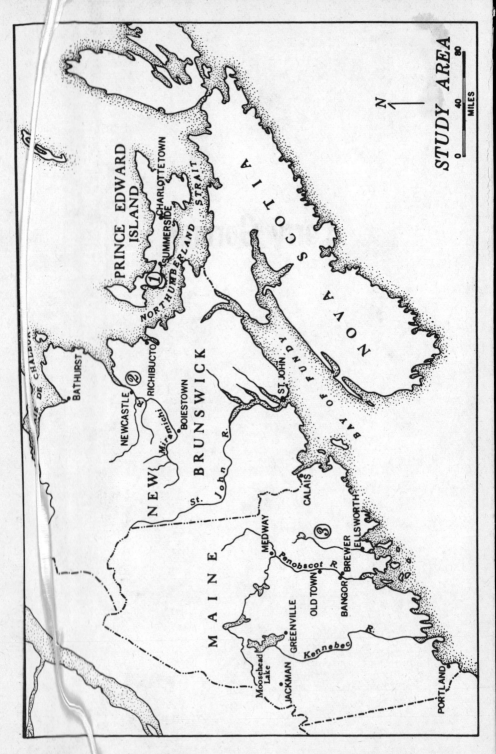

This map covers the general area where Larry Gorman lived and worked.
The numbers refer to more detailed maps of Prince Edward Island (1),
Miramichi (2), and Union River (3) in the text of this book.

Larry Gorman

the man who
made the songs

by EDWARD D. IVES

INDIANA UNIVERSITY PRESS

BLOOMINGTON   1964

Indiana University Folklore Series Number 19
Indiana University, Bloomington, Indiana

Publication Committee
Editor: Richard M. Dorson
Consulting Editor: John W. Ashton
Assistant Editors: W. Edson Richmond
and Warren E. Roberts

The Indiana University Folklore Series was
founded in 1939 for the publication of occasional papers and monographs by members
of the faculty.

for LOUISE MANNY
and CHARLIE GORMAN
two good friends

Contents

Preface   ix

Prologue   xiii

Introduction: "My Name is Larry Gorman"   1

   I: "That Garden in the Seas"   8

  II: Trout River   12

 III: "Along Lot Seven Shore": West Point to Miminegash   29

  IV: "And Came to Miramichi"   51

   V: "Down on the Union River"   79

  VI: The Henrys and the Lambs: Granite State to Tomah   101

 VII: "Poor and Neglected": Brewer and the End   109

VIII: The Larry Gorman Legend   138

  IX: The Ghost of Larry Gorman   149

   X: "That Sounds Like Gorman"   154

  XI: The Satirical Song Tradition   167

 XII: Conclusion   180

Epilogue   188

Appendix: A complete alphabetical listing of all the songs
written by or generally attributed to Larry Gorman   189

Notes   205

List of Works Cited   213

Index   219

MAPS OF PRINCE EDWARD ISLAND, MIRAMICHI, AND UNION RIVER FACE PAGES 8, 51 AND 79 RESPECTIVELY.

Biography will enlarge its scope by hanging up looking glasses at odd corners. And yet from all this diversity it will bring out, not a riot of confusion, but a richer unity. And again, since so much is known that used to be unknown, the question now inevitably asks itself, whether the lives of great men only should be recorded. Is not anyone who has lived a life, and left a record of that life, worthy of biography—the failures as well as the successes, the humble as well as the illustrious? And what is greatness? And what smallness?

Virginia Woolf, "The Art of Biography," in *The Death of the Moth and Other Essays* (New York: Harcourt, Brace and Co., 1942), p. 195

Preface

Certain special marks and notations have been used in this work, and it will be well to explain them now. An asterisk appearing before quoted material in the text indicates that what follows is transcribed *verbatim* from a tape recording. In such quotations, brackets indicate my conjectures in places where the speaker's words are not clear; where I have supplied words of my own to make the meaning clear, these words have been both italicized and bracketed. Oral material that I have not marked with an asterisk I have reproduced as faithfully as possible from notes taken in the field, but of course I cannot guarantee that my memory will be perfect in every case.

The texts for the individual songs have been given exactly as I found them, whether in print, in manuscript, or in oral tradition. The few collated and emended texts have been clearly indicated, and brackets and italics have been used in the same way as in the prose passages. Full notes on the changes are given in the Appendix.

My handling of the tunes requires a few words of explanation. For each song I give the melody for one fairly representative stanza and make no attempt to record the multitude of stanza-to-stanza variations. This study is not essentially musicological. My intention is to give the reader "the tune" to as many of the songs as possible and, without getting him mired in musical footnotes, still give him some feeling for how the song was sung, that is to say, for the style. The "sample stanza" seemed to offer the best compromise. Anyone interested in the detailed study of whole performances will find the original recordings of most of the songs easily available at reasonable fees from the Archives of Folk and Primitive Music, 014 Maxwell Hall, Indiana University, Bloomington, Indiana. The Archives Tape Library (ATL) numbers are given wherever possible.

With the exception of the two taken from Doerflinger's book, all the tunes in this book have been transposed to end on *g*. In traditional singing any one singer may pitch a song differently on different occasions, and another, as he is learning the song, will sing it where it is comfortable for him (or where it suits him); the key does not seem to be a matter of great importance. It therefore seemed to me that nothing would be lost by transposition and that the scale, mode, and range of each song could be more easily compared if all tunes were set in the same key. However, each tune is preceded by a catch-signature giving the original key and opening pitches. Meter and tempo are given as accurately as possible, but occasionally I have simply marked a piece as *parlando-rubato,* used only the dotted bar-line at the ends of phrases, and not attempted exact metrical transcription. A metrical signature in parentheses indicates what seems to be the basic meter.

The following special signs have been used:

Note slightly higher than written.

Note slightly lower than written.

Note slightly longer than given (less than half again the given length).

Note slightly shorter than given (a loss of less than half the given length).

Singer slides up or down to pitch.

Singer slides up or down from pitch.

Pitch not clear but determined from context when the same phrase is sung elsewhere in the song.

Breath pause of indefinite length (unless it is accompanied by a rest; then the pause is of the indicated length).

A break in the transcription where the singer stopped for conversation or to collect his memory.

 An extended hold (the length of the hold is indicated in the parenthesis).

 Original is sung one octave lower than written.

 Original is sung two octaves lower than written.

Since what I have done is to ransack an essentially oral tradition for the productions of an individual song-writer, I think the reader is entitled to know how I decided which songs are Gorman's and which are not. Each song presents unique problems, but there are three general kinds of evidence that guided me: ascription, content, and style. Let's discuss each of them briefly.

If I have a broadside with Larry's name on it, there need be very little doubt that he wrote that song, nor need we question those few songs where he has worked in his own name. Failing a signature of some sort, we have a lot of songs that other people say he wrote. General ascription — "Everybody knows Gorman wrote that" — is useful but not as reliable as ascription by people who were in some special position to know the facts: people who lived in the area where the song was written, people who knew the principals, or people who knew Gorman. One such informed ascription is worth dozens of the more general kind.

The content of a song can help in several ways. First of all, is the song about someone that Gorman knew or could well have known? Second, is it set in an area where he lived or worked? Third, if the song can be dated in any way, does that date square with what we know of Gorman's comings and goings? Finally (and this is necessarily vague), is the subject similar to others that Larry handled? Affirmative answers to any of these questions will certainly help to make a case for Gorman's authorship.

Style, on the other hand, is very little positive help, which is to say that I have found no mark of style that stamps a piece as undoubtedly Gorman's. On the other hand, as D. K. Wilgus has already pointed out, "the best evidence of style is negative."[1] If we had no other evidence that Larry did not write "Peter Emberly" (and we have plenty), the style is so different from that of his other work that we should be suspicious of it. Then too, a rank bit of botchery is not apt to be the product of a skilful poet like Gorman, but we cannot ascribe a piece to him simply because it is skilfully done.

These are my objective criteria, or as close as I've been able to come to them. I'll confess that oñ some songs I've used hunch. Time will tell how reliable my criteria and my sixth sense have been. I fully expect that the publication of this book will bring claims and counterclaims that are apt to alter the whole canon.

There are a number of people to whom I am extremely grateful. First I wrote a book which, under the guidance of Professors Richard M. Dorson, W. Edson Richmond, Warren E. Roberts and Dr. George List of the Committee on Folklore, Indiana University, became a dissertation. And now, with their further help, it has become a book again. I would like to pay my debt of thanks to them first of all, before I move on to settle some of the more specialized accounts I owe. First comes Bacil Kirtley, since he was the first person to read and criticize the original manuscript. My good friends Charles and Carol Andersen, who are less enthusiastic about woods song than I am, both read the original manuscript and made extremely helpful comments. Professor John E. Hankins proofread the entire final manuscript. Herbert T. Silsby II of Ellsworth, Maine, also read the final manuscript. Mrs. Nina Ross, formerly of Tyne Valley, Prince Edward Island, generously made available to me her notes on the history of that village. My debt to Dr. Louise Manny of Newcastle, New Brunswick, is clear both from the dedication and from the frequent references to her in the text. To all of these people, *gracias*.

Special thanks should also go to Louis T. Ibbotson and the staff of the University of Maine Library; to the Widener Library at Harvard University, particularly to Special Services Librarian Robert Haynes; to Miss Jean Gill and her staff at the Legislative and Public Library, Charlottetown, Prince Edward Island; and to Miss Helene Bellatty of the Ellsworth (Maine) Public Library. For financial support I am particularly indebted to the Coe Research Fund Committee of the University of Maine. It is no exaggeration to say that without their continued and generous aid I could hardly have begun, let alone completed, my work. My final trip to the Miramichi was made possible by a grant from the Indiana University Research Committee. I would like also to thank Harper and Row, Publishers, for permission to quote extensively from Holman Day's *King Spruce*.

There is no adequate way to express my gratitude to all the hundreds of people I have talked to or who have written me about Larry Gorman. Without their songs and stories there would have been no book at all. And to all those many people from Rumford, Maine, to Miminegash, Prince Edward Island, who gave me meals and hospitality while I was on the road, thanks. I have many pleasant memories.

My wife Bobby, who has borne up under all this hurrah quite well and who has shown everything from downright enthusiasm to strained but exquisite patience, deserves the highest tribute I can manage: the final paragraph all to herself.

Prologue [1]

A lumbercamp on the upper Sou'west Miramichi. With minor variations it is much like any other late-nineteenth-century lumbercamp in
the Northeast: a long, low, well-chinked log structure divided into two
large rooms by a third small one (the dingle, where the cook keeps his
supplies) between them. One of the large rooms is the cookroom, containing the big black cookstove and the tables where the men eat;
supper has been over for an hour or more, and there is a card game
going on now at one of the tables by the light of a smoky oil lamp. The
second large room, on the other side of the dingle, is the "men's part."
This room contains two long bunks, one on each side of the room,
just raised frames filled with layer upon layer of balsam boughs, the
results of many Sundays' "boughing up." For each bunk there are two
long spreads, one to go under and the other to go over the twenty-five
men who will sleep in it. Along the foot of each bunk runs a low bench,
the "deacon seat." In the center of the floor between the bunks is a big
ram-down wood-stove, and around and over this stove is the drying
rack, filled with the day's quota of steaming wet mittens, pants, shirts,
socks, and larrigans. Nearby, directly under one of the lamps, the men
have set up the grindstone, and a small group is gathered round it,
working or waiting their turns. Others are seated along the deacon
seat talking or tending to their own affairs. Heavy socks, wool pants,
suspenders, brightly colored shirts, red underwear — all are dressed
in some variation of this uniform. Some wear their hats, many are
heavily bearded; all are dead tired from a hard day's work in the woods.

It is not far from lights-out. A man in a black sweater yawns and
starts to stretch; then he stops midway. "Hey Fred," he calls, "give us
a song."

"Hell," Fred answers from the grindstone, which he is turning for
another man, "I sang last night. Get that new fella. Maybe he's got
something we haven't heard more'n a hundred times."

"You've heard every one *I* know a *thousand* times," says the new man, "and you don't want to hear *me* sing. C'mon Fred, give us 'The Lost Jimmy Whelan' again."

Several others look up and add their voices to the request. "Well," says Fred, "I don't mind. Wait a minute." He finishes his turn at the grindstone, walks over to the deacon seat, and sits down. Then he leans forward, elbows on knees, one hand holding the back of the other, and, looking at a point on the floor about five feet away, he begins to sing:

> Slow-ly I strayed by the banks of the ri-ver,
> A-viewin' those roses as evening' drew-hoo nigh...

On and on it goes, the voice clear and strong (Fred is a "singer"), speeding up and slowing down, holding notes unexpectedly, hitching, adding little graces here and there, filling the whole camp with that strangely beautiful song that better than any other seems to express the cold loneliness of the winter woods. All is still save for that voice.

Over at the far end of the cookroom, almost beyond the light shed by the cardplayers' lamp, a man sits alone beside the stove. He has been sitting there for some time, and while occasionally he glances over at the game, most of the time he has been looking (or not looking) up into the flickering dark of the low rafters. He runs his hand through his thick mop of reddish hair, then rubs the back of his neck abstract-edly, still looking off at nothing. He shakes his head disgustedly, gets up, and walks slowly across the room, hands behind his back, head down — a tall, spare, angular figure of a man lost in thought. He pauses to watch the card game. Suddenly he straightens a bit, and his eyes light up. He continues watching the players, nodding his head and smiling almost imperceptibly, obviously having reached some pleasant agreement with himself. Then he goes out across to the men's part, where he sits down at one end of the deacon seat and listens to the singing.

Fred has just reached the last verse:

> Oh, you are my dar-ling, my Lost Jimmy Whe-lan,
> I will sigh till I die by the side of yer grave.

He drops off to a speaking voice for the last few words, indicating that he is through now. In case there is any doubt, he lights his pipe, but he pauses in his puffing just long enough to look with good-natured menace at his best friend, who has just asked who in hell ever told him he could sing.

"Gorman!"

It is one of the cardplayers speaking, a big brute of a man; he has just entered the room and stands there just inside the door. "Gorman, I been watching you, and sure as hell you've been making a song. So let's have it, goddamn it! C'mon!"

Everyone turns to look at the tall man at the end of the deacon seat. "Yeah, come on, Larry, sing it for us," says another, and in a moment all hands are petitioning for the song. Gorman looks around the room and laughs. "Well, I guess I will, since you've found me out, Pete," he says, looking at the cardplayer, "but I don't say that you'll like it too well."

The big man measures the poet with his eyes. "I might not," he says, "and then again I just might. It's no odds to me what you say about me. You just sing it, Larry Gorman, and we'll see."

There is a general air of apprehension as Gorman clears his throat and leans forward to sing. The men look from one to another, smiling nervously, as he begins. He does not have a good voice, but it is high and true, and the tune is a familiar, lilting one that they all know. Suddenly someone guffaws; then all begin to chuckle, as they hear one of their number lampooned; the victim rubs his palms on his thighs and grins sheepishly around the room. The song moves on, and one by one the men find they are all woven into it — some little thing that each one of them has done or said, a way he has of holding his head, a little morsel of downriver scandal that had all but been forgotten or had not been known. The laughter continues; sometimes a man will wince or look at his neighbor and shake his head in amazement, but he is laughing. All the time, Pete is standing there waiting for his turn, and he doesn't have to wait long to discover that he has the place of honor: two double verses which discuss such varied matters as his broken nose, a team he sluiced three winters back, the size of his feet, and an interesting speculation on his affair with a bowlegged servant girl from Renous. Pete is not laughing, but everyone else is. The song ends with Gorman's pious hope that none has been offended.

Pete waits until things have quieted down. "All right, Larry," he says quietly. "I asked for it, and I should have known this is what you'd do after what I said the other night. I guess that's a pretty good song, too. But I tell you right now," he says, his voice rising in threat, "that if I ever hear of you singing that song downriver there isn't any place so far that you can go but what I'll catch you. That's all I'm saying."

Larry is silent for a moment; then he smiles. "I guess it's about time to climb into the bunk now," he says.

INTRODUCTION

"My Name Is Larry Gorman"

There was once a man named Larry Gorman. Initially, my modest plan was to write his biography and publish it along with as complete a collection of his songs as I could make. Since I am an academic by instinct and a folklorist by training, it was perfectly predictable that I would sometime begin to wonder what Larry's singular career could tell us about the vexed problem of folksong origins. To be sure, the great debate between the communalists and the individualists was focused on the ballads, even more specifically on the Child ballads, and it would be ridiculous to pretend that Larry Gorman's satires could provide conclusive evidence to settle it. Yet here was a man who was well-known among his peers and contemporaries as a maker of songs, and the songs he made went into oral tradition. Would not a study showing these songs in the context of his life shed some light on the creation of folksongs in general and the relation of the individual song-maker to his tradition? The answer is certainly yes, but, for reasons that will become more clear as the book progresses, it must be a carefully qualified yes.

No one theory of folksong origin is going to explain everything. Even the old doctrine of communal composition — which claimed that folksongs were created not by an individual but, in some mysterious way, by an inspired "singing, dancing throng" — may someday be shown to have some validity.[1] I know of no folksong that can be shown to have originated in just this way, but I did collect a long monicker song that was made up by three or four men who were working together in a New Brunswick lumbercamp one winter, which, if it isn't communal composition, is at least composition by *ad hoc* committee. Occasionally a cultivated writer would turn out something that got caught up in oral

1

tradition. John Gay wrote "Black-Eyed Susan," for example, and Seba Smith was the author of "Young Charlotte."[2] Certainly too, a good many songs were created by hacks in the employ of the urban broadside printers. Thackeray tells of one such hack, a young man named Oliver Goldsmith, who "wrote ballads, they say, for the street singers, who paid him a crown for a poem, and his pleasure was to steal out at night and hear his verses sung."[3] However, no small number of our traditional songs were created by individuals on the same cultural level at which traditional song flourishes; very likely traditional singers themselves, they created songs both within and for that tradition. A woodsman who created a new ballad about a comrade killed on the river-drive, who modeled his work on other woods songs, and who intended it to be sung by his fellow woodsmen would be a case in point. It is this sort of man that I will call a folk poet or, more specifically, a woods poet. And it is of the woods poet that Larry Gorman can tell us something.

Let me say at the outset that when I offer this definition of a folk poet, I am fully aware of its inadequacies. Certainly a term like "same cultural level" is too comfortably abstract. But I think it is best to keep an *a priori* definition general. We need to know a great deal more about individual folk poets before we can make any meaningful generalizations about them or even establish that they exist at all as a distinct species. My definition is only a rough map sketched on the back of an old envelope; we will see how well it works as we go along through the country and make our adjustments accordingly, but at least we can get started.

As I have said, there was once a man named Larry Gorman. I had heard of him, to be sure, but one evening in the spring of 1956, after I had sung some songs at a church supper in a small town some fifty miles north of Orono, I found myself face-to-face with an old river-driver who said he had known him. "Larry Gorman, 'the man who makes the songs?'" he said. "Why, he walked into a tavern where I was one night and someone said, 'Here comes Larry Gorman, the man who makes the songs.' Well, when Gorman heard that he started right in and made up a song that was thirty-two double-verses long, all about what was going on right in the tavern there, and every verse ended with 'Here comes Larry Gorman, the man who makes the songs.'"

When I went home that night, I dug out all I could find on Gorman. I reread the selections in Eckstorm and Smyth's *Minstrelsy of Maine* and William Doerflinger's *Shantymen and Shantyboys*. A few days later I found an article by Louise Manny in the old *Maritime Advocate*, and a friend put me on to Holman Day's novel, *King Spruce*, which had a whole chapter and more on Gorman. The stories certainly made him larger than life — the delight of the woodsmen, the despair of the bosses, and the Archpoet of the Northeast Lumberwoods — but no one really knew enough about him to satisfy my aroused curiosity, so I sent a letter off to my river-driver friend. His answer: "Larry Gorman was well before my time. That was a story I'd heard. Sorry." That was that. But, I reasoned, Gorman couldn't have died so very long ago, and he is supposed to have spent much of his life right near Bangor. Surely there were people still around who could remember him, but how was I to reach them? Knowing no better way, I published a letter in the *Bangor Daily News*.

I began to get replies within a few days. Arthur Dalton wrote from Rumford, saying that he remembered hearing his father tell stories about Larry back on Prince Edward Island. Several other people told me to read *King Spruce*. But, unlike Shelley, no one seemed to have seen Gorman plain. Then, returning from a week's vacation, I found among the half-dozen letters in the mailbox one addressed in a very spidery, shaky hand. I opened it and found the following note: "I knew Larry Gorman. He worked for my father. [Signed] Ralph Cushman, Ellsworth, Maine." Needless to say, I was on my way to see Mr. Cushman very quickly. I found him at his son's house down near Hancock Point. He was a man much bent over by his eighty-odd years, but his mind was clear and he spent the entire afternoon telling me (his voice vigorous and clean-edged) story after story not only about Larry but about Ellsworth back in the days when Jim Cushman and Roderick McDonald were feuding with each other along the Union River.

So it began. Then I heard from John O'Connor down in Portland: "Larry Gorman was my uncle," he said, and he sent me the only two original Gorman broadsides I have ever seen. The trip to Portland to see him gave me more than three closely written pages of notes on Larry and the Gormans. About a month later I met Billy Bell, who had moved to Brewer, Maine, from Prince Edward Island more than fifty years ago and remembered Larry's last years when he worked as a yard hand for the Eastern Corporation there in Brewer. He didn't take much stock in Larry's songs, but he certainly delighted in telling stories about him. Then there was blind Irving Frost from Bar Harbor. And Alden Mace of Southwest Harbor: I listen now to the tapes I made that evening, and the creak of his rocking chair is one with the drone of his voice and the tick and striking of the clock. When I asked him if there was much singing in the old lumbercamps, he answered, "Oh, yes, yes, yes, yes, yes!"

Another man called and said that the person for me to see was old Joe Tosh (i.e., McIntosh) down in Ellsworth. I phoned him, and when I asked if he knew Larry Gorman, the answer came back slow and quiet, like a man speaking from a dream, "I...knew...him...and...drove ...with...him...for...many...years." A few days later, I met Joe. He was over eighty, and in his prime he had weighed better than two hundred and forty pounds. He sat there in the parlor in a broken rocking chair, folding and unfolding his tremendous hands, occasionally smoking a cigarette and using a number-ten can for an ashtray. His wife stood in the kitchen door leaning against the pile of stovewood, and every once in a while, she'd prod his memory: "Tell him about Roddy McDonald and the eggs, Joe." His sharp little vignettes of Gorman gave me new facets of the man's character and suggested things that made the whole picture become a bit clearer.

Very soon I saw that I would have to make a trip through Miramichi and Prince Edward Island. I had published letters in papers all through the Northeast by this time, and the answers had come flooding in until I was corresponding with over a hundred and fifty people, many of whom claimed that they lived near men who had known Gorman. In the spring of 1957, I received a generous grant from the Coe Research Fund Committee of the University of Maine. Consequently, in June of that year, having muttered a prayer or two over my decaying Studebaker, I struck out north and east.

Spurgeon Allaby of Passekeag, New Brunswick, had written me months earlier, sending me two large packets of songs he knew, the leaves of each song carefully sewn together with white thread at one corner. In a heavy summer rain I drove up the dirt road to his farm and spent the afternoon listening to Mr. Allaby sing one song after another, stopping only for drinks of water or an occasional peppermint. He and his wife would not hear of my spending the night in a motel. It was the sort of hospitality I was going to find all through New Brunswick: from Bill Griffin, retired guide, and his wife in Boiestown; from Hugh Crawford of Blackville; from Louise Manny, who put me up for over a week while I made forays all through Miramichi; and from Mrs. Jared MacLean, her housekeeper, who kept me well-fed and told me of her late husband, who had been a splendid singer and song-writer himself.

I also spent an afternoon with John A. Jamieson of East Bathurst up on the Bay Chaleur. It was a grey day when I got there, one of those days that lets you know the cold is still there for all the sudden green, and as I drove up the Rough Waters Road, there was Mr. Jamieson out pruning his two rows of beautiful English cherry trees. They were in full bloom, and under that unrelieved leaden sky they were triumphant. I admired them with him for a while; then we went into the living room, where I set up my recorder. Mr. Jamieson lay back on the couch and, looking up at the ceiling, sang for me in a high husky voice that was still true and pleasant, though he was eighty-five years old. He sang two of Gorman's songs for me — "The Good Old State of Maine" and "The Winter of Seventy-three" — and told me what it was like to work for the Henrys in New Hampshire. Then he sang several more songs, though they were not Gorman's: "Young Jimmy Folger," "Napoleon Bonaparte," "The Plain Golden Band," and "The Bathurst Murder." Grandchildren and neighbors' children stood crowded in the hall and on the stairs, quiet save when one of them fell through the banisters.

The New Brunswick countryside was familiar to me as a continuation of what I was already used to in Maine. Prince Edward Island, on the other hand, was something new. I had talked to many Islanders before I made the trip, and they had all told me it was a beautiful place, but still I was unprepared for what I saw as I drove off the Borden ferry and made my way to Charlottetown on a misty day in mid-June. Everything was under cultivation, and fields of fresh-plowed red earth alternated with the varied greens of new plantings, all separated by spruce hedgerows. The farms looked as if they had just been scrubbed, and the apple trees were in full bloom.

If I had found New Brunswickers hospitable, I hardly know what word to use for the reception I got from people on the Island. The first person I went to see was Jim Pendergast of Charlottetown, a great figure of a man who in his long life had done everything from prospecting in the Klondike to farming and teaching school to prizefighting. He took me up to the west end of the Island, "West Prince" as it is called, and introduced me to many people who were to prove very helpful to me. He knew everyone, or, more accurately, everyone knew him. Wherever we went, he was greeted with "Hello, Jim," or "Hello, Mr. Pendergast." I couldn't have had a better — or pleasanter — introduction to the Island.

Charlie Gorman, son of Larry's older brother James, had written me saying he knew almost nothing about his uncle but that he would be glad to talk to me. His farm was over in Lot Seven, well up on a hill overlooking Northumberland Strait, and as I drove up the road to the house, I remembered all the things I had been told about how the family disliked Larry and would not talk about him. Charlie was in the kitchen, a tall, slight, bespectacled, retired farmer of eighty-four. "Now Mr. Ives," he began, "you probably know that my father didn't approve of Uncle Larry. Father wouldn't let us kids sing his songs in the house, and so I never cared much for him either. But that's all right now; I'll tell you all I know and won't keep anything back from you."

We liked each other immediately and I spent a delightful afternoon asking questions and listening to Charlie's considered, well-phrased answers: "Well, no, it wasn't exactly that, Mr. Ives, but, you see, my father ...." Then he thought of someone else who might be able to help me, so we got into the car and drove off. About a half-hour later, he said, "I know it sounds funny, Mr. Ives, because I've lived hereabouts all my life, but I'm completely lost. You couldn't lose me in a horse and wagon, but going this fast I just don't seem to recognize things at all." We finally found the house, but the lady we wanted to see was not home. "I had a feeling that this might be a water-haul," said Charlie, as we drove back to his place. A few days later, I took my wife over to meet him, and after we had sat and talked for some time, Charlie asked if we would mind if he sang us a song. We said we'd be delighted, and so he sang "Drive Dull Care Away," which, as he told me a year later, "seemed to suit the occasion":

> Life at its best is but a jest,
> Like a dreary winter's day,
> And while we're here with our friends so dear
> We'll drive dull care away.

I was to meet some other fine people on Prince Edward Island. David Dyment, for example, had known Larry before he left the Island, and the two had met for a visit in Brewer when Larry was an old man.

Mr. Dyment was ninety-four, and when I saw him he was in the little Tyne Valley hospital for a few days for a checkup, but there was nothing wrong with his mind. He had a lively sense of humor and was quick to pick up even the driest of remarks and dispose of them properly. Among the people we talked of was Angus MacAskill, the Cape Breton Giant; Mr. Dyment had had a book about him once, but he'd lent it to someone and never gotten it back. "If you ever find one, I wish you'd send it to me. I'll pay you back, but I'd like to have that book again." I wish I could have found a copy in time, but when I went back a year later, Mr. Dyment had died.

William Waldron of Tyne Valley was of an even age with Mr. Dyment. His daughter, Mrs. Nina Ross, had been writing to me for some time, urging me to come see him, and when I finally was able to, she wrote sadly that he had failed a great deal but to come anyway. When I arrived, she told me that he was very deaf and almost blind, so it was no wonder he did not hear or see me when I entered the room. "Father, here is the young man from Maine," shouted Mrs. Ross. "Oh, Maine!" he said, looking up suddenly and beaming at me. "Anyone from Maine is always welcome in this house!" He had me draw a chair directly in front of his; then he sat facing me, our knees touching and his hands on the backs of mine as he talked animatedly about the days when he had worked on the Union River or driven the upriver stage from Ellsworth to Aurora. I was to spend several more sessions with him because he had known Larry Gorman well and had much to tell me.

I had been writing to Edmund Doucette, in the town of Miminegash, for almost a year, and when I arrived at his door and told him who I was he just looked at me and gasped, "No." It seems that ever since I had started writing to Edmund, the whole town had been referring to me as "The Old Man" or as "Edmund's Old Man." After a few minutes' talk about the misunderstanding, we went over to Joe Tremblay's house, since Joe had electricity and I wanted to record some songs that Edmund was going to sing for me. I was to spend many pleasant hours there with the Tremblays and the Doucettes, and I learned a great deal, not only about Larry Gorman but also about good traditional singing. And one rainy evening, when the whole town was at Mass, I sat in Edmund's living room and watched through the window as the sharp roofs of the fishing stages disappeared into the dark. A horse grazed the sparse grass outside the gate. Then came the lights, as the people returned from church.

The more I looked for material on Larry Gorman, the more material I found on other satirical songmakers and poets, until I began to wonder just how much I was dealing with a unique individual and how much with a tradition. As I saw it, I would have to do a considerable amount of library work to see whether or not such a tradition existed; and then, assuming I found it, I would have to make another field trip, this one an intensive search in a limited area, to see how that tradition made itself manifest there. A year of folklore study at Indiana

University gave me the opportunity for the former; a grant from that university's research committee made possible the latter. A brief summary of the results of this work is contained in Chapter XI.

The quest for Larry Gorman has been fun. It has been enlightening, but it has also been exasperating and disappointing. When I began, I knew what I wanted to find, what I hoped I would find; often enough I didn't find it. Sometimes, in the evening, I would see that the only result of the day's work had been to destroy another cherished story or myth, and I would feel that perhaps I really ought to abandon the whole idea of writing a book about Larry Gorman. Yet there was something there. The cold light might dispel the fabulous shadows, but it revealed a spare, enigmatic man who was unquestionably flesh and blood. He was not always attractive, and those writers who would have their folklore serve some ulterior purpose of their own will find Gorman resistant to Bunyanization. He was an angular, cantankerous individual who lived his own lonely life, dying as obscurely as he was born, a disappointed man. But he made men laugh, and some few of his works survive. His story is worth telling, and I hope it will prove, to alter slightly Virginia Woolf's metaphor, a looking glass at an odd corner.

ONE

"That Garden in the Seas"

We landed there this day in four places for to see the trees, which are wonderfully fair and of excellent odor, and found that they were cedars, yews, pines, white elms, ash, willows, and many others to us unknown, all trees without fruits. The lands where there are no woods are very fair and all so full of peas, gooseberries, white and red, strawberries, raspberries, and wild corn, like rye, that it seems to have been sown and cultivated there. This land is of the best temperature that it may be possible to see, and of great warmth, and there are many turtle-doves, wood-pigeons, and other birds; there is no lack but of harbors.[1]

Thus spoke Jacques Cartier of his first visit to Prince Edward Island in 1534. However, those who came after him did not look inland; they looked to the sea, and as early as 1663 a Captain Doublet obtained a grant from Louis XIV to establish fisheries along the coast. Yet slowly other settlers came and cut back the forests and cleared the land. The French were the first to arrive, but in 1763 the Island of St. John (as it was called until 1798) was ceded to the British by the Treaty of Fontainebleau; and though some of the Acadians stayed, further settlement was mostly left to the English, Scotch, and Irish. The Board of Trade and Plantations in London divided the Island into sixty-seven lots of about 20,000 acres each and raffled them off to people who had claims against the Crown. It may not have been an ideal way to settle a new land, but it has supplied a handy method of identifying places; even today we speak of Lot Seven and Lot Sixteen, for example.

The west end was more slowly settled than was the central portion, the land not being as good or as easy to get at. But it was not land that caught the eye of William Ellis, partner in the shipbuilding firm of Chapman and Ellis of Bideford, Devon, England. In 1809, he crossed the ocean in search of timber for his shipyard, but a storm blew him

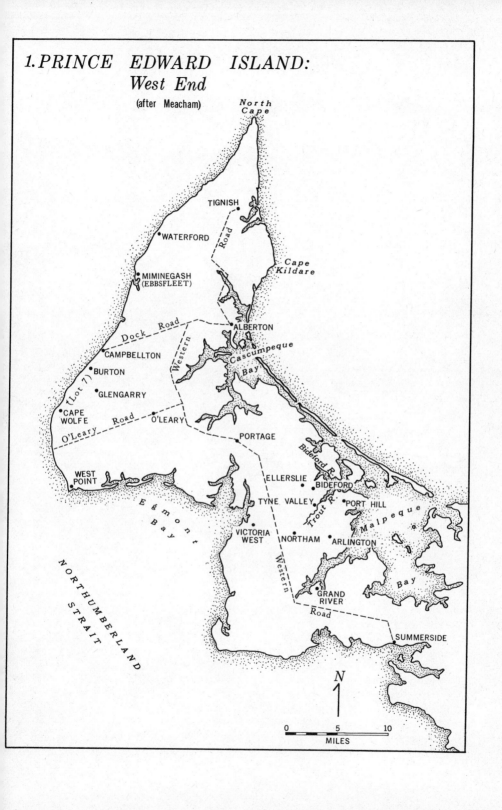

1. PRINCE EDWARD ISLAND:
West End
(after Meacham)

North Cape

TIGNISH

WATERFORD

Road

Cape Kildare

MIMINEGASH
(EBBSFLEET)

ALBERTON

Dock Road

Cascumpeque Bay

CAMPBELLTON

Western

BURTON

(Lot 7)

GLENGARRY

CAPE WOLFE

Road

O'LEARY

O'Leary

PORTAGE

Bideford R.

WEST POINT

ELLERSLIE

BIDEFORD

E g m o n t   B a y

TYNE VALLEY

Trout R.

PORT HILL

Malpeque

VICTORIA WEST

NORTHAM

ARLINGTON

Western

Bay

N O R T H U M B E R L A N D   S T R A I T

GRAND RIVER

Road

SUMMERSIDE

N

0   5   10
MILES

off his course and forced him into what is now called Richmond, or Malpeque, Bay. Seeking shelter, he sailed up one of the wide rivers emptying into the bay and dropped anchor near what is now the town of Bideford. As he waited for the storm to abate, he explored the area and found to his delight that he was in the midst of an immense forest of trees that was more than suitable for his needs. Five years later, "Grandfather Ellis" returned to the Goodwood River (as he had named it), bringing with him a whole shipyard crew, all necessary equipment, and a new partner, T. B. Chanter. They did their best to transplant Devonshire to Lots Twelve and Thirteen, even to using place-names like Bideford, Northam, and Port Hill. The maritime tradition of men like Raleigh, Grenville, Drake, and Hawkins was well carried on; during the great era of wooden ships, Bideford River was one of the leading shipbuilding areas of the Island, having at one time as many as six flourishing yards, and an astonishing number of ships was built here. By 1861 the two lots had a combined population of over a thousand.[2]

Among those who came to this basically English area in the first quarter of the century was a young Irishman from County Kilkenny, Thomas Gorman by name. Born in the town of Gowran about 1796, he probably left to seek his fortune in the New World when he was eighteen or twenty. We know he was here in 1825, for on January 8 of that year there appeared in the *Prince Edward Island Gazette* the following notice: "List of letters in the post office at Charlottetown. If not called for will be returned to Halifax." And under "Bideford Shipyard" we find the name of Thomas Gorman.[3]

He settled in Lot Thirteen on a hundred acres on the north side of Trout River (an arm of the Bideford River), built himself a house on a low point of land, and set to work in the shipyards and on his farm. The road along the western edge of his farm from the Bideford Road down to the river was known until very recently as the Gorman Lane, and it led to what was called "Gorman's Ferry," which for many years was the only way to cross from the Bideford side to Port Hill, the present-day road through Tyne Valley then being no more than a footpath. (The original ferry was a huge dug-out log that would seat three people.) So Tom Gorman left his name on the map. Not content with being a shipyard worker and farmer only, he became a storekeeper, too, for in 1835 the house is listed in one of the local papers as "Tom Gorman's store." Later he taught school, and in 1838 he was elected to the House of Assembly of Prince Edward Island, serving as a member from 1839 to 1842. The young Irishman had made his way, it would seem.

Some time before 1834, Tom Gorman married Ann Donahue, a small, vivacious, pretty girl about twenty years younger than himself. She had come over from the Old Country with her father and mother when she was about nine and the family settled in Miramichi just in time to get caught by the Great Fire of 1825. Whether her parents survived that holocaust I do not know, but Ann survived by standing all night in the water while flames roared about her, a terrifying experience for a

ten-year-old girl and a story she never tired of telling later on. How
Tom came to meet her there is no way of telling; perhaps he had come
over to Newcastle to work in the shipyards there, but after they were
married they returned to Trout River to live. "Oh, she was a lovely
woman!" said one who knew her, and she was a great favorite with the
neighborhood children (many of whom she had brought into the world,
for she was the local midwife). They used to love to call at her house
and get her to tell stories and sing songs for them, two things which
she enjoyed doing and did well. An avid reader, she had an able mind,
a sharp, ready wit, and a keen interest in politics all her life. When
she had to, Ann Gorman taught school for her own children, too; it was
not unusual for the local school to be closed for weeks at a time during
the long hard winters, and Mrs. Gorman always kept her children up in
their studies by holding spelling bees and the like in the parlor.

These two active, civic-minded, intelligent people and their many
children were well-liked and respected residents of Trout River, despite the fact that they were one of the very few Catholic families in a
Protestant community (they had to travel six miles to St. Patrick's
Church in Grand River whenever they went to Mass). In his later years
Tom Gorman is said to have been rather gruff and ill-natured, and the
neighborhood children often used to give him a bad time. There was
even talk about his being a Fenian with terrible designs upon all the
local Protestants, but it seems to have been just talk. The Fenian
scare was pretty general in the sixties, and since Gorman was almost
the only Irish-Catholic in the neighborhood, he was probably the only
person who could have been viewed with anything like proper alarm.
But whatever ill will old Thomas may have inspired at the last, it was
more than offset by his good-natured wife's popularity.

Thomas Gorman died on February 1, 1874, "after a lingering illness borne with Christian resignation."[4] For a short time, Mrs. Gorman kept the store in the old house, but soon she moved to the village
(now known as Tyne Valley), where she opened another store. Sometime around 1880 she moved her establishment to nearby Ellerslie, but
within ten years she went over to Glengarry in Lot Seven to live with
her eldest son, James. Right up to her death in 1907, she spent a lot of
her time traveling through Maine and eastern Canada visiting her many
sons and daughters.

The Gormans had thirteen children, ten of whom (five boys and five
girls) lived. The girls all married, and most of them settled down to
raise their families there on the Island. Of the brothers, James, the
eldest, is the only one who stayed at home. After his father's death, he
took over the farm in Trout River, but in the late eighties he and his
family moved farther west to a new farm in Lot Seven near Glengarry.
A tall, slow-moving man with a chest-length grey beard (it had once
been red), he was an unsuccessful farmer, but if his hand lacked skill
his mind did not. He was one of the organizers and leaders of the little
debating society in Tyne Valley. Later, over in Glengarry, he was a
justice of the peace, a solid citizen, and a very present help in time of

trouble. He had what one man called "that fantastic Gorman memory," never forgetting anything, be it a story or a political fact, and he could read through a newspaper, put it down, and tell everything that was in it. He was a great singer, too, with both an endless supply of songs and a fine, strong voice; Harry Thompson recalled hearing him do a beautiful job of singing "Annie Laurie" only a short time before his death at the age of eighty-six.

Three of the other brothers made their homes elsewhere. John, the youngest of them and the last to leave the Island, settled in California; he was the father of the Most Reverend Thomas K. Gorman, Roman Catholic Bishop of Dallas-Fort Worth. Charles went to Montreal and worked for a newspaper there. Thomas, like Charles was a newspaperman; at the age of nineteen he obtained control of the *Summerside Progress* and was its editor for a couple of years. Then he moved to Toronto, where he joined the staff of the *Mail*. Later he worked his way up to editor-in-chief of the *Montreal Herald,* and finally became editor of the *Ottawa Free Press*. Surely here was a son who brought honor to his father's name, a worthy Isaac for old Abraham.

And then there was Lawrence. He was the second son, "and Larry," said his nephew John O'Connor, "was all the Gorman characteristics rolled into one." Wanderer, mill-hand, swamper, river-driver, writer of embarrassing verses, his hand against all men — he was Ishmael to Thomas' Isaac.

TWO

Trout River

Lawrence Gorman was born in the summer of 1846, and, like most of the boys around Trout River, he probably grew up "living off the shore." Lobsters were plentiful there, and the boys used to lash a hook to the end of a stick and just go out and snag them out from under the rocks and weeds; a bushel of lobsters was a short afternoon's work. Clams and oysters were in abundance and easy to come by. There was plenty for a boy to do, and if things got really dull, he could always go down to the shipyards and get in the way. Larry attended the little school in the village, where, according to Mrs. Ernest Ellis of Tyne Valley, he is remembered as "friendly but much given to playing tricks."

What did he look like? No photograph of him has, so far as I know, survived, but if we put together all the little bits of description from here and there, we can block out a rough likeness. He was about six feet tall, well built, with a straight back and a good pair of shoulders; but he tended to be spare and angular, a tendency which became more marked as he got older. He was "a fairly good-looking man," one woman said, "but he wasn't handsome." He had a large mop of unruly reddish hair, a Roman nose, and a strong, squared jaw. "He looked a bit like Henry Ford — *that* kind of a face," said John O'Connor. Usually clean-shaven, he sometimes had a mustache, sometimes a chin-whisker, but rarely a beard. His speaking voice was inclined to be high and unpleasant.

Larry Gorman probably began being Larry Gorman at an early age. He loved jokes, was a good mimic, and had a flair for hitting people off in pencil caricatures. He was curious about everything, and to satisfy this itch he read a great deal. He was especially curious about

12

people and was regarded by many of his neighbors and fellow workmen
as downright nosy. Add to these features the already-mentioned Gorman memory; he never forgot a thing he might be able to use in a song,
so when he wanted to roast anyone he could rummage around in a
rather well-stocked larder and come up with the proper ingredients for
his sauce.

It is almost impossible to establish any sort of chronology for
Larry's comings and goings on Prince Edward Island and in the Miramichi region of New Brunswick. It was perfectly customary for young
men from the Island to go to the mainland for the winter (either to
Maine or New Brunswick) to work in the woods and then, after the
spring drives, return home. Then they would spend the summer working on their farms or hiring out as fishermen. They would keep this up
until for some reason (usually marriage) they settled in one place or
the other. Larry seems to have followed this tradition. There are no
records, but it is a safe guess that he started traveling to the mainland
when he was about eighteen (roughly 1864), and for the next twenty
years the only dates I can establish show that he must have gone back
and forth quite regularly, which makes it more difficult to assign dates
to particular songs. The easiest way to classify his verses from the
Island and Miramichi is by the area in which they were written, re-
membering that they may have been composed any time between, say,
1860 and 1885.

How old he was when he discovered that he had a talent for making
up songs, we do not know. Lots of people made up songs back in what
Doerflinger calls "the happier days before movies, radio or TV."[1] It is
said that he started making up poems on the neighbors when he was
just a boy, but none of these early efforts seem to have survived. However, when his father died in 1874, Larry spent a good part of his time
living with his mother and, presumably, helping her keep the store.
For a while Mrs. Gorman's was the only store in Tyne Valley, and she
had things pretty much her own way, until Forbes and Coles opened up
a store directly across the street from her in 1879. One of Larry's
earliest extant songs deals with his mother's store. There was an old
woman who lived just off the Western Road in what was called the
Hardscrabble Road district, and she used to come in to Tyne Valley to
trade at Mrs. Gorman's. Evidently she often ran up a considerable bill
and always wanted to pay in barter. One day (so the story goes) she
came in to trade while Larry was behind the counter. She recognized
him and told him that she certainly didn't want any songs made up
about her. Larry took her order, made up her bill, and came right
back at her with a long parody of "The Shan Van Vogh," a well-known
Irish patriotic song (the title, by the way, means "poor old woman" in
Gaelic). We do not have to believe the story, but it might not be far
from the truth. The version I give here was sent to me by Edmund
Doucette of Miminegash, P.E.I. Mrs. Lawrence Murphy of Campbellton, P.E.I., sang the tune for me.

The Shan Van Vogh

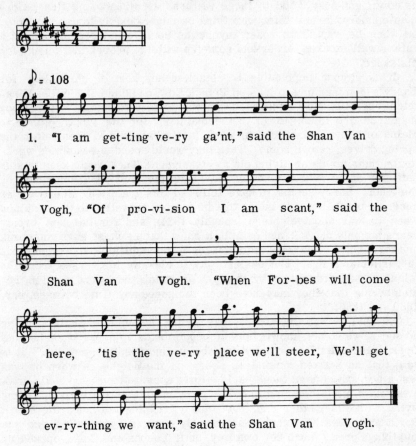

The Shan Van Vogh[2]

1. I am getting very gaunt, said the Shan Van Vogh,
   Of provision I am scant, said the Shan Van Vogh,
   When Forbes will come here, it's the very place we'll steer,
   We'll get everything we want, said the Shan Van Vogh.

2. I wonder when he'll start, said the Shan Van Vogh
   I wish he would be smart, said the Shan Van Vogh
   My provision's getting scarce, and with hunger I am fierce,
   I am keen to make a start, said the Shan Van Vogh.

3. Such parties as we owe, said the Shan Van Vogh
   We'll not pretend to know, said the Shan Van Vogh
   We'll give them just a nod, when we meet them on the road
   Whilst to Forbes we'll go, said the Shan Van Vogh.

4. We must keep our secrets dark, said the Shan Van Vogh
   If we want to make our mark, said the Shan Van Vogh
   To handle our cards well, a good story we must tell
   We'll promise hemlock bark, said the Shan Van Vogh.

5. We'll promise him a sleigh, said the Shan Van Vogh
   And half a ton of hay, said the Shan Van Vogh
   We'll promise him some meat, some barley and some wheat
   Just before we run away, said the Shan Van Vogh.

6. I've just come in to deal, said the Shan Van Vogh
   Have you any Indian meal, said the Shan Van Vogh
   I mean to pay you soon by the latter end of June
   With a carcass of fresh veal, said the Shan Van Vogh.

7. I want some cotton spools, said the Shan Van Vogh
   And a set of candle moulds, said the Shan Van Vogh
   I'll pay you with the hide of the little bull that died
   All full of warble holes, said the Shan Van Vogh.

8. I want a pair of boots, said the Shan Van Vogh
   If the payment only suits, said the Shan Van Vogh
   A pair both good and strong, I'll pay you before long
   My husband's digging roots, said the Shan Van Vogh.

9. I want to get a hood, said the Shan Van Vogh
   Have you any very good, said the Shan Van Vogh
   I want a bunch of tape, and I'd like a bonnet shape
   And some extract of logwood, said the Shan Van Vogh.

10. I want a yard of crepe, said the Shan Van Vogh
    Some matches and a pipe, said the Shan Van Vogh
    You'll have no need to fret, for your pay you're sure to get
    When the berries will get ripe, said the Shan Van Vogh.

11. I want some yellow dye, said the Shan Van Vogh
    And some concentrated lye, said the Shan Van Vogh
    I have no money now, I give my solemn vow
    But I'll pay you bye and bye, said the Shan Van Vogh.

12. I want a new tea tray, said the Shan Van Vogh
    If you'll trust me for the pay, said the Shan Van Vogh
    If I am only on my legs, I will bring you down some eggs
    When the hens begin to lay, said the Shan Van Vogh.

13. I want to get a hat, said the Shan Van Vogh
    With the crown perfectly flat, said the Shan Van Vogh
    I want some kerosene, and a package of Roseine
    To dye rags for a mat, said the Shan Van Vogh.

14. I want to get a broom, said the Shan Van Vogh
    And I want a fine tooth comb, said the Shan Van Vogh
    With some manila rope, and a cake of toilet soap
    And a bottle of perfume, said the Shan Van Vogh.

15. I want some cotton tweed, said the Shan Van Vogh
    And an ounce of turnip seed, said the Shan Van Vogh
    I want a lamp and flue, and I'd like a box of blue
    And I think that's all I need, said the Shan Van Vogh.

16. I want some cotton print, said the Shan Van Vogh
    If you'll only give consent, said the Shan Van Vogh

I am now in great distress, for I want a flashy dress
To attend the Sacrament, said the Shan Van Vogh.

17. I want a pound of tea, said the Shan Van Vogh
If we only can agree, said the Shan Van Vogh
I want two water pails, and a pound of shingle nails
And that will do for me, said the Shan Van Vogh.

18. I want a mustard can, said the Shan Van Vogh
And I want a frying pan, said the Shan Van Vogh
Some sugar and some rice, some soda and some spice
Some pickles and cayenne, said the Shan Van Vogh.

19. I want a water jug, said the Shan Van Vogh
And I want a chamber mug, said the Shan Van Vogh
I am troubled this last year, with one that's got no ear
And it's awkward for to lug, said the Shan Van Vogh.

20. Now tell me what is due, said the Shan Van Vogh
I hope you will not sue, said the Shan Van Vogh
Just run up my account and tell me the amount
That's all I ask of you, said the Shan Van Vogh.

I have heard a different story explaining the song. George L. McInnis of Vancouver heard it this way from ninety-six-year-old John Foley, also of Vancouver, who had grown up in Larry's neighborhood and knew him well:

There was a man in the neighborhood...who had a Store and Fish Buying establishment; and an old Irish woman with a rich brogue came to the joint for a fish that her husband asked for, he being sick and having a craving for such food. She also was in need of oil of some sort for the old man's boots, or her own maybe. Foley said she took a long time explaining it all and Gorman and some others were listening; and as soon as the old dame left Larry started a rhyme, Foley could only remember a few lines of it, it went thus.

I came down to get some oil, said the shan van voch;
I'm afraid my boots will spoil, said the shan van voch;
And it is my husband's wish
I'd come down and get a fish,
I can either fry or boil, said the shan van voch.[3]

One day young David Dyment went into Mrs. Gorman's store to buy a pencil. Having made his purchase, he was about to leave when Mrs. Gorman called him back. "Did you know that Lawrence once made up a song on an auction your grandfather held?" she asked. Dyment said he did not. "Well," she said, with a smile, "I'm going to give you a copy of it." With that she handed him a broadsheet from a pile of her son's songs she always kept around. When I talked to Mr. Dyment in 1957 he could still recall two verses of it:

The first that was sold was a large breeding sow,
The next was put up was an old hornless cow;
And then came a gander and two old geese,
They were set up and sold for a dollar apiece.

"And that was a good price," said Mr. Dyment.

> The farming utensils were none of the best,
> They were made by two men who have long gone to rest:
> The late Harry Waldron and Johnny Hopgood,
> No doubt but they made them as well as they could.

"Remember that this was in the days when you couldn't buy farm tools mail-order," he added; "they were always made by the local black-smith. The hay-forks all had the square, hammered tines."

Larry also worked in the shipyards in the Bideford River-Trout River area, and here for the first time we encounter a story that will become increasingly familiar: people were scared to death of him and his songs. I was told that one Donald Buchanan, who had the reputation of being a fighter and who was a big powerful man, used to work with Larry in the yards. "And I was terrified of my life of him," he said, "I was scared he'd make up a song about me." Evidently he did make up a long song about all the men who worked in Yeo's yard, but only the legend of the song survives (it is supposed to have been "a rough one").

This song brings us to the Yeos themselves, a very considerable family indeed in the Bideford-Trout River area. The father, James Yeo, came here in 1818 from Cornwall County, England, to work for Chanter and Ellis. Frank Sweet of St. Eleanor's, P.E.I. told me the story this way:

*Old Jimmy Yeo came out, him and the wife, to this country, and all he had was twenty-five cents when he landed here, and he went and bought a drink of whiskey with it. And he had overalls on and he went up and he got a job with Brown (Brown was running a little store in Port Hill; I used to hear the old fellows telling it). And old Jimmy Yeo had no schooling, but his wife was a book-keeper....And he went in partnership with Brown then, and it was Mr. Brown and Yeo. And after a few years it was Mr. Yeo and Brown, and after a few years more it was Mr. Yeo and no Brown at all....And do you know that...from Sum-merside here to Tignish he run six shipbuilders....And as I was going to tell you, for six months he'd never go to bed. He'd go into a tavern or halfway house and have a few drinks and get a lunch and lay down in a chair and sleep for a couple of hours and then he'd go out in the saddle again—rode always in the saddle. And I've heard my poor old father say that he's seen him go past Cas-cumpecque (that's where the road used to go then—there was no Western Road then) and he'd be sound asleep in the saddle going by [with] the horse walking along. Yeah, he was quite a bird. But he made big money here one time and then he got into the government.

James Yeo the elder died in 1868, old and full of days, but his story is still part of the tradition of "West Prince." And if "Old Jimmy" was the block, certainly "Little Jimmy," his eldest son, was the chip. Born a hunchback, he more than compensated for his blemish by his tremen-dous energy. Like his father before him, he was very active in poli-tics; and when The Island accepted Confederation in 1873, he and J. C. Pope were the first representatives from Prince County to the Domin-ion House of Commons in Ottawa, an office which he held until his re-tirement in 1891. As an MP, merchant, justice of the peace, ship-

owner, and farmer, he was constantly on the move; and he was both
a hustler and a pusher — demanding much of himself and those who
worked for him — the type to run when he could have walked.

Larry Gorman never took kindly to hustlers, and he detested
pushers, particularly if they tried to push him. The very fact that he
and "Little Jimmy" were in the same neighborhood made it likely that
something would happen, and, sure enough, when Yeo was running for
office, Larry struck:

The Bully of Lot Eleven

I am the bully of Lot Eleven,
My name is Robert Ramsay;
Oft times in my youth I have sold
Both wormwood and tansy.

Mr. Yeo, don't you know,
Is sure of his election;
To Ottawa he has got to go
To fight for our protection.

I have fought for Yeo through thick and thin,
Upon it I kept stumping;
When the battle it is won,
Surely I'll get something.

One day "Little Jimmy" was in Port Hill, and he had some business
to take care of at his brother-in-law William Richards' shipyard on the
Bideford side of the river, seven miles away by land. He got a ride
over with a friend who also had business at Richards', but Jimmy finished his business first and, not wanting to wait around, began looking
for a quicker way back. For what happened then, let the woman who
sent me the story tell it in her own words:

He spied Larry just leaving the wharf to row about three miles to Yeo's wharf
so he ran and jumped aboard. Larry's dory was flat bottomed and sharp stern
like the Cape Cod dories of today. Little Jimmy was no more than seated till he
started swaying to the swing of the oars and saying, "Faster, Larry, faster."
Finally Larry could stand it no longer and stood up and threw the oars far out on
the tide. Then [he] said, "Row, Mr. Yeo, row," and he lay back to enjoy nature.
Jimmy tried paddling with his hands [and] then got out on the sharp stern and
paddled with his feet. Every so often Larry would raise his head and call out,
"Paddle, Mr. Yeo, paddle." Finally someone from Yeo's shipyard saw them and
came out and rescued them.

Some days afterward, the Yeos gave a party. Probably they wer'en't
planning to invite Larry anyhow, but perhaps "Little Jimmy" used this
way of getting back at Larry; at any rate he was not invited. The next
day there was a new twenty-verse song making work lighter in the
shipyard. Only a few verses have survived, and some of those in gar-
bled form:

1. Twas on the fifth of November
    That Little Jimmy Yeo he gave a party;
    They all attended just like it was intended
    . . . .

2. There was Mr. Dick Best with his wife from the West,
   She was dressed up in ribbons and looked mighty gay.
   . . . .
   . . . .

3. Mrs. Yeo in her hurry sent forth Sarah Murray
   And invited her brother Sandy;
   But Sandy objected just as we expected
   For his teeth wasn't shaped for eating candy.

4. There was Sarah Jane Yeo with her face all aglow
   And her sister just eighteen year old;
   They say they are dashes, the both of them mashes
   (I can't say for certain, it's just as I'm told).

5. When supper was over, like sheep in good clover,
   Our stomachs being full to the collar and tie,
   And now we have parted and home we have started
   To leave Mrs. Yeo and her family goodbye.

6. . . . .
   Now come sing this ditty, it won't take you long,
   If ever you make a spree and don't invite me
   As sure as the devil, I will make a song!

That last line is evidently the truth, but only half of it; he couldn't be bought off simply by inviting him to the party. He would come and sit back quietly, never dancing but observing everything that went on; later he would deliver himself of a poem, working in references to everyone there and to all that had transpired. People were really frightened of him, and, Lord knows, his satire could be vicious, but often enough it seems to have been pretty good-natured. Take the following, for example, "The Spree at Summer Hill." First he describes the fiddler:

> His elbows all were greased with gin
> And his heart and soul were warmed within;
> He picked up the fiddle and the bow he drew
> And the dancers like chain lightening flew.

Then came a description of the dancing and the dancers: "*It was really funny all through...," said Mrs. Frank Sweet, who recalled these few fragments of the song. "Some of the fellows, their eyes were bulging out, and some of the girls — the way each one swung...and one tripped the other." There was a lot of drinking and before long a fight started:

> They shoveled and they pushed and they kicked and shoved
> Till Sally's hoofs got on the stove,
> Upset the kettle down on her feet
> Which caused that lady to retreat.

And out in the yard, someone paid a visit to the goose pen:

> He threw the old gander o'er his back
> Till every joint in him did crack;

&"'Twill bring me fifty cents, I guess,
'Twill help to pay my school assess."

One time John Plestid of Arlington was holding a "work frolic"; everyone worked around the place during the day, and then in the evening there was a party and dance. The party had not gone on for very long before Plestid discovered that he was running out of drink, and it was just at this time that Larry Gorman and a friend arrived. Since they had not worked, they were not entitled to take part in the festivities; but many of the people there implored Plestid to give Larry something to drink so that he would not write a song about them. He acquiesced, and Larry felt called on to offer a toast:

Here's to you, Mr. Plestid,
You gave us liquor while it lasted;
We hope next time you have a frolic
You won't run short of alcoholic.

One of Gorman's best-known songs on the Island was "Bachelor's Hall." A man who lived some five miles from Trout River evidently had begun to cast about for a wife. Whether he ever actually placed an ad in the paper I do not know; but he did let it be known that he was available and, if he did say so himself, a pretty good catch. Larry heard about this situation and hit the gentleman off in a poem said to be about twenty stanzas long. I had received many fragmentary versions of it, but I despaired of ever finding a reasonably complete one until Mrs. Cyrene McLellan of Grand River sang me the following one afternoon:

Bachelor's Hall

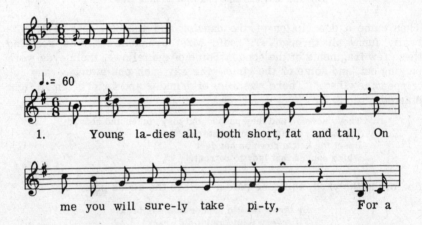

1. Young la-dies all, both short, fat and tall, On
   me you will sure-ly take pi-ty, For a

bach-e-lor's hall   is   no place at all,   And the

same I'll ex-plain in   my   dit-ty-------.

Bachelor's Hall

1. Young ladies all, both short, fat and tall,
   On me you will surely take pity,
   For a bachelor's hall is no place at all
   And the same I'll explain in my ditty.

2. Folks boast of a life without any wife
   They tell you it would be much cheaper
   And you they'll persuade, the great riches they made
   By hiring a frugal housekeeper.

3. But that's all a hoax, all those silly folk
   Their outlays are much more extensive
   And their story don't believe for they did me deceive
   And I find that it's much more expensive.

4. If you'll listen to me or just come and see,
   I'm well fitted out for housekeeping;
   And the angels of love that flew as a dove
   To my bedside they nightly come creeping.

5. So now, imps divine, if you'll only be mine,
   Or just take a look at my welfare;
   And if you say no, it's away I will go
   In order to seek a wife elsewhere.

6. I've a comb and a glass, both mounted with brass
   Some soap, a towel and two brushes;
   My mirror will show from the top to the toe,
   And a mattress made out of bulrushes.

7. I have two iron steads, I have two feather beds,
   Some blankets, some quilts, and two pillows;
   I have two hives of bees, I have many fruit trees
   And for ornaments, two weeping willows.

8. I've a hen and a cock, I've a stove and a clock,
   I have turkeys and geese by the dozen;
   I've a cat and a dog and a two-hundred hog
   That I purchased last spring from my cousin.

9. I have salt and fresh meats, I have cabbage and beets,
   I've a large carving knife for the table;
   Cups, saucers and bowls, and new candle molds,
   I've a frying pan, saucepan and ladle.

10. And a box of white sand I keep always on hand,[4]
    All packed away safe for the winter;
    I've a broom and a mop for to wipe every slop,
    In your fingers you'll ne'er get a splinter.

11. My story don't doubt, I'm well fitted out,
    My house is both papered and plastered;
    I have knives, I have forks, I have bottles and corks,
    I've a lamp and a new pepper caster.

12. But the best of all yet is my new chamber set,
    My two sweet canaries in cages;
    I've a bowl and a jug and another large mug
    With the gilded flowers all round the edges.

13. In the summer so gay you can see every day
    My lambkins so nimbly sporting;
    And the fierce iron horse with its serpentine course
    You will see it go by my door snorting.

14. I have a large farm, I've a house and a barn,
    And a rich patch for rising tomatoes;
    And I spared no expense in building a fence
    For to keep the hogs from my potatoes.

15. And so now, imps divine, if you'll only be mine
    Or just take a look at my welfare,
    And if you say no, it's away I will go
    In order to seek a wife elsewhere.

16. So now, ladies all, come each when I call,
    Come Peggy, come Betsy, come Nancy;
    When I see you all, both short, fat, and tall,
    I will surely see one that I fancy.

James Pendergast of Charlottetown had these two verses not included in Mrs. McClellan's version:

Some folks of our day will disdainfully say
Self-praise is no recommendation,
But my houses and land as you understand
Are opposite Northam flag station.

I have harrows and plows, I have sheep, I have cows,
And they're a stock that I take a great pride in;
I have ten gallon kegs all chock full of eggs,
A horse and a carriage to ride in.

Any courtship that had something even slightly offbeat about it was
evidently an irresistible subject for Larry. There was a girl in a
nearby town who was being courted by two fellows, one of them a tailor.
Some say that there were three fellows after the girl and that one of
them was Larry Gorman. At any rate he made a song about her, "The
Arlington Maid." One of the suitors starts after her, whipping his
horse on:

1. He started her off at the race of a hound;
    I'll swear to my life that she ne'er touched the ground,
    I'm sure that she went twenty feet to a bound
    In pursuit of the Arlington Maid.

Finally she makes her choice:

2. "I'll go with the tailor," said she, "I suppose;
    He will make the best husband, sure everyone knows.
    And he'll be so handy to cut baby's clothes,"
    Replied the sweet Arlington Maid.

The last two verses tell of the loser's sorrow:

3. And when I am dead, let it not be neglected
    To show that I still died in love,
    Here over my grave let a tower be erected
    And write these inscriptions above.

4. In hygrific letters have it written plain,
    Saying, "Here lies the corpse of young Albert MacLean.
    Cruel Cubit's sharp pangs put an end to my life,
    And I died for the Arlington Maid."

The Arlington Maid

♩. = 63

2. "I'll go with the tai-lor said she, "I sup-pose;

He will make the best hus-band, sure ev-ery-one knows. And

he'll be so han-dy to cut ba - by's clothes," Re-

plied the sweet Ar-ling-ton Maid.   3.   And

when I am dead let it not be ne-glec-ted To

show that I still died in love, Here

o-ver my grave let a tower be e-rec-ted And

write these in-scrip-tions a - bove. 4. In

hy-gri-fic let-ters have it writ-ten plain, Say-ing,

"Here lies the corpse of young Al-bert Mac-Lean. Cruel

Cu-bit's sharp pangs put an end to my life, And I

died for the Ar-ling-ton Maid."

Not even Larry's own family was safe, as his brother James dis-covered to his sorrow. James had procured a horse that had belonged for years to the local Presbyterian minister. Evidently the animal had seen its best days, but Larry felt that his brother was abusing it by lending it to the neighbors, working it too hard around the farm, and making it take the whole family on the twelve-mile round trip to St. Patrick's Church in Grand River on Mass days. The story goes that he even rented it out to McKay and McNibben to turn the bark grinder in their tannery in Tyne Valley, but that once they had harnessed the animal to the pole it stiffened out its legs and refused to budge. Larry made up a song about all this, which seems to have been one of his most popular, if evidence of wide oral circulation is any index. And when David Dyment visited Larry in Brewer he asked him to sing it for him; Larry obliged, claiming that the song was his own favorite. The amazingly complete text given below was sent to me by James Pendergast of Charlottetown, P.E.I., who in turn had received it from Lawrence McNally of Summerside. The song had been typed out as separate quatrains. I have numbered the stanzas as I have in order to show what I believe to be the basic stanza pattern. If I am correct, then the first half of stanza 2 is missing.

The Horse's Confession

1. Come brother geldings, lend an ear
    And listen to my story;
    In these few verses you will hear
    And it's for me you'll feel sorry.

    Though I am all brown with sweat,
    My skin was once as black as jet,
    That time I was the Parson's pet,
    'Twas then I was in my glory.

2. For seeing horses every day
    That's fed so well on oats and hay
    And sport about in harness gay
    It makes me melancholy.

3. When I came to this country
    I met with great disaster;
    It was a fatal blow to me
    The day I changed my master.

    Though I dearly loved the first,
    The second one I've oft-times cursed,
    The third proved to be far the worst;
    You can tell that by my pasture.

4. They take me down to Crapaud,
    More times to Lot Eleven;
    I'm driven in to Summerside
    And back to Lot Seven.

    This is the way that I am used,
    Kicked and cuffed and badly bruised,
    It's no great wonder I'd refuse
    To grind bark for MacNevin.

5. Those brats of boys get on my back,
    They really do provoke me;
    They tie a rope around my neck,
    It's tight enough to choke me.

I'm seldom driven by a man,
I'm always in a caravan;
It's Cooper's boy or Ed McCann
That's always sent to yoke me.

6. Another thing I've got to tell —
I'm subject to a colic;
And before I am right well
They lend me to White Alec.

Oh he is the boy to make me fly,
It's the truth I don't deny;
And he takes me to a place where I
Hear nothing spoke but Gaelic.

7. When he gets me it's his delight
To canter me and run me;
Instead of coming home that night
He keeps me over Sunday.

He is the boy to make me jump,
He leaves great welts upon my rump,
He keeps me tethered to a stump
From Saturday to Monday.

8. Another thing that grieved me sore
And broke my heart forever,
Instead of going to my own church
They take me to Grand River.

When many a hungry hour I've passed,
Not tasting either hay or grass,
I stand out there 'til after Mass —
Oh Lord, don't it make me shiver.

9. I see the crowd assemble there
Dressed in their silks and satin,
But what still comes worse to me
Is the Mass is sung in Latin.

There's many a thing I've left untold,
I'm oft-times wet and oft-times cold;
For all these reasons I've been told
I've good reason to complain, sir.

I am puzzled by the line "And back to Lot Seven," since the other references are to the Trout River area, but perhaps we should attribute it to the vagaries of tradition, perhaps to a bit of conscious improvement on somebody's part.

Other members of the family were stricken too, especially two brothers-in-law, Michael Monaghan and Luke Hughes. Monaghan, who had married Bridget Gorman, was the subject of at least two songs. He had been twice married before he met Bridget, and Larry seized on this point, nicknaming him "Brigham." Hughes, who had married Julia Gorman, was a poet too, "and he was every bit as good a poet as Larry was," said Charlie Gorman. Either of the next two songs may be his. Charlie said they were, and so did Harry Thomson of nearby

Glengarry. However, others claim they are Larry's. The first, "Luke and His Rambles," doesn't sound like a song a man would make about himself, and it does sound like the sort of thing Larry did to perfection. Yet poets have satirized themselves, so we'll have to leave the matter undecided. It was quite a long song, I was told, but only fragments of it have survived:

> One morning as Luke he was tasting the juice
> His tongue in his head it hung very loose;
> He gave the old woman some dirty abuse,
> Which didn't go well in the morning.
>
> Old Aunt Kitty came in on a hop,
> I saw her advance to a large boiling pot;
> Says I to myself, "Things look rather hot,
> And I'd better jog off in the morning."

Another informant gave me the following stanza:

> As I was coming out over soapsuds and muck,
> I met an old peddler with fish in his truck,
> I bade him good day and wished him good luck,
> At five o'clock in the morning.

Her comments on this stanza are worth repeating: "Immediately it placed the woman as a poor housekeeper as only lazy women threw dish water out the door. And coming out at five o'clock — no decent girl would sit up that late, so perhaps it's no wonder his songs wasn't valued."

"The Pack of Hounds" was sent me by G. R. Rowe of Brandon, Manitoba, by way of Alan Mills. Rowe said it was by Gorman, but Charlie Gorman insisted it was by Luke. Again, we only have a fragment. The song is about two bailiffs who used to arraign people for debt at a certain price:

The Pack of Hounds

> 'Tis of a noble pack of hounds
> I purpose now to sing
> . . . .
> . . . .
>
> Somewhere up West I'm told there're two,
> Their names I'll write some future day,
> Were reared on smelts and gaspereaux
> In a den somewhere about the Brae.
>
> One had a dusky cat-owl's eye,
> His back a hump of roguish round,
> A withered whisker thin and dry,
> And just the snout that suits the hound.
>
> He sneaks about your barn by night,
> Conceals himself all in the hay,

And in the morning's dusky light
He suddenly pounces on his prey.

His comrade next of beagle-breed
With Irish-wolf is slightly crossed,
He's little known for feats of speed,
But the hold he takes is seldom lost.

There was another man in the neighborhood whose wife had died, and Larry felt that he was looking for a replacement all too soon. He made a gay, lilting song that started like this:

If she's gone, let her go,
I will soon get another;
There are lots of pretty girls
At the head of Grand River.

Further along he described the kind of girl the man had found:

She can dance to a pipe,
She can dance to a fiddle,
She's as neat around the waist
As a cow around the middle;
She has two rows of teeth
And a tongue in the middle.

The man, of course, was furious, but the song caught on and was very popular.

THREE

"Along Lot Seven Shore":
West Point to Miminegash

When James Gorman bought a farm near Glengarry in 1889 and moved his family there to live, he found that the name of Gorman was already quite familiar to the people of Lot Seven. In fact it was notorious almost all the way from West Point to North Cape. Larry had been there first and written songs about practically every one of James's new neighbors. It hardly made life easier for the new arrivals; and James, a very kind and conscientious man, was made even more exasperated than ever with his brother. "You can understand how it was," James's son Charles told me; "we had to live with those people, and by that time Uncle Larry was away down in Maine."

Larry never had a home, properly speaking, in Lot Seven; it was just one of the areas he struck in his wanderings. He worked as a hired man on several farms — for Peter Doyle and for Art Dalton's father in Burton, for example. In Waterford he worked for Patrick Fitzgerald and boarded there with him. One day Mrs. Fitzgerald passed by his door and heard Larry mumbling to himself. She went downstairs and told her husband that he had hired a crazy man. Patrick laughed: "Oh no, that's the way Larry makes up all his songs," he said.

But his main employment along this shore was in fishing. There was always plenty of such work to be had during the busy summer season; men who did not own their own boats (and Larry never did!) would hire with someone, either for a flat rate or on "shares." If a man worked shares, he would, of course, first establish what his share was going to be; he might, for example, agree to work for half the fish he himself caught, the rest going to the owner of the boat. There might be anywhere from one to five men hiring to go out in a particular boat. If they were handlining for mackerel, each man had a "berth" and kept his fish separate from those of the others. If they were setting trawl lines for cod or ling, they would set out the long back lines, from which would hang as many as a hundred short hook lines (the "gain-jun") about six feet apart. Later, they would haul them back in and take off the fish. When the boat was back on shore, the men would get busy and clean the catch, teaming up to split, gut, salt, barrel, and finally store the catch in the "stage." And overhead and all around the air was full of screaming gulls circling and dipping down for the offal.

This brings us to another song, one which several people have said was Larry's own favorite. A man Larry fished for was a great whistler, and he had developed the trick of imitating the sea gull's cry:

> When I stand up and begin to whistle
> You'll see all the gulls around me fly,
> And in the sand they seem to nestle,
> From whence they call me the Gull Decoy.[1]

Larry did not think up the name, but when the fellow "made little of him" and (some claim) did him out of wages, he spread that name and the rumored deeds of the bearer over three Atlantic provinces and the State of Maine! Over on the Miramichi, for example, it is well known as the song for which Larry was run off the Island. The best version I have collected was sung for me by Spurgeon Allaby of Passekeag, New Brunswick. Mr. Allaby, by the way, had never heard of Larry Gorman, nor did the song's local allusions mean anything to him.

The Gull Decoy (I)

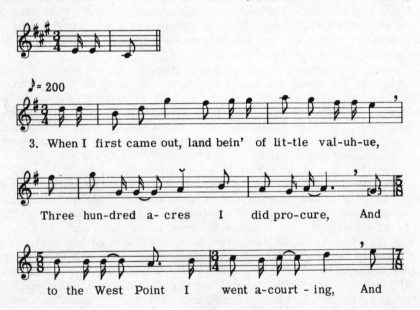

♩= 200

3. When I first came out, land bein' of lit-tle val-uh-ue,

Three hun-dred a-cres I did pro-cure, And

to the West Point I went a-court-ing, And

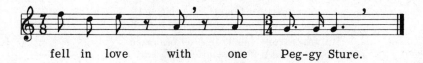

fell in love with one Peg-gy Sture.

The Gull Decoy (I)

1. I am a man from the County Kerry
   And Pat O'Reilly it is my name;
   I was born and bred in the land so early,
   I was noted for many's the deed of fame.

2. When I first came out I was much respected
   By every man, woman, girl, or boy,
   But it is of late I've been much dejected
   To hear them call me the Gull Decoy.

3. When I first came out, land being of little value,
   Three hundred acres I did procure,
   And to the West Point I went a-courting
   And fell in love with one Peggy Sture.

4. Now her old parents being so delighted
   That on me she had a glancing eye;
   Oh, her old parents being so delighted
   She fell in love with the Gull Decoy.

5. I raised my children to my own notions
   The oldest of them I called him Ike;
   I always intend to give them tuition
   To drink and swear and to kick and fight.

6. Oh the other day we got in a tussle,
   'Twas then his mettle I meant to try,
   But he threw me down and did me guzzle,
   He chewed the thumb of the Gull Decoy.

7. I have no books or I have no papers,
   I have no money to win or lose,
   But every Sunday when I get up
   I run about for to hear the news.

8. I stay at home 'til I get my breakfast,
   I then run down to my son Pat's;
   I stay with him 'til I get my dinner
   And then go up to my nephew Matt's.

9. His aged uncle, he does me honor
   The minute on me he casts his eye;
   He takes me in and he reads the paper,
   He reads the news to the Gull Decoy.

10. He first begins at his evening process,
    The "miscellaneous" I love best;
    He reads to me the Highland Journal
    The "heathen progress" and all the rest.

11. I then run home fully delighted
    For I always meant to win my post,

For fear that I might get benighted
And at the bush I might meet a ghost.

12. All earthly spirits that get benighted
My heart and conscience does terrify
To think that I have been such a wicked rover
And now to be christened the Gull Decoy.

13. To my own church I have been neglectful,
My mind being on every thing that passed;
To my Christian duties I've been neglectful,
It's been forty years since I went to Mass.

14. My oldest brother I did him torture,
I tortured him 'till he had to fly,
All on account of the girl he married,
And still in anger I did rage.
To the place where his child was buried[2]
I went by night and dug up the grave.

15. Of all my actions and my bad doings,
I set a dog on an orphan boy,
And many the other cruel and dirty action
Which adds more grief to the Gull Decoy.

James Pendergast of Charlottetown knew a different tune:

The Gull Decoy (II)

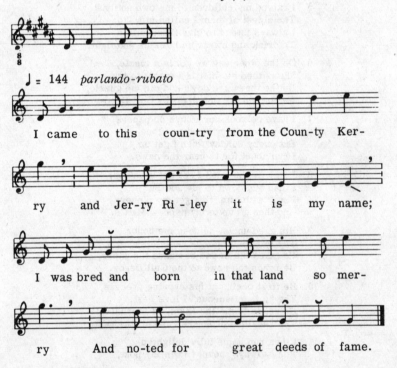

♩ = 144 *parlando-rubato*

I came to this coun-try from the Coun-ty Kerry and Jer-ry Ri-ley it is my name;
I was bred and born in that land so merry And no-ted for great deeds of fame.

I came to this country from the County Kerry
And Jerry Riley it is my name;
I was bred and born in that land so merry
And noted for great deeds of fame.

And Steve Murphy of Alberton had still a third, to my mind the best of
the lot. It has the variant opening line, characteristic of a number of
folk-tunes I have collected here in the Northeast.

The Gull Decoy (III)

1. Oh I'm an I-rish-man   from the Coun-ty Ker - ry,

Oh   Pat-rick Ri - ley   it   is   my   name.   I was

bred and born   in   a   land so   mer -ry   And

no -ted for   ma-ny a   deed of fame   2. When

I   came here   land was   lit-tle val - ue,   Three

hun-dred a - cres   I   did   se - cure,   And

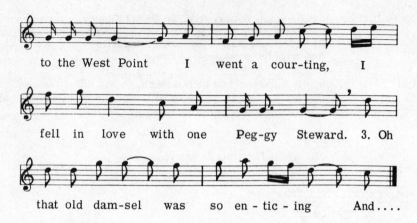

to the West Point   I   went a cour-ting,   I

fell in love with one   Peg-gy Steward.   3. Oh

that old dam-sel was   so en - tic - ing   And....

[*Continue, repeating tune for stanza two for each succeeding stanza.*]

The Gull Decoy (III)

1. I'm an Irishman from the County Kerry,
   Oh, Patrick Riley it is my name;
   I was bred and born in a land so merry
   And noted for many a deed of fame.

2. When I came here land was little value,
   Three hundred acres I did secure,
   And to the West Point I went a-courting
   I fell in love with one Peggy Steward.

And Frank O'Holleran of Bloomfield Station, P.E.I., added this stanza:

When I'm dead and my friends all round me
There'll be no tears but a sob and sigh,
But all their tears will be unavailing
For none can pray for the Gull Decoy.

He also said there was a final stanza that ended "Like a horse they'll bury the Gull Decoy." There was evidently a family plot on the farm, and since, according to the song, he had been "neglectful" of his "Christian duties" he could scarcely be buried in holy ground.

How much of what Larry says in this song is fact, how much is simple gossip, and how much is straight fabrication, there is no longer any way of telling. I have met people who have told me that the Gull Decoy was a fine man who did not deserve the treatment Larry gave him; I have met others who claim Larry was justified. Knowing what we do about Gorman, however, we can be sure that if he once got hold of a sharp bit of scandal, he would not bother to check his sources. He was out for blood in this song, and scandal could cut deep. In stanza fourteen, for example, he may have heard (as I did) the following story:

the Gull Decoy had hounded his brother for marrying a Protestant; and when the brother's child died and was buried in the family plot, the Gull Decoy dug up the body and left it on his brother's doorstep. The brother reburied the child on a hillside facing the Gull Decoy's house, marking the grave very plainly so that it would be the first thing the Gull Decoy would see on stepping out of his front door in the morning. And as for the Gull Decoy's having "set a dog on an orphan boy," we can be sure, at the very least, that Larry has worked his material to a fine edge. Veracity was all very well in its way, but for Gorman's purposes it was not a necessary consideration. Whatever the facts behind "The Gull Decoy" may be, it was one of Larry's most popular songs, known even in some places where he himself was unknown.

The "Gull Decoy's" son, Michael, was not only a fisherman but just about the best cobbler on the West End. He made excellent fishing boots back in the days before rubber boots came in, and there was a local saying that went "A mackerel line, a hook, and a pair of Mick Riley's boots and you're a fisherman." Larry used him for a target, too, in at least two songs. The first one is as much about the father as it is about the son. All but the last stanza was sung for me by Jim Pendergast:

Michael Riley

3. He took me to a raf-fle Where he gave me too much rum; We got in-to a squabble and I chewed my fa-ther's thumb; And when I proved his cham-pi- on how migh-ty proud I

felt.   Ev -er since that   time - - - I've

worn   the   dia - mond   belt.

Michael Riley

1. My name is Michael Riley, I'm a cobbler by trade,
   Many a pair of brogans I've cut and never made;
   My father is a pagan who lives in yonder bush,
   From morn to night he whistles like a bird they call the thrush.

2. He wears a belt around his middle and a linsey wooly coat,
   And he nickers while he's laughing like a rocky mountain goat;
   I was my father's favorite, he gave me extra feed,
   And when I arrived at manhood, I did him as proceeds:

3. He took me to a raffle where he gave me too much rum —
   We got into a squabble and I chewed my father's thumb;
   And when I proved his champion, how mighty proud I felt;
   Ever since that time, I've worn the diamond belt.

4. The Cape Wolfe pugilists I did beat them all,
   Like Samson with the Philistines, I slew them great and small.
   . . . .
   . . . .

5. When I go to a tavern [I] like a foaming spout
   When they get tired of me [it's] then they throw me out;
   I leave for home in anger to accomplish my desire,
   I take my wife and children and throw them on the fire.

The second song concentrates more on Mick, but Larry spread the vilification around a bit, just to make sure that no one felt left out:

Mick Riley

1. 'Twas in the summer season in the year of seventy-six,
   'Twas with a crazy cobbler I went to learn some tricks;
   To spend the summer fishing along Lot Seven shore,
   Where foaming billows madly leap and breakers loud do roar.

2. But to my sad misfortune it proved an awful day
   Instead of human beings, they're more like beasts of prey;
   They'll cheat you and backbite you and give you lots of chaw, —
   They'd kill you, skin, and eat you if it wasn't for the law.

3. It's in the summer season he runs a fishing craft,
   It's elegant and pleasing, it's called the *Ocean Lark*.
   He goes a-pickarooning, sometimes a prize he gets;
   He goes to Richibucto and steals the Frenchmen's nets.

4. It's in the winter season he runs a cobbler stall;
   He makes a scanty living with his hammer and his awl.
   For five rude and saucy offspring and a broken-hearted wife,—
   Who's allotted for to spend with him a sad and tortured life.

5. . . . .
   . . . .
   And while the life is in him to carry on that game,
   Until at length he'll find himself in Hell's eternal flames.

Larry also went fishing with the "nephew Matt" of "The Gull Decoy," Matt Howard. Early one season Matt lost an anchor; his wife, when he told her, said that she would pray every day to the Blessed Virgin Mary for its return. Months later, he and Larry hauled in their nets and, sure enough, there was the anchor, corroded but still recognizable. We can imagine the transports of joy and thanksgiving at home when Matt reported his luck to his wife, because some time later someone asked Larry how the dav's fishing had gone and he replied,

> 'Tis to the Virgin we must pray
> And every day must thank her;
> Matt went out to fish today
> And caught his little anchor.

If Larry was not exactly a model of Christian virtue, if he was not always "in love and charity" with his neighbors, if he often seemed not to understand the Master's admonition about the mote and the beam, nevertheless he was a good Catholic all his life. Lot Seven was predominantly Catholic, but some Baptists had come in and set up a church out on the Nauvoo Road. The story goes that some of the people out that way did not have very high moral standards; two old fellows are said to have swapped wives, one throwing in a good heavy bunk chain to even the trade. Larry made up a song about the Baptists and their new pastor, and for a tune he took that of a hymn that he is supposed to have heard these people singing. The hymn, by the way, is "Near the Cross," a Fanny Crosby production with the tune by William H. Doane. It was first published in *Bright Jewels* (1869), which can perhaps help us date the present parody.[3] The version I give here is a composite:

Larry Gorman

The Baptists

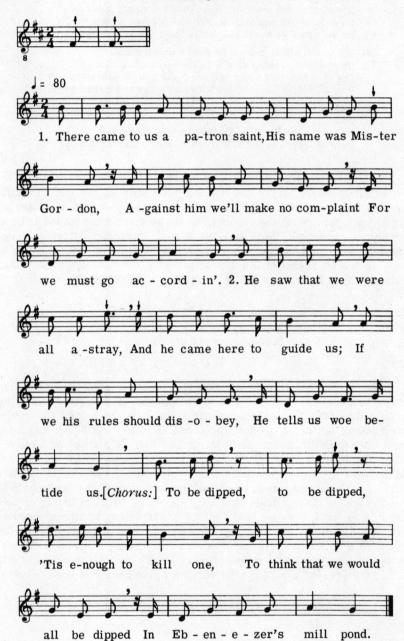

1. There came to us a   pa-tron saint, His name was Mis-ter

Gor - don,   A -gainst him we'll make no com-plaint For

we must go   ac - cord - in'. 2. He saw that we were

all   a -stray, And he came here to   guide us; If

we his rules should dis -o - bey, He tells us woe be-

tide   us.[*Chorus:*] To be dipped,   to   be dipped,

'Tis e-nough to   kill   one,   To think that we would

all   be dipped In Eb - en - e - zer's   mill pond.

The Baptists

1. There came to us a patron saint,
   His name was Mr. Gordon;
   Against him we'll make no complaint,
   For we must go accordin'.

2. He saw that we were all astray,
   And he came here to guide us;
   If we his rules should disobey
   He tells us woe betide us.
   Chorus: To be dipped! To be dipped!
   'Tis enough to kill one!
   To think that we would all be dipped
   In Ebenezer's mill pond.

3. Here comes this holy man of God,
   Gathering up his lost ones,
   Preaching to his famous squad,
   The Morrills and the Crossmans.

4. The Baptists they are very thick,
   They think they have the right time;
   They raise from every bush you kick,
   Especially in the night-time.
   Chorus: To be dipped, *etc.*

5. The Baptists they're a nervy crew
   When they do get together,
   Stemming out to cold Nauvoo
   Despite cold wind and weather.

6. On Sunday evening [*the girls*] go to church
   Escorted by their father,
   But on the way returning home
   A young man they would rather.
   Chorus: To be dipped, *etc.*

Down in Miminegash there was a fellow by the name of Michael McElroy, a fisherman who also ran a lobster-packing factory. It was evidently a good-sized establishment including, besides the factory itself, a kitchen, a dining room, and the big "ram-pasture," sleeping quarters for the hands. McElroy hired many men both to fish for him and to work in his factory. According to the man who told me his life story McElroy prospered for a long time until the market failed and he lost everything. He then went out to Alberta to work in the wheat harvest one year and started all over again. Eventually he owned two businesses there, which he sold to return to the Island and live in comfort for the rest of his days. Industrious, thrifty and stern, he was just the sort of man who was anathema to Larry.

No one person ever seems to have suffered more abuse at Larry's hands than this McElroy. It is claimed that he did Larry out of some wages, but whether the injury was real or imagined, Larry was angry and went after McElroy with every weapon at his command. He jabbed at him with quips, sniped at him with little verses, and gave him broadside after broadside from the heavy artillery of his *ad hominem*, his most fearful weapon. He even made use of a secret weapon: his hitherto unknown ability to cartoon. He drew pictures of McElroy and his family and gave them all long tails. One picture which made the rounds showed on one side fat, healthy fishermen coming to work for McElroy and on the other side the same men leaving him, all skin and bones and some on crutches. Clearly, Larry did not feel that McElroy spread a good table, and Larry liked to eat. He showed his disapproval in a more characteristic way one time when McElroy had some buyers from England down at the factory and brought them in to dinner. Everyone ate at one long wooden trestle table, and as they were preparing to sit down McElroy (why I'll never know!) asked Larry to say grace. Larry looked down at his plate and said,

> Oh Lord above, look down on us
> And see how we are forgotten
> And send us meat that is fit to eat
> Because by Christ, this is rotten.[4]

Larry disliked the ram-pasture, and when he woke up one morning and saw someone he didn't know sleeping on the floor (all the bunks were full), he is supposed to have fired this one off extempore:

> A stranger to the pasture came
> And slept upon the floor;
> He certainly made a great mistake
> For there are fleas galore.

Gorman is supposed to have made up thirty-four separate songs on McElroy. In Miminegash, when Larry wasn't working, he would never be with the rest of the men; he'd be off by himself somewhere, perhaps down on the beach, making up a song. When he returned, he would sing it. No McElroy songs survive in entirety, but bits of them still turn up. The narrator in one is evidently McElroy himself, giving us a hard luck story:

> Hail, fishermen assemble, sad news to you I'll tell;
> I just received a circular and I hear that lobsters fell.
> I just received a circular, and in the same did state
> The prices they are bringing would scarcely buy the bait.

Here is another fragment that keeps appearing:

> When he wants to get a joke out,
> His slanderous tongue he'll poke out,
> And some dirty words he'll croak out,
> You can hear him far and nigh;
> Like the wild beast of the jungle,
> You can hear him growl or grumble,
> You can hear him growl or grumble,
> That reptile McElroy.

And yet another:

> I will tell you my belief McElroy:
> You're a liar and a thief, McElroy;
> You'd resemble much the beast
> Of the jungles of the East
> If you only had a tail, McElroy.

But perhaps the most abusive of them all, in fact probably the most vicious thing Larry ever wrote, is the last and longest of the fragments:

Michael McElroy

1. Hail fishermen, for your own sake
   I pray you all a warning take,
   And unto me a promise make
   While going to seek employ;
   And if you should fish another year
   Or ever happen to come here,
   Of one great bogus, pray keep clear;
   He'll rob and starve you all I fear,
   His name is McElroy.

2. He has a wife that's much the same,
   Who glories in the swindling game;
   Were he to rob both blind and lame,
   She'd laugh and shout with joy.
   His knavish tricks she does inspire,
   She'll counsel with him and conspire,
   She'll make the balls for him to fire,
   This Mistress McElroy.

3. How holy and divine she looks,
   When reading some pious and moral books,
   While many a curious yarn she cooks
   About some girl and boy.
   God's holy laws she will impeach,
   His pardon seldom she'll beseech,
   With prayer and catechism teach
   This Mistress McElroy.

4. This McElroy is quite a fop,
   A proud, suspicious, naughty pup,
   His head is tapering at the top,
   Like some wild goose decoy.
   . . . .

There were some ten or twelve more stanzas that have been lost.

As I have said before, Larry was a great reader. One night at McElroy's he walked into the kitchen and sat down to read by the kitchen lamp. However, the cook, having finished her work for the night, simply picked up her lamp and walked out, leaving Gorman there in the dark. He evened the score by writing a poem with a neat *double entendre*:

I'm a poor and blighted old maiden,
I'm banned from the pleasures of life;
I try to look nice and engaging,
But no-one inquires for a wife.

In order to show my high breeding,
A stranger I treat like a tramp;
When he calls in to have a night's reading,
I always refuse him my lamp.

On the Dock Road not far from Miminegash lived James O'Brien and his brother, Michael. "Big Jim" was just what his nickname implied: plain-dealing and expansive. His brother, I was told, was quite a different sort; people used to call him "Sweet Michael" because he had a reputation for being "cute." Larry stayed for a while with Big Jim and worked for Michael, who thought it would be pretty funny if Larry made up a song about Jim. Larry refused; "I'll never make up a song about Jim O'Brien or any other man who uses me like that," he said. One Sunday morning not long after that, while the Jim O'Briens were at church, Larry made up a song. Young Harry, who had not gone with his father, told me that he watched Mr. Gorman pacing slowly and steadily back and forth between the living room and the parlor, his hands behind his back and his head down, too absorbed in what he was doing to notice he was being watched. Every once in a while he would stop, walk over to a high desk in the living room, write busily for a moment, and then go back to his pacing. All signs pointed to a squall in the offing, and it broke before long.

Michael had evidently been looking for a wife. It is said that he went so far as to advertise, telling what he had to offer and what he wanted in a woman. Whether he did or not, the situation was a familiar one to Larry; he had the technique well worked out in "Bachelor's Hall," so all he had to do was adapt it to the immediate subject. He adapted it all right, and gave it an unexpected fillip. The version I give here was sung for me by Edmund Doucette of Miminegash:

Michael O'Brien

1. Come all you girls both short and tall, I pray don't be so

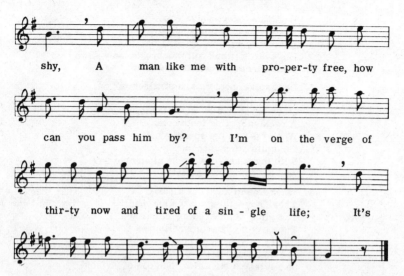

shy, A man like me with pro-per-ty free, how
can you pass him by? I'm on the verge of
thir-ty now and tired of a sin - gle life; It's
time that I should make a vow that I should have a wife.

Michael O'Brien

1. Come all you girls both short and tall,
   I pray don't be so shy;
   A man like me with property free —
   How can you pass him by?
   I'm on the verge of thirty now,
   And tired of a single life;
   It's time that I should make a vow
   That I should have a wife.

2. I got house and barn, a stock and farm,
   And what more do they want,
   With sixty acres in one block
   With fifty chains in front?
   My house is built in the latest style
   And well finished out and in,
   With a heavy finishing around the eaves
   And a grand look-out in front.

3. My barn is built on the medium size
   With tiles of the best,
   And the tempest of the snow and rain
   From against my hay and grain.
   The doors are new and painted blue,
   The small ones in two halves,
   That I might close the lower half
   Against my pigs and calves.

4. I got horse and wagon, two bobsleighs,
   A harrow and a plow,
   A fattening pig and two runabouts

With five calves and a cow.
I have a bull, a famous beast,
Your very eyes would charm;
His search [i.e. *sire*] was bought away down east
I think from a well-stocked farm.

5. I got stove, pot, pans, a strainer can,
   A bucket, and a broom;
   Stove brush and towel, a looking glass,
   A rack and a fine tooth comb.
   When I get on my sporting suit,
   I'm quite a fancy chap,
   With my brand-new dress cloth overcoat
   And my fine south sealskin cap.

6. When I go to a ball or a party
   There's one thing makes me mad:
   The girls won't keep my company,
   They say my breath smells bad.
   I'll try in vain their hearts to gain,
   But they won't believe my life;
   So I'll take a stroll for the good of my soul
   And see my neighbor's wife.

Larry Gorman was not a big drinker, but he would drink and, what is more, he would occasionally get drunk. One night at a party, he was pretty full and went outside to get some fresh air. He passed out, and a little later some girls found him asleep under a hedge. They decided to play a joke on him. "Let's bury the beast alive," said one, and she grabbed a shovel and covered him over with dirt. It was a mistake. She forgot the old proverb, "If you eat with the devil, use a long-handled spoon," and she had leisure to discover that a short-handled spade was no substitute. Larry found out who she was, his memory supplied him with a few wisps of gossip (the girl had "gotten into trouble"), and his invention provided a fitting vehicle. He was even able to work in his much-married brother-in-law, Mick Monaghan, whom he detested. I don't know who "old Dunn" was. The following version is taken from a manuscript copy given me by Mrs. Harold Doyle of Campbellton, P.E.I.

Dame Bruin

1. One night as Dame Bruin she went to her bed
   She scarce had retired on her pillow
   When the Masculine voice, she heard close to her head
   Of Satan — That nasty old fellow,
   She spied old King Satan, so hairy and black
   With a long claw and foot, and a hump on his back
   Saying — Let you be sleeping or be you awake,
   You must rise, and come with me, Dame Bruin.

2. Poor Bruin arose with a terrible yell
   She asked — Is that you old King Satan?
   He says it is I — you know very well

And this long time for you I've been waiting.
Once to spare you — it was my intent,
But now I see plainly, you'll never repent
And now to take you I am fully bent.
So Hasten! Make ready — Dame Bruin.

3. Poor Bruin was now in a terrible stew
Her screams they were loud & alarming.
Oh spare me! Oh spare me! for one year or two
Until I have revenge upon Gorman.
With him I've had dealings, he thus did me wrong
He has hurt my feelings, and has made a song.
But I hope I shall catch him before very long
If you will but spare me, King Satan.

4. He says all your pleadings of no use shall be
To take you this long time I've intended.
But each time I came for you, you had some excuse.
But still you have never repented.
Your time is being up now a long time it's true.
This is the fourth time I have come for you
And out of sheer pity each time let you go.
But I'll spare you no longer Dame Bruin.

5. She says when I'm there — Shall I live by my trade?
Or shall I have a situation?
No, shovelling brimstone with a short handled spade,
He said shall be your occupation.
You will find nothing there but hardship and toil.
Fire, smoke, brimstone, and Kerosene oil,
And cold tar at your nose, shall so furiously boil.
I will not deceive you Dame Bruin.

6. She says to King Satan where I shall be there
I fear that I shall be lonesome
But as for the shovelling I don't at all care
To the same, I am quite well accustomed.
For I buried Gorman as you read in his song
And six years ago I have buried my young
If it had been proved for the same I'd been hung,
But no one could prove it, said Bruin.

7. He said if you handle your spade pretty fair
It will be a great deal in your favour
And I'll guarantee all the time you are there
That you never shall want for a Neighbor
And when you all get together you'll have glorious fun,
There'll be Monaghans, streals, yourself and Old Dunn.[5]
Each one with a club smashing brimstone
To keep you a 'shovelling Dame Bruin.

8. Now the next time I come, I'll have you to mind
By no one shall I be prevented
In order that you shall be easy to find,
My mark on your rump. I shall print it.
Before I come for you, I'll give the alarm.
Nine days before, there shall be a great [storm][6]
So Farewell for this time Dame Bruin.

Did Gorman write "Prince Edward Isle, Adieu"? In 1956 I thought he did, in 1957 I was sure he didn't, and now, while I still doubt his authorship, it is not a matter on which I stand foursquare or even threesquare. Before discussing its authorship, however, let us look first at its background and then at the song itself. The proprietors of the sixty-seven lots into which the Island of St. John was divided in 1767 were supposed to see to the settling of the land, but very few of them were interested in anything but a quick profit and almost none of them went to the Island to live. Thus the system brought with it all the evils of absentee landlordism. Many of the farmers who had made homes on the Island still felt that they owned their land and were rightfully resentful when rent collectors or land agents came around and took away what they had worked hard to gain. Oftentimes, of course, the agents themselves were manifestly unfair. There were many land riots, and the "land question" was a leading issue in election after election. It was not fully resolved until 1875, two years after Confederation, when the Compulsory Land Bill forced proprietors to sell their land to the Provincial Government, which in turn resold it to the tenants, often advancing them the money to pay for it.

Confederation itself is another point taken up in "Prince Edward Isle, Adieu." There was strong feeling on the Island against becoming part of the Dominion, much as there was in Newfoundland before 1948. But a coalition government in 1870 carried a measure authorizing the construction of a railroad that would ultimately run the whole length of the Island from Souris to Tignish. Public opinion was against the railway, yet work was begun right away. People began to worry that the province could not bear the financial burden of the railroad alone, and many who had been strong anti-confederationists now began to look to Confederation as economic salvation. Thus it was that in 1873, Prince Edward Island became part of Canada.

We can date the song, then, sometime between Confederation and the Compulsory Land Bill. The version I give here was sent to the Charlottetown *Guardian* by Mr. J. A. Gillies and was published in that paper on November 13, 1950. The tune I give was sung for me by Mrs. Frank Sweet of St. Eleanor's, P.E.I., but since almost every other tune I have collected for "Prince Edward Isle, Adieu" is almost identical to this one, we can safely say that this is *the* tune.

Prince Edward Isle, Adieu (I)

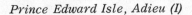

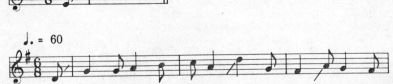

2. There is   a band all   in our land that moves in pomp and

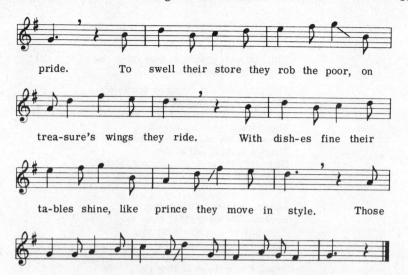

pride.   To   swell their store they rob the poor, on

trea-sure's wings they ride.   With dish-es fine their

ta-bles shine, like   prince they move in   style.   Those

are the knaves that made us slaves and sold Prince Ed-ward's Isle.

Prince Edward Isle, Adieu (II)

1. Come all ye hardy sons of toil
   Pray lend an ear to me
   Whilst I relate the dismal state
   Of this our country.
   I will not pause to name the cause
   But keep it close in view;
   For comrades grieve when they must leave
   And bid this Isle adieu.

2. There is a band within this land
   Who live in pomp and pride;
   To swell their store they rob the poor;
   On pleasures' wings they ride.
   With dishes fine their tables shine,
   They live in princely style.
   Those are the knaves who made us slaves,
   And sold Prince Edward Isle.

3. The Father's boy, his only joy,
   Must bid a sad farewell;
   They're parting here, no more to meet
   On earth, for who can tell.
   Far from this Isle, in prairies wild,
   In countries now that's new,
   Content they stay, and bless the day
   They bid this Isle adieu.

4. Our daughters fair, in deep despair,
   Must leave their native land;
   To foreign shores they're swiftly borne,

As I do understand.
The tide it flows, they all must go
There's nothing else to do!
While parents grieve as they must leave
And bid this Isle adieu.

5. Through want and care and scanty fare,
   The poor man drags along;
   He hears a whistle loud and shrill,
   The "Iron Horse" speeds on;
   He throws his pack upon his back,
   There's nothing left to do;
   He boards the train for Bangor, Maine,
   Prince Edward Isle adieu.

6. The reason why so many fly,
   And leave their Island home;
   Because 'tis clear, they can't stay here,
   For work to do there's none;
   In other climes there's better times,
   There can't be worse 'tis true;
   So weal or woe, away they go,
   Prince Edward Isle adieu.

7. In days of yore, from Scotland's shores
   Our fathers crossed the main;
   Tho dark and drear, they settled here
   To quit the "Tyrant's" chain;
   With hearts so stout, they put to rout
   The forest beasts so wild;
   Rough logs they cut, to build their huts
   Upon Prince Edward Isle.

8. With ax well ground, they levelled down
   The forest far and wide;
   With spade and hoe the seed they sowed,
   The plow was left untried;
   With sickle hooks they cut their stooks,
   No "Buckeyes" were in style;
   They spent their days — their ashes lay
   Upon Prince Edward Isle.

9. The place was new, the roads were few,
   The people lived content,
   The landlords came, their fields to claim;
   Each settler must pay rent.
   So now you see, the turning tide
   That drove us to exile,
   Begin again to cross the main,
   And leave Prince Edward Isle.

10. But changes great have come of late,
    And brought some curious things;
    Dominion men have brought us in,
    The Isle with railways ring;
    There's maps and charts, and towns apart,
    And tramps of every style;
    There's doctors mute and lawyers cute,
    Upon Prince Edward Isle.

11. There's judges too, who find a clue
    To all the merchants' bills;
    There's school trustees, who want no fees
    For using all their skill;
    There's law for dogs, for geese, for hogs,
    At this pray do not smile,
    For changes great have come of late,
    Upon Prince Edward Isle.

12. So here's success to all who press
    The question of Free Trade;
    Join hand in hand, our cause is grand;
    They're plainly in the shade.
    The mainland route, the world throughout;
    Take courage now, stand true,
    My verse is run, my song is done,
    Prince Edward Isle adieu.

When Mr. Gillies had this song published in the *Guardian*, he said he did not know who wrote it, and for about a month after that the paper was full of letters claiming that Larry Gorman wrote it, that he didn't write it, that Larry Doyle of St. Peters wrote it — claim and counter-claim, but nothing was really decided. For every person who has told me Larry Gorman wrote it there has been another to say that he didn't. Around the Campbellton-Lot Seven area several people told me that the song was written by one Fitzgerald, the first schoolteacher in Camp-bellton. Yet Billy Bell, of Brewer, Maine, says that he has talked to Larry about that particular piece and asked him questions about specific things he said in it; he can even recall having seen a broadside of the song with Larry's name on it. And Joe MacDougall of Alberton, P.E.I., told Helen Creighton that he used to visit Larry Gorman when he lived in Brewer and got a lot of songs from him (many of them on printed broadsides). "*I remember one that I learned from him himself," he said. "It was 'Prince Edward's Isle Adieu.' He made that one here." Obviously the ascriptive evidence is just plain contradictory, but there the matter stands. We probably never will be sure who wrote the song. There is nothing in the style that would gainsay Gorman's authorship. If I have a reason for doubting it, it is that the subject is not the sort that Larry was likely to handle. His satire was usually personal, directed at individuals; it was occasionally social, dealing with the foibles of women, for example; but it was never political, and "Prince Edward Isle, Adieu" is basically political, dealing with a much larger issue than Gorman ever tried to handle.

Just when Larry left Prince Edward Island never to return we do not know, but it appears to have been in the early or mid-eighties, when he was between the ages of, say, thirty-five and forty. Why did he leave for good? We have the story from several sources that he *had* to leave because of a song he had made, "The Gull Decoy" usually being named as the song. It is perfectly possible that there came a time when he found it the better part of valor not to cross Northumberland

Strait to the eastward again, but we have no reason to believe that any
one song was to blame. The reasons were more likely economic.
Larry had been travelling back and forth from the Island to the Miramichi woods for many years. Probably, he was lured to Maine by the
better wages he could make there; and once there, he certainly would
have found it much more difficult to return to the Island in the summers. Also, he probably found that in the summers he could make
more money in Maine as a mill-hand than he could have as a fisherman
or a farmer back on P.E.I., where fifty cents was a good day's pay.
Further, he had no proper home on the Island, and he had had a falling-
out with his brother James. Reasons enough for not returning. But
who can tell — perhaps Larry *had* caught a whiff of tar and feathers.

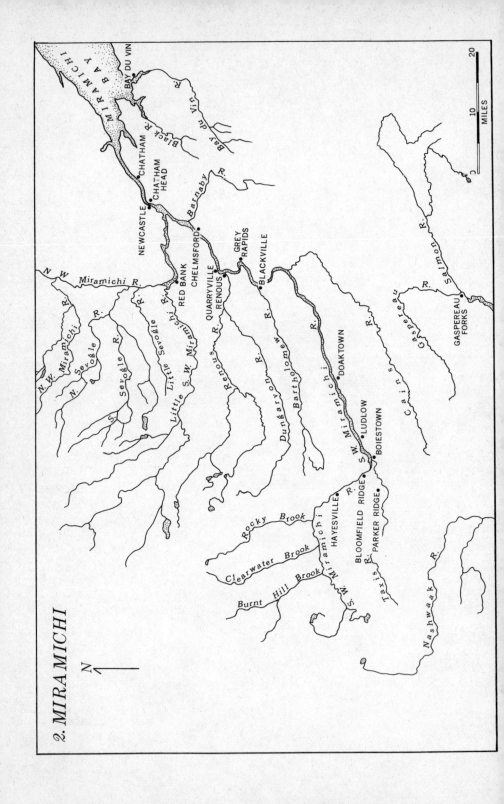

2. *MIRAMICHI*

FOUR

"And Came to Miramichi"

"Miramichi: From Doon and Shannon, from Clyde and Dee, they spread their poverty over the rich acres. They sowed their children broadcast upon the untested soil." So reads the inscription on Lord Beaverbrook's memorial to the Miramichi pioneers that stands in the town square of Newcastle, the once-important lumber port and shipbuilding center located just below the junction of the two main branches of that great river.

And it is a great river, by far the largest river lying entirely within the province of New Brunswick. With its many branches and tributaries, it drains the whole central portion of the province: the Northwest Miramichi, with its main branch, the Sevogle, comes down from the north and is joined by the Little Southwest Miramichi at Red Bank, and from here it flows east until it comes to Wilson's Point, where it joins the main southwest branch. The "Sou'west" is the largest and most important of the branches; it stretches all the way across the province, until its headwaters almost touch the St. John and the Tobique. It comes down through the great central wilderness, picking up the water of many feeders as it flows eastward and then southward to Boiestown, a settlement which in the year 1830 had (according to Cooney) two sawmills, one gristmill, one forge, one washing mill, and "one respectable hotel" (which was probably not Duffy's).

Just below this town the river passes the little cemetery where Peter Emberly is buried, that young Island boy the story of whose untimely death in 1881 was made into a song that is still sung all over the Northeast:

Nearby the city of Boiestown
My mouldering bones do lay,
Awaiting for the Saviour's call
On that great Judgment Day.

At Boiestown (or, to be more accurate, just above Hayesville) the
river changes from a rough, narrow, wilderness stream to a smooth,
wide river in a gentle, broad, well-settled valley. In its northeasterly
journey of some sixty miles it picks up several more sizeable tributaries before it joins the "Nor'west" at Wilson's Point and the two
rivers flow past Newcastle and Chatham into a wide bay; then, beyond
the line of islands at its mouth, the Miramichi joins the Gulf of St.
Lawrence and the Atlantic Ocean.

Miramichi (as the whole region is called) has a long tradition. In
the seventeenth century it was part of the great seigneury of Nicholas
Denys, and we know that there were Acadian settlements there. One on
Beaubair's Island was practically wiped out by scurvy and famine in
the winter of 1757-58, and many of the survivors fled after the fall of
Louisburg in June of 1758. The first English-speaking settler was that
enterprising Scot, William Davidson, who came here in 1765 and began
to export fish, furs, hides, and, of course, masts and spars for His
Britannic Majesty's dockyards. Soon the lumber industry began to
boom, or, as that florid historian Robert Cooney put it, "Like the opening blossom that gradually discloses its sweets, and unfolds its beau-
ties, the latent resources of Miramichi now began to germinate."[1] At
Davidson's death in 1790, Messrs. Fraser and Thom took over the
main part of the lumber trade, and in 1792 they sent out two ships, the
Friends Adventure and the *Blackitt,* containing the first great square
timber ever to be exported from Miramichi. Very early the lumberwoods began to claim its own, for one of the inscriptions on a poor
grave on Wilson's Point (it is now a Provincial Park known as The En-
closure) reads, "In Memory of/ Donald Munro he/ died by the fall of a
tree/ in Febr. 1804." The population swelled as wave after wave of
Scotch, English, and Irish came to work in the woods and in the small
but promising shipyards in such towns as Newcastle and Chatham.
Everything was coming along beautifully until the dry fall of 1825
brought the horror of the Great Fire.

There were fires all through the Northeast that fall, but the "Miramichi Fire" was certainly the worst of them. Even Cooney, no slouch
when it came to bogging a metaphor, felt inadequate to the situation;
living about a mile from Newcastle at the time, he described the fire in
part thus:

The earth seemed to stagger as if it had reeled from its ancient foundations. The
harmony of creation appeared to have been deranged; and about to revert into
original chaos. *Earth, Air, Sea,* and *Sky;* all visible creation seemed to conspire
against man; and to totter under the weight of some dreadful commission they
were charged to execute. The river, tortured into violence by the hurricane,
foamed with rage and flung its boiling spray upon the land. The thunder pealed
along the vault of Heaven; the lightening rent the firmament in pieces. For a

moment all was still, a deep and awful silence reigned over everything. All nature appeared to be *hushed* into *dumbness;* — when — suddenly a lengthened and sullen roar came booming through the forest, and driving a thousand massive and devouring flames before it. Then Newcastle, and Douglastown, and the whole Northern side of the river, extending from Bartibog to the Nashwaak, a distance of more than 100 miles in length, became enveloped in an immense sheet of flame, that spread over nearly 6,000 square miles.[2]

And the ballad commemorating the fire is still part of the repertoire of singers from Prince Edward Island to Maine.

The fire ended the masting trade, but in its wake came the great shipbuilding era; hundreds upon hundreds of ships came down the ways in Newcastle and Chatham in the yards of such firms as Johnson and Mackie and Gilmour, Rankin and Co. Louise Manny has discovered records of over five hundred of these ships with such evocative names as *Sword Fish, Indian Queen, Annie Laurie, Knight of Snowdoun,* and *Royal Arch.*[3]

The lumber industry had its great development during the era of wooden ships and lasted well beyond it down into the early twentieth century. The work pattern was about the same in Miramichi as it was in Maine. In the fall the men would go into the woods — not only local men but men from Prince Edward Island, Newfoundland, Nova Scotia, Maine, and, of course, from all over New Brunswick. They would work until late March or April, the choppers and sawyers bringing the tall spruce down, the teamsters hauling the long logs off to temporary gathering places or yards, where another crew piled the logs on great "two-sleds" (a sled with two sets of runners — one under each end of the load of logs) and hauled them off to the landings on the edges of the nearest drivable stream. Then in April or May the driving crews would begin their work. They would break up the landings, rolling the logs in and following them downstream, working hard with peaveys and pickpoles to keep them from jamming. Should a jam form, someone would have to take a crew and work it loose, hoping that when it broke they would all make it to shore alive, for a man stood little chance if he fell into that grinding mass of huge sawlogs. If he didn't make it, the best he could hope for was that whatever was left of him after the river had done its work would by some chance get a decent burial, but probably he would never even be found. Still the drives came down, Death always the extra man in the crew — down Fifteenmile, Burnt Hill and Clearwater, down The Sisters and Rocky Brook, and then down the main "Sou'west" to Hayes' Bar above Hayesville. Here all the individual operators turned their drives over to "The Corporation," which took the whole works down to the head of tide just below Quarryville, picking up other drives as they came out of the rivers along the way: the Cains, the Bartholomew, and the Renous (with its tributary, the Dungarvon). At "The Old Squaw," the Southwest Boom Company took the drive over. The boom itself, a great chain of logs strung end to end, within which the loose logs from the drive are confined, stretched for miles along the south bank of the river down to about where

Chelmsford is today, and the company's job was to keep it full and working. At the sorting gaps, boom crews separated logs according to their owner's marks, rafted them together, and staked out the rafts for the mill crews to take over and tow downriver. It was a long drive with a long history; the boom was still at work in 1957, though the drive brought down only a few million board feet of logs. Since 1958 there has been no drive at all.

When Larry Gorman began travelling over to the mainland I do not know, but it is very likely he began his life as a woodsman in his late teens, that is to say, sometime around 1863 or 1865. That was about the age when many boys like Larry would have started working in the woods, and, further, the American Civil War made a vacuum in the Maine woods which was filled by men from the provinces. It may be that Larry made his first trip to Maine at this time, but work would have been easy to get anywhere, and our first traces of Gorman on the mainland occur in Miramichi.

Boys from the west end of the Island usually caught a ride on a fishing schooner across to Richibucto or Miramichi. Our first record of Gorman that can be called a record at all is one of his songs, "The Winter of Seventy-Three," which tells of his leaving the Island and coming to Chatham, where he found work in Jabez Snowball's sawmill and lived in a boarding house in the area still known as "Sawdust Hill." But soon the mill shut down, and Larry headed upriver to Indiantown (present-day Quarryville). From here, portage teams used to go back in to the woods camps along the Little Southwest, the Renous, the Dungarvon, and the upper main Southwest; Larry met up with one of these teams and — but the song tells its own story. The version I give here was sung by Nick Underhill of Northwest Bridge, New Brunswick. Nick learned the song as a very young man while he was tending skidway in the woods for Arthur Underhill on Underwood Brook, a tributary of the Dungarvon. "*That's where I learned 'The Winter of Seventy-Three,'" Nick said. "Elderly man there, Hughie Dickison, I would take to be around about my age now, sixty, and he used to sing it...and he knew Gorman personally, he told me, when he was around Blackville... He said, 'I learnt that song from him; I knew him personally, Larry Gorman.'"

The Winter of Seventy-Three

♩.= approx. 50 *parlando-rubato*

1. It   be-ing ear-ly in   Sep-tem - ber in eight-een se-ven-

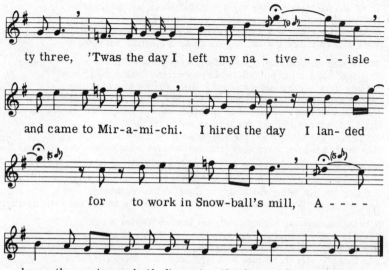

ty three, 'Twas the day I left my na - tive - - - - isle

and came to Mir-a-mi-chi. I hired the day I lan- ded

for to work in Snow-ball's mill, A - - - -

large three sto -ry buil-ding at the foot of Saw -dust Hill.

The Winter of Seventy-Three

1. It being early in September in eighteen seventy-three,
   'Twas the day I left my native isle and came to Miramichi;
   I hired the day I landed for to work in Snowball's mill,
   A large three-story building at the foot of Sawdust Hill.

2. I worked away for three long weeks with a discontented will,
   But I soon made my acquaintance with the folks of Sawdust Hill;
   On the tenth day of November when the mill it did shut down,
   Which caused a general scatter and the men go walking 'round.
   I heard of those who wanted men, and it put me in good cheer,[4]
   And I packed my kennebecker[5] and for Indiantown did steer.

3. When I arrived at Indiantown being quite fatigued from tramp,
   I fell in with two portage teams[6] bound for McCullam camp;
   They said that I might ride with them, that's if I did desire,
   And that if I would come along, they thought I would get hired.

4. Oh I rode with Willy Derringham, a verse for him I'll make;
   He drove a team of ro-uns [i.e. *roans*] that he brought from the Grand Lake.
   The horse he weighed twelve hundred pounds, a noble beast to haul,
   And the mare she was a beauty, although she was but small.

5. Now I being at my journey's end, and hungry, tired, and cold,
   The face of Billy O'Brien was the first I did behold;
   And so glad was I to see him, and I asked who was the boss;
   He pointed to a little man whose name was Charlie Cross.

6. So I hired the next morning and concluded for to stop;
   Along with Joseph Fullyerton they sent me for to chop.
   Charlie Cross and Guy McCullam they both cruised the woods all round,
   And thought they might do better down in MacIneary's Ground.

7. So we all packed up quite early and that place we did forsake,
   And moved out to another camp situated by a lake;
   Along with Archie Woodworth there, a silly young gaw-gaw,
   They placed me on the landing for to haul a cross-cut saw.

8. There was one big Island man along among the rest,
   Two feet across the shoulders, in proportion 'round the breast;
   He was very big but not awful cute, Jim Whelan was his name;
   On the second of March he cut his foot and he marched off downstream.
   He took with him five pound of gum [i.e. *spruce gum*] their favors for to gain
   But all the thanks he got for it, they said that he was green.
   He blowed the roost upon me and he said I'd made a song,
   And proved me out a traiteer [i.e. *traitor*] for which many the man was hung.

9. Now we being there and set to work, good lumber which we found.
   The spruce they stood in bunches, they were handsome, stout, and sound;
   But Guy not yet being satisfied, at Charlie Cross did say,
   And he says, "We must forsake this place, there's no use for two-sleighs."

10. It being on our way a-going out past Barney Taylor's camp,
    I fell in with Patrick McLaughlin and I hired for to swamp;
    For to work for Patrick McLaughlin, 'tis very hard they say,
    For there's only three men to a team and they drive ten turns[7] a day.

11. So now the crowd has all gone out and I'm left to watch the camp,
    And the martins and the lucifees [i.e. *loup-cervier*] go skipping o'er
       the swamp;
    The cruel winter is over and thank God I'm still alive,
    And if the weather proves favorable I mean to stay up and drive.

12. So now to conclude and finish as my ballad I must end,
    I hope I have said nothing wrong to those shantyboys offend;
    When those logs are in the Southwest Boom I hope youse all to see;
    Some will go to Andy Conners' and have a glorious spree.

Several people have suggested that this song commemorates Gorman's
first trip to Miramichi, and they may, of course, be right. Notice,
however, that he does not claim this as his first trip, and the song
seems to be by a man who already knew something about the region.
Further, it is unlikely that Gorman waited until he was twenty-seven to
make his first trip into the woods. Nor can we interpret this song as a
celebration of his *final* break with the Island either, since, as we have
seen, there is ample evidence that he was on the Island at different
times *after* this date. "The Winter of Seventy-Three" tells of one of
Gorman's trips to Miramichi from his "native island" but there is no
certainty that it was either his first or his last.

His fame spread rapidly in Miramichi. Louise Manny tells the
story of his going to work for Hutchison; evidently the men had not
been paid, and Larry had just made up a verse celebrating that fact at
the expense of Richard Hutchison. One evening in camp he sang it:

> Here's young Hutch,
> He don't say much,
> But tells us to keep sober,
> We'll get our money by and by,
> When these hard times is over.

What he had not noticed was that his victim, "whose temper," as Miss Manny says, "is still a Miramichi tradition," was standing right behind him. All were waiting for Larry's annihilation, but Hutchison was intelligent enough to realize that there were few things more dangerous than Gorman wounded, so all he said was, "That's a good song, Larry! D'you know any more?" [8]

Not everyone had Hutchison's perspicacity. Larry made up a song about two fellows who took an obvious woodsman's revenge on him; they met him at a place called The Devil's Back (up the Renous River) and beat him up. Within a few days, there was a song going round about two ruffians who had beaten Larry Gorman on The Devil's Back. It was worse than the first one, and presumably the third song would have been worse yet, but evidently the men had learned their lesson.

Silas Curtis of Blackville told me the following story:

One time Larry was going up along the Nor'west on his way into the woods. He stopped at a house to see if he couldn't get put up for the night. The woman said no she couldn't put him up at all. "Well," Larry wanted to know, "would you give me something to eat?" She thought a long time about that before she finally said yes, she'd feed him, and she gave him a bite in the kitchen. They talked a little and in the course of things she asked him his name. And he told her. "Oh," she said, "I've heard of you. You're the man who makes the songs. Now look," she said, "will you do something for me?"

"What's that?" asked Gorman.

"Well, my husband died not long ago and I haven't got a verse for his tombstone."

"Oh," said Larry, "I could make one all right. What was his name?"

"Teazle," she said.

So Larry began:

"Mr. Teazle died of late,
Just arrived at Heaven's gate —"

"Oh that's fine, fine," said Mrs. Teazle.

"Well," said Larry, "that's all I'm going to make now, but if you'll put me up for the night I'll finish it in the morning, before I leave."

So she put him up for the night. And the next morning she gave him breakfast. She didn't say anything about the verse during breakfast, but just as he got ready to leave she mentioned it to him.

"Oh, yes," he said. "I'll finish it up now. Let's see, how did I start it?

Mr. Teazle died of late —"

"Yes?"

"Just arrived at Heaven's gate —"

"Yes, yes?"

"Along came Satan just like a weasel
And down to Hell he dragged old Teazle."

Then Larry left. [9]

Whether or not "Morris Ellsworth" is by Larry Gorman is still an open question. In 1949, Louise Manny thought it was his and included it in her article on Gorman. [10] Now she has changed her mind. I have heard it credited to him, but that is a slender reed indeed. All I can do is give the song as I heard it and point out that there is nothing in the style of the piece that can bar it from the Gorman canon. The subject of the song, Morris Ellsworth (or Ellworth, as I have heard it on the Island), came from up above Waterford on the west end of P.E.I., and it is quite possible that Larry knew him from there. In the song, he makes him the type of the poor, scared, green jack, the sort of Island boy that immortal Miramichi River foreman meant when, as a jam got ready to haul, he bawled out, "Green hands ashore! Island men up a tree!"

Morris Ellsworth

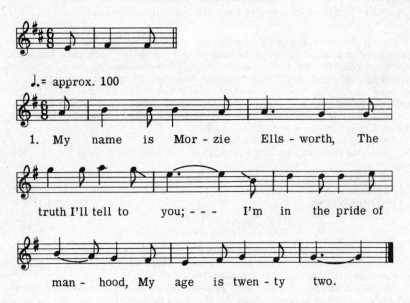

1. My name is Mor - zie Ells - worth, The truth I'll tell to you; - - - I'm in the pride of man - hood, My age is twen - ty two.

Morris Ellsworth

1. My name is Morzie Ellsworth,
   The truth I'll tell to you;
   I'm in the pride of manhood,
   My age is twenty-two.

2. I left the darling of my heart
   On that fair Island shore;
   Here's adieu to my aged parents
   I never will see them more.

3. On the fourteenth of October,
   Our vessel put to sea
   For the Province of New Brunswick
   And the port of Miramichi.

4. We landed in Newcastle,
   In the lumberman's rendezvous,
   And hired there with McIneer
   To join his winter crew.

5. The wages being three pounds a month,
   On that we did agree —
   My time it being to serve him
   Was six months faithfully.

6. He gave to me a sheathing belt, [i.e. *sheath and belt*]
   Likewise a bowie knife,
   A battle axe and carabine,
   For to defend my life.

7. Oh, woe be on the morning
   When I did undertake
   A voyage into the forest
   For gold and riches' sake.

8. A voyage into the forest,
   Just at the break of day;
   I found myself surrounded
   By birds and beasts of prey.

9. There's the lynx, the mink, the dingbat,
   And the roving caribou;
   The muskrat and the otter,
   The savage owl there too.

10. There's the celebrated rabbit
    From the polar regions came,
    And many other animals
    Too numerous to name.

11. 'Twould fill your flowing ebb of life
    And your heart's blood run cold
    To see the work of nature
    Done by the mink and mole.

12. 'Twould fill your flowing ebb of life
    And your heart terrify,
    To see the wicked robins
    That through the forest fly.

13. But if I live through this winter,
    All danger do survive,
    There's a harder job ahead of me,
    I've got to stop and drive.

14. To see those tall and scraggy rocks
    All on that eastbound shore,
    Where rippling waters loudly press
    And cataracts do roar.

Louise Manny says that some singers, notable among them the late Traven Aitken, Lord Beaverbrook's brother, used to sing this song as part of "Peter Emberly." That this confusion easily could have come about is made clear by looking at the first three stanzas of a copy of "Morris Ellsworth" printed in 1888:

Farewell Prince Edward Island,
Farewell ye purling streams
Where all my childhood's days I've spent
Does now appear in dreams.
All nature has lost its charms for me
Since I am doomed to roam
Into this land of slaver-ee
Far from my native home.

Farewell warbling songsters,
All in the hawthorn trees
To greet each early morn
All in the twilight breeze.
Thoughts of your music make me sad
Since I can find no rest,
While in this land of tyranny
In bondage I'm oppressed.

Farewell my aged father
My honored mother too,
My sisters and my brothers,
To you I bid adieu.
Fond memory recalls to mind
Those happy scenes of yore,
Beneath that old paternal roof
Which I behold no more.

Oh the 14th of October, etc....[11]

The satire then gets broader and broader as the song goes on, but
compare the three stanzas quoted above with three stanzas from a
typical version of "Peter Emberly":

Farewell unto my dearest friend
I mean my mother dear
She reared a son that fell as soon
As he left her tender care
Little did my mother think
When she sang sweet lullaby
What country I might travel in
Or what death I might die

Farewell unto my father too
It was him that drove me here
I thought him very cruel
His treatments were severe
It is not right to press a boy
Or try to keep him down
It will oft times drive him from his home
When he is far too young

Farewell to Prince Edward's Island
That garden in the sea
No more I'll walk its flowery banks
To enjoy a summer breeze
No more I'll watch those gallant barques
As they go sailing by
With their streamers floating in the air
Above their main masts high

This is as good a place as any to scotch once more the idea that Larry Gorman *wrote* "Peter Emberly," although Doerflinger has already told the story of how that song came to be written by John Calhoun.[12] It was quite natural, as he points out, that this song about a boy from "Prince Edward's Island" would get into the Gorman canon, especially in Maine, where Gorman was well known and Calhoun was not. But there seems to be more to it. For example, according to Irving Frost, who had worked for years along the Union River in Maine, when Larry was asked where he was from he would answer,

> I belong to Prince Edward's Island,
> That garden in the sea;
> No more I'll walk its flowery banks
> Nor enjoy its summer breeze.

This verse is an adaptation of one of the stanzas of "Peter Emberly." Of course, Gorman was not saying that he wrote the song, but this does show one way in which the song became associated with his name. Also, we have just seen that on the Miramichi "Peter Emberly" and "Morris Ellsworth" were sometimes sung as one song, which certainly helped to compound the confusion. Further, when Jim Lynch and his friend took their red-eye over to South Brewer to listen to Larry sing, one of the songs he sang was "Peter Emberly."[13] Lynch showed some surprise, saying that he had always heard that John Calhoun wrote that song. Larry got very annoyed and said that Calhoun was a goddamned liar; *he* wrote that song, although Calhoun was in the same camp at the time. In fact, Larry went on, Peter's mother had put a curse on him for making that song. If Larry did say that, there is more red-eye than truth in it, because his nephew, John O'Connor, recalls Larry telling him that he did *not* make up that song. "Some people say I did," he said, "but I didn't."

We come now to what many people, including me, consider just about the best song Larry Gorman ever wrote, "The Scow on Cowden Shore." The general circumstances are clear enough: Larry was working for the Southwest Boom Company.[14] But why "Cowden," and what was the "scow"? Cowden had a farm on the south side of the river just about eleven miles up from the Newcastle bridge. I have stood on his old shorefront there, and the fact that it was well inside the boom and about a mile-and-a-half above the boom-house and sorting gaps first led me to believe that when he wrote the song, Larry was working with a crew on a rock scow, repairing the old cribwork "blocks" that helped the boom hold in the logs.[15] Further investigation has shown me that I was probably wrong. I have it from two different sources that the old Southwest Boom ended just about at Cowden's farm. There was no boom-house then and the crew slept in a tremendous scow that was anchored offshore and outside the boom. After the company extended the boom downriver and built the boom-house, the scow was no longer needed.

Nick Underhill's uncle, Thomas Vickers, had worked on the boom
with Gorman, "*and he said he was a self-styled man," said Nick. "He
said he didn't go to no entertainments or nothing, circus or anything;
he didn't approve of that at all. He was more of a man to stay by himself, quiet man, but he seen *everything* that was going on." If he didn't
see everything, he saw plenty, and he has left us an incomparable picture of life around the boom. The significance of much of the local
allusion in this song is irretrievably lost now, but the life of the piece
is still there. There are supposed to be some thirty or more stanzas
in all, but no one to my knowledge knew more stanzas of it than the late
Fred McMahon of Chatham, whose version follows as it was recorded
by Louise Manny for the Beaverbrook Collection. He gives us Dan
Brown with his triple problem of wine, women, and song; he gives us
Whinny Gillis who, as one man said, "had a little place just up the
road"; and, best of all, he gives us Larry Gorman himself in a realistic
self-appraisal — cocksure, playfully arrogant, with all the pride of a
poet in his craft and power.

The Scow on Cowden Shore

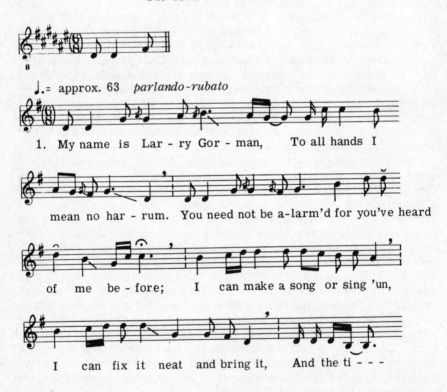

1. My name is Lar - ry Gor - man, To all hands I
mean no har - rum. You need not be a-larm'd for you've heard
of me be - fore; I can make a song or sing 'un,
I can fix it neat and bring it, And the ti - - -

tle that I'll give it is "The Scow on Cow - den Shore.

The Scow on Cowden Shore

1. My name is Larry Gorman, to all hands I mean no harm;
   You need not be alarmed for you've heard of me before;
   I can make a song or sing 'un, I can fix it neat and bring it,
   And the title that I'll give it is "The Scow on Cowden Shore."

2. I have got many's the foe and the same I do know,
   So amongst them all I go, and it grieves their hearts full sore;
   For I know that they could shoot me, cremenate [?] or prosecute me,
   But they kindly salute me round the scow on Cowden shore.

3. There was men from many places, of many different races,
   With pale and swarthy faces, I cannot name them o'er;
   Island men and Restigouchers, there's Nashwaakers and Pugmooshers,
   All assembled here together round the scow on Cowden shore.

4. There was men from Oromocta, some more from Rooshibucta,
   From Fredericton town and Bathurst, and MacDonalds from Bras D'Or;
   There's night ramps and gallivanters, there's swift runners and
       rafcanters [?]
   All work for daily wages round the scow on Cowden shore.

5. There was the two young Joyces with their unhuman voices,
   Kept making peculiar noises till their throats got quite sore;
   Oh for Indian Devil, they would be far more civil
   Than those uncultivated rubbage round the scow on Cowden shore.

6. There was the Widow Whinny, she sold ale and cokaninny,
   To get the poor fool's penny she sold apples by the score;
   She sold whiskey, gin and fly beer, some odd porter, ale, and cider,
   Which made them whoop and stagger round the scow in Cowden shore.

7. Dan Brown and Bill Buggy, one night got very groggy,
   The night being dark and foggy and we heard a teejus roar,
   They were some intoxicated, and get somewhat agitated,
   All hands they did upright it round the scow on Cowden shore.

8. Dan Brown, when he begins, he's a curious little man, oh,
   He'll study and he'll plan 'till he gets to Whinny's door;
   On he'll drink beer and whiskey, until he gets pretty frisky,
   And then he'll turn quite sozzy to the scow on Cowden shore.

9. Dan Brown's a splendid singer and in dances he will swing her
   He'll bring to her good tidings of a new bank bill or more;
   Oh, she'll laugh and she'll be funny, when she knows he's got the money,
   She'll call him her darling honey from the scow on Cowden shore.

10. "The True Lover's Discussion," is once more brought in fashion,
    She'll keep quietly hugging, while he sings it o'er and o'er;
    For his voice is so melodious, that the ladies they'll join in chorus
    And their echoes all sing o'er us round the scow on Cowden shore.

11. Dan Brown and Johnny Leighton on the women they go a-waiting,
    They go out on a Sunday with Miss Vickers and Kate Poor;
    It's all to gain insight for all hands they mean to invite
    You're welcome to a clean by [?] round the scow on Cowden shore.

12. Some of the blokes spend good few dollars in fine shirts and paper collars,
    And in good whiskey wallers til they fight and get them tore;
    Oh they'll fight and they will wrangle and each other they'll badly mangle,
    They're called hard men to handle from the scow on Cowden shore.

13. Oh some they go a-courting while others they go a-sporting,
    They go into a circus to view scenes of days gone o'er;
    In the like I take no pleasure, so I sit down at my leisure,
    And I daily take their measure from the scow on Cowden shore.

14. So now my song is ended and I hope no-one is offended
    The like I never intended and your pardon I'll implore;
    So you humble, mild, and witty, I pray on me take pity,
    And join me humble ditty from the scow on Cowden shore.

Sometime in the mid-seventies Gorman moved further upriver. He evidently settled in Renous for a while where (when he wasn't in the woods) he lived and worked at Patrick McLaughlin's place. Later he moved to Blackville, where he lumbered for Hugh Underwood and, when in town, stayed in the men's quarters out behind Underwood's house. I talked to no one in Blackville who could actually remember seeing Gorman around town but plenty of people remember hearing their parents and neighbors speak of him. Hugh Underwood's son (over eighty when I spoke to him) remembered his father laughing and joking about different things Larry had said or done, but he added that the general opinion seemed to be that "Gorman was sort of a useless fellow, pretty raggedy, and not much given to work of any kind."

What prompted Gorman to write the next song, "Mary Mahoney," is not known. The "Archie" of this song is supposed to be (and probably is) the "silly young gaw-gaw," Archie Woodworth, mentioned in "The Winter of Seventy-Three." But several people have doubted Gorman's authorship on stylistic grounds ("It just doesn't *sound* like him!"), and certainly it is much more of a straight narrative than is his typical product. Still, Larry could well have written this story of the young man who could not tell oroide from real gold and the sharp-eyed servant girl who could. Many people along the Miramichi attribute it to him, but since Louise Manny has often played it on her radio program and ascribed it to Gorman, such evidence is anything but reliable. However, my sixth sense tells me that this song is vintage Gorman, and I'm leaving it at that. Here it is as it was recorded by Louise Manny for the Beaverbrook Collection from the singing of Thomas W. Coughlan of the South Nelson Road:

Mary Mahoney

♩.= approx. 104 *parlando-rubato*

1. Come all you jol-ly lum-ber-men and lis-ten un-to

me. I'll sing you of a pret-ty fair maid that

lived in Mir-a-mi-chi. Her name was Ma-ry Ma - ho-

ny, a sweet and come -lye maid, And the heart

of ma-ny's the lum- ber-man I'm told she has be-trayed.

Mary Mahoney

1. Come all you jolly lumbermen and listen unto me,
   I'll sing you of a pretty fair maid that lived in Miramichi;
   Her name was Mary Mahoney, a sweet and comely maid,
   And the heart of many's the lumberman I'm told she has betrayed.

2. This brisk young youth mere for a cruise came down to Indiantown[16]
   And he fell in love with this fair maid as soon as he came down.
   To start a conversation he thought it not amiss,
   He stepped up to this fair maid, saying, "How do you do, miss,"
   She said, "Young man do go away, don't irritate me so,
   For I'd only fool my time away if I would talk to you."

3. Poor Archie has retired to rest, he lay upon the clothes,
   His heart it beat like lightning fleet, he could find no repose,
   His heart it beat like lighting fleet as he rolled from side to side,
   Sayin' "That girl I wished I never saw, since she'll not be my bride."

4. He arose by day next morning, downstairs did nimbly creep,
   His landlady accosted him: "Young man how did you sleep?"
   "I did not sleep, dear madam," he said, "for love torments me so,
   And I am afraid your servant maid will prove my overthrow."

5. His landlady she laughed at him and looked at him for shame,
   Saying, "If you want to gain her heart, I'll put you on a scheme,"
   She packed him up for Newcastle, and what did he buy there
   But five dollars worth of jew-la-ree to gain this lady fair.

6. He packed up all his jewelry, for Indiantown did steer,
   Gay gold rings like wide tear drops he purchased for his dear,
   This fair maid was soon to know and to her sad surprise,
   After wearing them a day or two found they were or-i-eyed.

7. She quickly flew into a rage, saying, "What a lie you told,
   It's when you bought those rings for me you said they was pure gold;
   You need not come from Fredericton to tell me such a lie,
   Or buy me rings for pure, pure gold when they were or-i-eyed."

8. Now come all you jolly lumbermen and listen unto me,
   Before you go a-courting be a judge of jewelry,
   Have it examined carefully, see that it lifts a hair
   Or else you'll never gain the heart of any lady fair.

Up and down the river in the seventies and eighties there travelled a little stern-wheel passenger boat, the *Andover;* one day she'd travel up to Red Bank on the Northwest, the next day she'd go up the Southwest. The local blades had a song they used to sing about it, a parody of a popular tune:

> The *Andover* came to Bay du Vin,
> Good bye, my lover, good bye;
> She certainly took the passengers in,
> Good bye, my lover, good bye.

By no stretch of the imagination could it be called a romantic craft, but Larry worked it into one of his most "romantic" songs, "Young Billy Crane." According to Herbert Hinchey, he made up this song in 1877 about a Blackville girl who had had an unfortunate affair. Larry may have had some more or less tangled personal motives for deciding to "song" this girl, since, some years later, he speaks of her in a letter as "my old girl," but perhaps we shouldn't read too much into that remark. [17] For his model, Larry took the well-known come-all-ye pattern in which a girl dons men's clothing to follow her lover;[18] then he kidded the corners off it. The language is highfalutin romantical, and the devices are standard: "Cubit's chain," "admired by earls and squires," "skin milk-white," etc. And now that she has been betrayed, she'll dress herself "in man's attire" and go on board "some gallant ship." Then in "that great ark" she'll sail until she gains her lover, who has gone not to "India's burning sands" or "the wars of Germany," but on board the little *Andover* as it butts its way up and down the Miramichi.

Young Billy Crane[19]

♩ = approx. 100

1. Ye gods of love, look from a-bove on a

bro-ken heart-ed maid Who

by false Cu-bit's burn-ing flames and

dart that I'm be-trayed. I am

left be-hind with a heart con-fined, bound

down in Cu-bit's chain, All

by a thought-less young man whose

name was Bil-ly Crane.

Variants:

Young Billy Crane

1. Ye gods of love, look from above on a broken hearted maid,
   Who by false Cubit's burning flames and dart that I'm betrayed.
   I am left behind with a heart confined, bound down in Cubit's chain,
   All by a thoughtless young man whose name was Billy Crane.

2. My name is Nellie Harrison; the truth I'll tell to you.
   I'm in the prime of womanhood, just turning twenty-two.
   I've been admired by earls and squires and many's the lovesick swain,
   But 'twas beyond their art to gain my heart till I met young Billy Crane.

3. Now the lad that I love dearly, he's of a medium size.
   His hair is light, his skin milk-white, two dark and rolling eyes.
   He dresses neat from top to feet, speaks elegant and plain,
   And many's the maid he has betrayed, that false young Billy Crane.

4. The last time that my love was here, 'twas twelve o'clock at night.
   The wind was still, the sky was clear, each star was shining bright.
   He came to my bed window, tapped lightly on the pane.
   I soon arose, put on my clothes, let in false Billy Crane.

5. What passed within our room that night I never mean to say.
   We kissed and hugged and talked of love until the break of day.
   He promised he would marry me when he'd return again,
   But never since have I sot eyes on false young Billy Crane.

6. Now, since I've learned where he has gone, much pain have I to endure.
   He shipped on board of the *Handover;* he's cooking there for steward.
   And I hear that he has placed his mind all on some fairer dame,
   And onto me has proved unkind, that false young Billy Crane.

7. Now, happy, happy is the maid that has my love ensnared!
   She must have been some angel bright, all in her view appear.
   She must have been neat, genteel and sweet, on her character no stain,
   To interrupt my intercourse with false young Billy Crane.

8. Now, on board of some gallant ship or bark I mean to go straightway.
   I just declee [majestically] in that great ark I'll rock with yielding sway.
   I'll dress myself in man's attire, I'll scorn the raging main;
   I mean to ride the swells and tides till I gain young Billy Crane.

While the last two songs have been about particular girls, Larry generalized his complaints in the next song, "Barren Town" or "Byrontown." It may be questioned why this song is included in this chapter at all, since both Miss Manny and Mr. Doerflinger claim that Larry wrote it after he had gone to the State of Maine.[20] The only evidence I

can find for such an assertion is the following stanza in Jared Mac-
Lean's version of the song:

> But love has blinded all mankind
> From the days of Adam down,
> So that's the way in the State of Maine,
> Likewise in Byrontown.[21]

I have already said that Larry may have made a trip or two over to the
Pine Tree State as early as the sixties, but even if he had never been
there, the stanza might only be a way of saying that women are the
same everywhere. There are adequate reasons for believing that the
song originated in Miramichi. First, all extant versions of the song
have been found there, and it has never been found in the State of
Maine. Second, where is the town he speaks of? The only Byron in
Maine is so far from where Larry Gorman is ever known to have been
that we need not consider it. However, on the Miramichi, there is a
Bryenton about ten miles upriver from Newcastle. But Everett Price
of Blackville, who sang the song for me, identified the place immediately; it was not Byron— but Barren Town, he said, by which Larry
meant Renous, because it was very sparsely settled at the time. We
are pretty certain that Larry did at one time live in Renous, so here
the matter rests, at least for now. Mr. Price sang the song for me as
follows:

Barren Town

black, the   white,   they   dress a - - -

like,   all   in   their   glor - ious

land - - - - - - - - .   There's the tall   and

slim   both   thick   and   thin   in

ev - ery   shade   and   style - - - ,

There's the   young   and   old,   both

hot   and   cold,   these   young   men

to   be -   guile.

Barren Town

1. In Barren Town of high renown
    That's where I do belong;
    To speak my mind on womenkind

I've now composed a song.
If you'll agree and come with me,
Mind what I say is true,
And these ladies gay we will betray
And give them half their due.

2. Now the first of all is the big and the small,
As you may understand;
There's the black, the white, they dress alike,
All in their glorious land.
There's the tall and slim, both thick and thin,
In every shade and style;
There's the young and old, both hot and cold,
These young men to beguile.

3. To a ball they'll go, as you all know —
Next day they are half dead;
Saying, "Mother dear, I feel so queer,
There's a pain all in my head!
My back does break, it will surely bake —
This day I dearly rue;
And my back again does ache with the pain,
Till, alas, what can I do?"

4. Now they'll marry a man, it's if they can,
And keeping house they'll go;
Till all at once they'll shove on style,
Let the wages be high or low.
And it's all for a cake they cannot bake —
It is fun to see their pies —
And they'll swear that the flour is poor and sour,
And the dough it will not rise.

5. Now an organ sure you must secure
All for your lady dear,
And a sewing machine to hem and seam,
To keep their work so clear;
And a late style hat, they must have that,
No matter what you say,
And a brand new shawl they'll have this fall
When you your debts can't pay.

Larry's love of making up songs about parties had come with him from Prince Edward Island, and we hear the same things about him in Miramichi that we did on P.E.I.: he would come to a party, sit there taking it all in, and then (either at the party or the next day) make up a satirical song about what had gone on. The women were scared to death of him and would often run and hide when they saw him coming. Unfortunately (or perhaps fortunately at that) none of these songs survive except the one he was reputedly run out of Blackville for — "Donahue's Spree" — and even this song exists more as legend than fact. Every singer I talked to in Miramichi knew of it. Some even knew a few lines or a stanza, but no one could sing it all. I had resigned myself to publishing a reconstruction, but just before this book went to press Jim Wilson kindly sent me the following version which he had

recorded from an old friend of his, Irvine van Horne of Bloomfield
Ridge, N.B. *"I learned that in 1927...," Mr. van Horne said. "I
learned that from Fred Fairley. I was working with Fred [*in the
woods*] swamping main roads, and he used to sing it and I'd get him to
sing it over so I could learn it all, and that's how I come to know it.
'Christ,' he said, 'ain't you ever going to learn that?'" Learn it he did!
And thirty-six years later he sang it splendidly for Jim Wilson.

While the song itself never names its victim, legend names him
Israel Brown. The setting is a party (a "racket") at Donahue's, the
"lad in the corner" is probably Larry Gorman, and Mrs. Mackenzie
kept a rooming house in Blackville. I don't believe the song needs any
further introduction.

Donahue's Spree

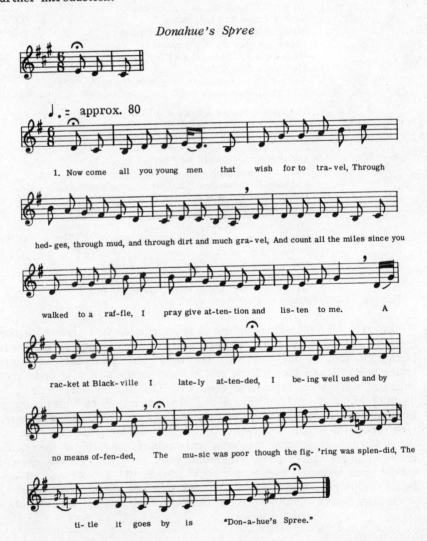

Donahue's Spree

1. Now come all you young men that wish for to travel
   Through hedges, through mud, and through dirt and much gravel,
   And count all the miles since you walked to a raffle,
   I pray give attention and listen to me.
   A racket at Blackville I lately attended,
   I being well used and by no means offended,
   The music was poor though the figuring was splendid —
   The title it goes by is "Donahue's Spree."

2. Now there was a lad there whose name I'll not mention,
   To give him a warning it is my intention;
   By unproper means trying every invention
   To gain the fond hearts of all that he'd see.
   He strove every nerve to gain their affection
   (It wasn't his person's such powerful attraction),
   But at the same time there was future to fraction (?)
   For his [i.e. *this?*] lady killer at Donahue's spree.

3. Now from dark until daylight this lad he was sporting,
   Sometimes with her dancing, more times with her courting,
   From kitchen to parlor he was her misfortune
   Saying, "Jenny my darling, you're pleasing to me."
   His head on her bosom he fon-de-lye pressed,
   With flattering speeches and slobbering kisses,
   More times he would play with her brown curly tresses,
   He seemed so affected at Donahue's spree.

4. Now the next agin' strangers he kin-de-ly warned her:
   "Do you see the lad that sets there in the corner?
   The kind that he is, love, I mean to inform you:
   He's come here tonight to try what he can see.
   And when he has backing it's harder to scare him,
   But now he's alone you have no need to fear him,
   But take my advice, love, and don't you go near him,"
   He told his own darling at Donahue's spree.

5. "Now when he get married you'll find me quite able
   To empty out Jerry and clean out the stable;
   I know there'll be times, love, you'll feel something feeble,
   I know in my heart I love no-one but thee.
   The thought of you, fair one, it keeps me from sleeping,
   Each night to my chamber like you could come creeping,
   My gold and my silver goes ring-a-jing-jingle,"
   He told his own darling at Donahue's spree.

6. "Now for emptying pots, it's a job that do please me,
   Two years I have emptied for Mrs. Mackenzie,
   The boys are so jealous they fain would revenge me
   Because they ain't got such a billet as me.
   Now I take a commodity under my jacket,
   Steal out through the kitchen and make little racket,
   And set it down easy in case I might crack it,"
   He told his own darling at Donahue's spree.

7. "Now as for blacksmithing I am very handy,
   At shoeing of horses I'm just a jim-dandy;
   I counsel I'd feed you on apples and candy —

Our lips then for kissing how sweet they would be!
I flatter you not, love, or mean to deceive thee,
I can make a cant-dog, a crowbar or peavey,
A knife or a fork or a spoon to dip gravy,"
He told his own darling at Donahue's spree.

8. "Now I'm fit to complete any job I go doing,
For tempering axes, likewise bobsled shoeing;
Now wedding with me, love you'd never be rueing
For I am a genius you plainly may see.
I can make a tooth that goes into a harrow,
Put a tongue in a bell for a cow that went farrow,
And sharpen a plow on Renous for old Sparrow,"
He told his own darling at Donahue's spree.

9. "Now I think for this night, love, we must be declining,
The next time we meet we will talk of combining;
The stars of the morning so brightly are shining,
I think it's high time we were shankin' the lay [i.e. *shaking the leg*].
To your castle this night, love, I mean to escort you
For fear some bold ruffian might catch you and hurt you;
Ma'am, while I am with you I'll die or support you,"
So off they both started from Donahue's spree.

10. Now when he got back he got courting Miss Mountain,
And all the short while he was jumping and bouncing.
"A lad that come near us I'd give him a trouncing
[*That would blacken his eyes whosoe'er*] he may be."[22]
He said, "Fairest lady, you're fairer than Venus;
Woe be to the lad, love, would dare come between us;
Besides, with a needle you're very ingenious,
My pride and my fancy of Donahue's spree."

One such song per citizen would be enough, it might seem, but
Larry favored poor Israel with another. Considering that another
songwriter, Joe Smith, later made up a song about Israel's sister
Laura, the Browns had no reason to love music![23] Either Israel had
been stealing things from around Andy McCormick's place, or Andy
thought he had, or Larry made the story up out of the whole cloth.
Whichever it was, Larry wrote a piece called "The Old Prowler," in
which he pictured Brown as a dog. Unfortunately all we have are fragments. Mrs. Alan MacDonald of Black River Bridge, N.B., sang me the
tune with one stanza:

The Old Prowler (I)

♩. = approx. 36

He   bor-rowed a trap and he   rigged a dead-fall,

And there he lay wait-ing to   hear the lad bawl,

And   now he's gone home with a   ve-ry   sore paw,

And it's sel-dom he   gets there a   bone for to   gnaw,

Sing-ing   fol   the did-dle ay,   fol   the

did-dle -air- o - ay   too - ral - i -   ay.

The Old Prowler (I)

He borrowed a trap and he rigged a deadfall,
And then he lay waiting to hear the lad bawl,
And now he's gone home with a very sore paw,
And it's seldom he gets there a bone for to gnaw.
    Singing fol the diddle ay, fol the diddle-air-o-ay too-ral-i-ay.

The following version is a composite but most of the lines were recited by Silas Curtis of Blackville:

The Old Prowler (II)

1. Straight over to Andy's the dog he did go;
   I asked them his name but they said, "We don't know.
   He comes every night and he comes all alone,
   And he won't go away 'til we give him a bone."

2. So they threw him a bone and he gnawed it a while,
   And then turned it over and picked it in style,
   So then he went off with his tail hanging down,
   And they tell me that dog's name is Israel Brown.

(Apparently the prowler returns):

> 3. A ham or good mutton that hung on a hook,
>   He said, "In my plunder I have struck good luck."
>   . . . .
>
> 4. [Mrs. McCormick was aroused from her sleep in a dream,
>   And says to her husband, "There's a dog in the cream!"]
>   "Tomorrow," said Andy, "I'll borrow a trap,
>   And if you come back I will catch you my chap."
>
> 5. So he borrowed a trap and he rigged a deadfall,
>   So he waited a while and he heard the lad fall,
>   And now he goes off with a very sore paw,
>   And it's seldom he gets there a bone for to gnaw.
>
> 6. [If I had a dog that was given to roam,
>   It'd be better to feed him and keep him at home;
>   When all good people are home and asleep,
>   He's out stealing cowbells or out stealing sheep.]
>
> 7. [When you pick a pup, pick one like Brown;
>   His tail stands up, his ears hang down.]

After Larry left Blackville, his next move seems to have been up-river to the town of Ludlow. He stayed there for only a short while, but it was long enough to make up at least one song about a man named Dave and his skinny wife Fanny. Dave was just crazy about his dog Jeff; he had even docked his tail in what was, he felt, the latest fashion. Larry went to a party at his place, and, in his usual style, took no part except to watch as everyone drank. Evidently Dave was pretty annoyed about the song Larry made up; it is perhaps just as well that Everett Price could only recall these two stanzas:

In Eighteen Hundred and Seventy-nine

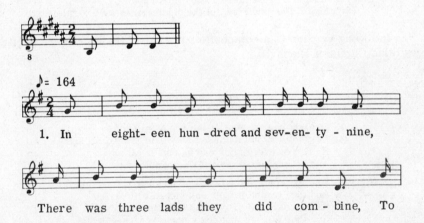

1. In   eight- een hun -dred and sev-en- ty - nine,

There was three lads they   did   com - bine, To

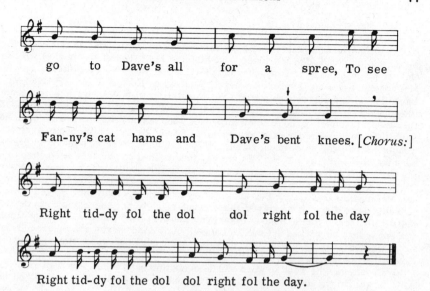

go   to   Dave's all   for   a   spree, To see

Fan-ny's cat   hams   and   Dave's bent   knees. [*Chorus:*]

Right   tid-dy fol   the   dol   dol   right   fol the   day

Right tid-dy fol the dol   dol right fol the day.

In Eighteen Hundred and Seventy-nine

1. In eighteen hundred and seventy-nine
   There was three lads, they did combine
   To go to Dave's all for a spree
   To see Fanny's cat hams and Dave's bent knee.
       Right tiddy fol de dol dol, right fol de day
       Right tiddy fol de dol dol, right fol de day.

2. Up jumped Jeff, brisk but frail,
   A broken jaw and half a tail;
   He yelps and barks and seems to say,
   "I've been a whopper in my day!"
       Right tiddy fol de dol, etc.

Some time after this, Larry was up around Hayesville, where he set his cap for a local belle, but she would have nothing to do with him. Disgusted, Larry did what we might expect: he made a song that scandalized her so fearfully that her brother ran Larry right out of the country. The one man who knew the song refused to sing it for me, claiming it was just too rough.

It is time now to recapitulate. Everett Price is far too young ever to have known Larry Gorman along the Miramichi, but in his sixty-odd years of guiding (he was one of the finest fly tyers on the "Sou'west," by the way), he seems never to have forgotten anything he heard. How much of the following saga is based on what Larry says in his songs, how much of it is gossip, and how much of it is irreducible fact, there is no way of telling. The account is coherent and interesting, and it forms a fitting coda for this chapter. I had asked Everett how Larry came to Blackville:

*He didn't come [*directly*] to Blackville [*from Prince Edward Island*]. He came down here to somewheres below here. I believe he went to work around a mill down there first. And then he worked there for a while and he worked in the woods and he didn't like the place, and him and his pal shifted and they went to another place. And so anyway, they didn't think too much of that either.... [*Now*] McLaughlin was a big lumberman here. He lived on Renous River — Patrick Mc-Laughlin.... And somewhere on the road they fell in with McLaughlin's tote team (they used to tote all their provisions from Newcastle up by horse) and they asked this there teamster if he...knew any place they might get some work. Well, he said, they might get work with McLaughlin. "And," he says, "I'm pretty sure you would." So, as the story goes, he says, "You can go right on with me. I'm pretty sure that he'll give you work." So anyway they walked on and they used to get on the wagon and drive a little piece and eat a little salt codfish and keep on that way 'til they got to the camp. And I just forget who was taking charge of that camp for McLaughlin that time. But anyway they got work...and they stayed there. And this here Gorman he stayed there, hung right to her and come down on the drive with them — that's Renous River, you know.... And there was a long time, you know, that he worked around McLaughlin's.... And he got shifted around and he...worked over here with Underwoods out here — Underwoods was logging... And that's the way he come into Blackville.

Well, anyway, he went to work and he made this song about Israel Brown, you see. Israel Brown come from the Island...and he was a big husky man. And he made this damned song about this "Donahue's Spree." By God this old Brown would have killed him if he'd got hold of him.... He was an ugly man and he'd do it.... He'd of killed him. So Gorman had to get out of here to save his life. And he went up the river — the only retreat there was — and he went up and fell in with this Foster up there. Well he was around up there quite a while, Gorman was...in Ludlow. But that's the only song that I know that he made up there [i.e. "*In 1879*"]. He learned them — he learned them this "Gull Decoy," the singers there, but not "The Scow on Cowden Shore," they didn't learn that. But he learned "The Gull Decoy" and he learned them this "Donahue's Spree," for I've heard the old fellows singing them. And then he made this song about Lyons there. And him and this Bill Foster started, they claim, in the night and moved on and they went over to Maine. And that was the last time that Foster ever was seen. He never come back afterward, nor Gorman never come back.... But Foster's wife stayed here and the two children.... Oh times was awful hard here then. There was...fifty dollars afloat in the State of Maine at that time for every one there was here. And there was better possibilities there.

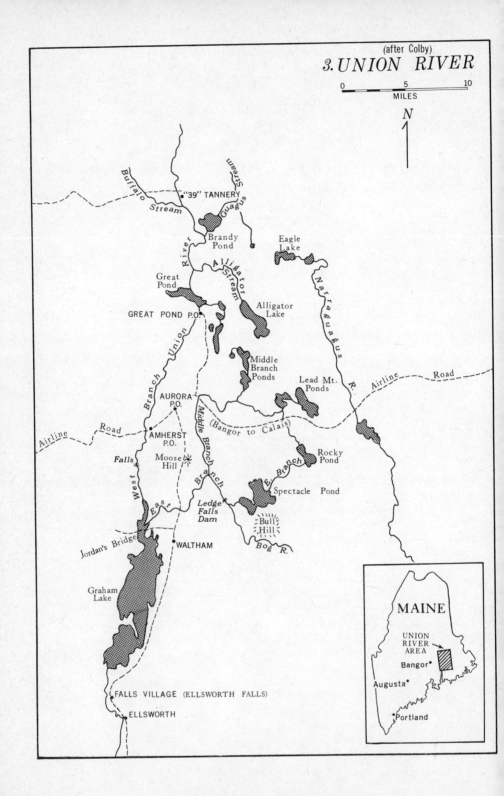

0   5   10
MILES

N

Buffalo Stream

Guagus Stream

●"39" TANNERY

Brandy Pond

Eagle Lake

River

Alligator Stream

Great Pond

Alligator Lake

GREAT POND P.O.

Narraguagus R.

Branch Union

Middle Branch Ponds

Lead Mt. Ponds

Airline Road

AURORA P.O.

Middle Branch

(Bangor to Calais)

Airline Road

●AMHERST P.O.

Rocky Pond

Falls

Moose Hill

E. Branch

Spectacle Pond

West

East

Ledge Falls Dam

Bull Hill

Jordan's Bridge

●WALTHAM

Bog R.

Graham Lake

MAINE

UNION RIVER AREA

Bangor●

Augusta●

●Portland

●FALLS VILLAGE (ELLSWORTH FALLS)

●ELLSWORTH

FIVE

"Down on the Union River"

Union River is not a big river. The headwaters of its longest branch, the West, are only about fifty miles from the sea. The main stream isn't even a river any more; it is Graham Lake, made in 1923 when the Bangor Hydro-electric Company built a dam at Brimmer Bridge above Ellsworth Falls that flowed the whole thing back for fifteen miles, well above Jordan's Bridge and the junction of the East and West Branches. But above the lake the three branches and their many feeders are just about what they always have been: wilderness streams flowing through miles and miles of swamp and cutover timberland.

It was not a particularly friendly country to those who first came there. The early proprietors of the land, notable among them the wealthy William Bingham of Philadelphia, were insistent that it be settled by farmers — not a very realistic policy, since the whole area was, and still is, almost entirely woodland. It was never very good farmland, and those settlers who did come in the late eighteenth and early nineteenth centuries suffered terrible hardships, particularly during the years before the War of 1812 when eastern Maine was almost completely cut off from its markets. But in 1820 a new land agent took over, and he saw things rather differently. As Herbert Silsby puts it, "John Black got out his big axe and convinced practically everybody that lumbering could produce large homes and a pretty comfortable living."[1] More and more settlers came, and almost every able-bodied man went into the woods, felled the great pines — and, when they were gone, the spruce — and drove them down the river. Soon some of the upriver towns began to cut in on the swag. Amherst had not only a large tannery that employed thirty-five men but also a sawmill, a clapboard mill, a gristmill, and two shingle mills. There was even a big

79

tannery way up in township thirty-nine, more than seven miles back in the wilderness above Great Pond; it was cheaper, it seems, to haul the hides twenty miles overland through the woods from the Penobscot than it was to haul the hemlock bark out. But most of the new prosperity came from cutting timber and driving the sawlogs down to the mills in Ellsworth.

The Union River drive was different from the Miramichi drive or the great drive on the Penobscot. It was smaller for one thing, the whole Union River itself being no larger than some of the major tributaries of these other waterways; and for another, each of the three branches was contracted for separately. On the West Branch, the main drive would start way back on Buffalo Stream, but there would be smaller drives coming down Partridge Brook, Guagus and Little Guagus Streams, and Alligator Stream. At Great Pond, the logs would be put into a boom and warped across to the outlet by headworks, a capstan on a raft. Here they would be sluiced through the dam and sent on their way down through Amherst to Jordan's Bridge outside Mariaville. Once a drive was through Jordan's Bridge, it was considered "in." From here on, the Ellsworth Boom Company took over, keeping the logs moving through more than twelve miles of deadwater and delivering them to the mills in Ellsworth. "*Union River was an awful small river for what business there was done on it," Ralph Cushman told me one day, and certainly the figures bear him out. Although the Union River carried in a given year only about one-fourth as many board feet of lumber as the Penobscot, it brought down, in proportion to its size, five times the volume of its big sister twenty miles to the west.

What Bangor was to the Penobscot, Ellsworth was to the Union River. As a sawmill center, it was perfectly situated, for from Falls Village to the Main Street Bridge, two miles downstream, the river dropped eighty-five feet. Seven dams were built to take advantage of this power potential, and there were a total of eleven gang-saw mills, nine single-saw mills, eight shingle mills, five box mills, and three clapboard mills, many of these running with day and night crews through the busy summer season. And all the time there would be a steady procession of teams carrying the lumber to the wharves. H. M. and B. Hall at one time kept twenty-five double-horse teams hauling their lumber to the wharves, each team making four daily trips. "*And I'd like to tell you," said Ralph Cushman to me one afternoon, "that when *I* can remember, they was two strings of teams on that hill there where the church and the county buildings are — one string going up, one pair of horses right behind the other, on one side of the street... and just the same thing coming down!"

There were eighteen wharves and docks running down the shore as far as Tinkers Cove, and sometimes the schooners (many of them Ellsworth-built) would be lying there three and four abreast taking on lumber; they'd roll the lumber right over one vessel to the others, often piling up huge deck-loads when the holds could take no more. Then, since the river was narrow and tricky, the ships would have to be taken down to the sea in single file by the famous towboat, *Little Round Top*. "*Some days she'd tow out both tides, night and morning," said Ralph Cushman, "but most every day that towboat would tow out one string of vessels, and I think one time there was as much as a dozen vessels towed out. I tell you it was a busy place!"

Like most towns having the combination of woodsmen, river-drivers, sailors, and (as I was told) West India rum for twenty-five cents a gallon, Ellsworth saw more than its share of wild sprees. Evidently both before and after the Civil War the situation was extremely bad, with organized gangs, many riots, and frequent fights along Water Street (then known as "Rum Row"). But the town hired an ex-Civil War officer named Andrew Spurling and told him to clean house. "The General," as he was called, cracked down hard, and when the drive came in, he and two special deputies handled the whole thing easily, whereas before his arrival fifteen special policemen had been needed to keep order. At any rate, Water Street in Ellsworth was quieter than Haymarket Square in Bangor, which still allows for plenty of whiskey.

So in the 1880's, Ellsworth was a thriving city of over five thousand, having in addition to its lumber and shipping establishments four carriage shops, four harness shops, two sail lofts, a foundry, its own newspaper, and a railroad station. In short, the Union River valley was truly a microcosm of Down East, and Ellsworth was, as Wasson said, its busy London.[2] And one day early in the decade, a lean, leisurely, amiable menace parked its heavy kennebecker at a Paddy Lane (Grant Street) boarding house and got a job at Cushman's mill. Larry Gorman had arrived.

Ralph Cushman recalls seeing Larry at his father's mill on the lower dam, working at what was just about the most menial task there: tending the sluice that brought the wastewood down from the mill. His job was to pick out the slabs and edgings as they floated by; he threw the pieces that were worth saving up where the teams could get them, and the rest he threw over the sluice to the river bank, where they would be burned as waste come a rainy day — all in all a wet, undesirable job. Occasionally Jim Cushman would come down and give the sluice-tender an extra dollar, saying, "Don't say anything about it," but Larry never found fault with his work there. Actually, it was just the sort of work he specialized in; it required almost no thought and left his mind free for those more important matters that constantly occupied it. In fact, he never seems to have held a skilled job. When mill work gave out, he went to haying; Captain E. N. Hodgkins of Orono remembers that Gorman hayed for a man named Greeley down in Trenton in the late eighties, and in the evening he would often sit in the front parlor and sing (Captain Hodgkins particularly recalls him singing "The Banks of the Gaspereaux" one night). Leon Brown remembered Larry's doing the same sort of work at Dorr's up at the Falls Village. He delighted the children there by making up and singing songs about them as he worked along. In the woods he was never much more than a swamper, and on the drives he was no great shakes. Here we see

Larry on a skilled job where quickness and alertness were required,
and though he could go on logs he was never a quickwater man, never a
really good river-driver. Even in the deadwater he was an awkward
hand. Joe Tosh remembers seeing him fall off a log one time: "He
scrambled up on the bank and stood there letting the water drain off
him," Joe said, "and damned if he didn't fall right over backwards into
the river again. I don't remember seeing anyone else ever do quite
that."

When Larry worked at the sluice at Cushman's he wore a pair of
oilskin pants, but when he went to church on Sunday he was as dapper
as any man in town with his gentleman's brown gloves, brilliant cravat,
and his cane with a head carved in the shape of a human foot. One
woman, who was a child at the time, remembers: "He'd come in the
door and with those great long strides of his it wasn't more than half a
dozen steps before he was in his pew. Then he'd hook that cane over
the pew in front of him and put his hat and gloves beside him on the
seat. And his voice rang out over everyone else's in the response. In
the Rosary, his 'Holy' would resound through the whole church and he'd
hiss the 'Pray for ussss' in the Litany. We kids used to snicker at
him, but we'd always pick up his verses and learn them." There is no
agreement as to just *how* dressy he was. One man said, "He was a
dandy, a regular dude!" but Miss Mary Gaynor demurred: "Larry
Gorman wasn't over-dressed," she said. "He just dressed very well,
that's all. It was his *manner* that was so elegant." And evidently this
is so. He loved the little formalities and hated (may he forgive me!)
to be called Larry. Mary Gaynor told me that one day she met him on
the street and, knowing that his wife was ill, she asked, "Good morning,
Mr. Gorman. How is Mrs. Gorman today?" He replied that she was
not feeling well at all. Later in the day, a friend, very much amused,
told Miss Gaynor that she had just met Larry and he had talked of
nothing but what a real lady that Miss Gaynor was. "She didn't just
come up like most people and ask, 'Larry, how's Mary today?'" he
said. Everyone had a good chuckle over that one.

Opinions about Larry varied a lot. When I asked one man what
people thought of him he said they "didn't think anything about him at
all" — he was very quiet and colorless, never drinking or raising hell.
Ralph Cushman claimed he was "a nice, agreeable man"; and the
daughter of a man who knew him well said that he was wonderful company, a marvellous mimic and storyteller. But there is one attitude
that was much more generally held, especially among the women in his
neighborhood: he was a nuisance. If there was one thing in life he
loved as much as making songs, it was visiting and gossiping. "He'd
come calling about half past eight," a woman told me, "and he'd stay
underfoot until noon sometimes, just stretching out his legs in front of
the stove and talking. And that wasn't like what the other men would
do." Often if a woman saw him coming she would duck and not answer
the door at all. Nor was he popular with his fellows, the mill-hands
and woodsmen; about the most encomiastic statement I could get was a

grudging, "Oh, we liked him well enough." Joe Tosh put it this way: "Larry just wasn't the kind of guy you'd choose for a pal."

Always, of course, he was the observer, the poet. Many people were a bit afraid of him, and everyone joked about being careful not to incur his displeasure in any way. Occasionally someone took umbrage at a song Larry had made about him. William Waldron of Tyne Valley, P.E.I., recalled seeing Larry take a tongue-lashing from a fellow he had "songed" there in Ellsworth. "That man called him all sorts of fearful things and all but threatened to kill him. Larry just stood there, not blinking any more than a toad, until the fellow was finished. Then he just walked away." And so Larry Gorman, whether he liked it or not, was a man who walked by himself — not only in the Wet Wild Woods but also in Ellsworth.

Sometime early in his stay in Ellsworth, Larry was involved in a railroad accident. The story is not absolutely clear, but he was working on a train which was getting a load of gravel at a pit just east of the Ellsworth Cemetery; somehow he was critically injured. Ralph Cushman, who was a young boy at the time, tells the following story:

*They told...that Larry Gorman was hurt so bad he couldn't live. Well, of course, I was at that age then that if I heard that a man couldn't live, well, he couldn't live. I don't know whether it was the next winter or two or three years after, but it was quite a while after, I went down the street one day (I guess I was going to Sunday School) and I met Larry Gorman right on the bridge right there in Ellsworth. And you don't know what a feeling come over me! I thought he was dead! If I hadn't been so scared of the water I guess I'd of jumped right into the river.

Unfortunately, the railroad has no official record of any accident back that far, but unofficial word keeps coming in. Larry's nephew John O'Connor recalls that his uncle had almost died in a railroad accident, but he thinks it happened up around Great Works, just south of Old Town. And, at two removes, from Prince Edward Island via Manitoba, comes the following note: "On one occasion in New England a train wreck occurred. Considerable damage was done to the rolling stock including the passenger cars. Fortunately all passengers escaped injury but one. He was Larry Gorman, who was pulled from the wreck in great distress. For weeks he hobbled about until a cash settlement was arranged from the railroad, after which Larry Gorman improved with amazing rapidity."[3] Until more information comes to light, we can only guess, but this accident may explain how Larry came into enough cash to allow him to make his next move.

In 1887, Larry did a surprising thing: he bought a house up on Cork Hill. Where he ever got the money (unless he got it from the railroad accident we have just talked about) there is no way of telling, but he is said to have been "pretty nigh," so perhaps he had saved it up. But on June 23, 1887, he bought the house at 16 Union Street (at what is now the corner of Bayview Avenue) from Colin McKenzie, who lived right next door. He evidently paid cash, $800.00, and for his money he got a good-sized house in fair shape with an attached shed, a barn, and about a quarter of an acre of land. The house has since been torn down, but the old McKenzie place is still there.

In no time at all, Larry and McKenzie were scrapping. It was always something; once McKenzie noticed that his potato patch had been raided, and a neighbor woman whispered to him that she had "seen Larry Gorman in there with a bag." Larry denied it, of course, and the story is highly improbable; theft was not his style at all, but the incident caused bad blood between them for a while. Larry was an Irish-Catholic, McKenzie a Scotch-Presbyterian; and they used to get into violent doctrinal arguments. Sometimes they would not speak to each other for weeks; then they would forget about it until next time. And when Larry was home and not fighting with McKenzie, he might be seen leaning on the fence which separated his place from that of D. H. Eppes. Eppes' daughter can still remember seeing him there, talking and singing softly to her father's horses. She used to love to go over and talk to him about life upriver in the lumbercamps, and he would take off his hat, run his hand back through his hair, and answer her in a brogue so thick she never could get all he was saying. She does remember his being enthusiastic about camp cooking, though: "Those riz biscuits — as big as *that*! Man size, they were!"

On March 23, 1888, Larry sued Henry L. Rowe, one of Ellsworth's leading lumbermen and just about the biggest man on the East and Middle Branch drives, for $252.86. There is nothing to say why, except for two promissory notes dated August 14, 1886, one for $199 and the other for $53.86. It is quite possible that Rowe owed Larry back wages, but we can't be sure. At any rate, the matter was settled quietly at the April term of court, 1889, which probably means that Larry got his money.[4]

Joe Tosh met Larry one day after he had bought his house and said that all he needed now was a woman to take care of it for him. "Yes," Larry said, "I've got the cage; now all I need is the bird." Still, for four years he lived there all alone except for those times when his mother came down from the Island to visit him. Then on November 5, 1891, Larry married an attractive widow, Mary Mahoney (*née* O'Neal), the Reverend T. F. Butler officiating. The surprise caused by his buying a house was slight compared to that occasioned by his getting married, but nothing at all compared to the surprise many people evidenced at Mary Mahoney's marrying him. "How we all laughed at Mary for taking Larry," one woman told me, but evidently they were happy together during the five short years before Mary was taken sick. She died of dropsy on June 19, 1896.

After Mary's death, one of her sisters came to keep house for Larry, and while Larry had thought a great deal of his wife, he did not care for her sister at all. Charlie Gorman remembers a letter that Larry wrote home to his sister Ellen in which he described the woman and his troubles with her. "I wish I had that letter now," he said. "Everybody was laughing over it, it was so comical. He really carded her to a peak."

Larry seems to have worked on the Union River drive nearly every spring he was in Ellsworth, that is to say, for almost twenty years. Sometimes he worked for Jim Cushman and sometimes he worked for Roderick McDonald, both of whom took charge of big drives on that river. Competition was strong on the Union and as Jim Cushman's son Ralph said, *"A man that didn't get up in the morning was the fellow that come out behind. He had to be on to all the other fellow's tricks."

No one, it appears, got up any earlier in the morning or had more tricks to be on to than did the aforementioned Roderick McDonald, who is still remembered as just about the hardest driver Union River ever knew. Born in Scotland in 1830, he came to Ellsworth and started working for the Grant Lumber Company as mill-hand, woodsman, and driver. He soon became a foreman, and it wasn't too long before he began to contract for different logging operations himself. He took crews into the lumberwoods, he had managed the drives on all three branches for more years than anyone can remember, and he did a lot of work improving the river by building dams and sluices.[5] He was demanding and parsimonious, and the stories about him are traditional by now. Take, for example, the story about the eggs. I have heard it several different ways, but the following is typical. One morning Roderick approached his cook, Del Avery. "Mr. Avery," he said, "do you know any of the farmers round here?" Avery allowed that he knew several. "Well, then," said Roderick, "I want you to get out and rustle up enough eggs for dinner." Then he turned to the men: "By the jollys, boys," he said, sniffling a couple of times as was his wont, "we'll have eggs for dinner today!" Later, when the men got out on the logs, he called Avery aside and told him to forget about those eggs. That night at dinner he questioned the cook about it and chided him before the men for failing to get the eggs. When Del began to remonstrate, Roderick cut him off with, "Now Mr. Avery, tomorrow morning for sure you get out and bring back some eggs," again cancelling the order later on the sly. It was a little hard on Avery, but he seemed willing to play along; and Roderick would feed his men on codfish and beans actual and eggs anticipated for several days.

Then there is the story of Joe Hennessey's thumb. Joe was one of the biggest men in Hancock County, standing, they say, nearly six-foot-seven, and he had tremendous hands with thumbs that can be modestly spoken of as outsize. On the drive, when the crew had biscuits and molasses, it was the custom for each man to thumb a hole in his biscuit and pour the molasses in, but when Joe Hennessey came up for his turn, Roderick stepped in. "Now there, Joe Hennessey, don't you use that awful big thumb of yours! You use your little finger or you'll ruin me!"

There are plenty of other stories about Roderick McDonald, but whatever else people said about him, they always admitted that he "got his logs out." He drove his men hard and struck an even harder bargain, but he got the job done as no one else did. One of his most famous exploits occurred the time he had a big drive all landed and ready to go

up in Township Thirty-Four on the headwaters of Partridge Brook, a
tributary of Little Guagus. A heavy rain came and took out his dam,
leaving him no water to start his logs with. He rebuilt the dam but
could not get enough flowage back, so he was hung up with just about
every cent he had tied up in those logs. However, he was only a few
rods and a slight horseback from Eagle Lake, the source of the Narraguagus River, and the difference was in his favor. So he set his
whole crew to work digging a channel from the lake into the brook
above his dam, and in no time at all he had Narraguagus water flowing
into Partridge Brook, giving him all the head he needed to get his drive
out. "And that," explained one man to me, "is how the first pickerel
got down into Great Pond."

Even when he was too old to take charge of the drives or cutting
operations himself, he could not keep out of the woods. He would
wander from one camp to another, and go out in the woods just to watch
the men work. In early December of 1907, he started from one camp
to walk nearly fifteen miles to another, but he never got there. They
hunted all through the area but could find no trace of him. It was not
until the next fall that a boy who was out after partridge found Roderick's bones leaning up against a stump not far from Great Pond Settlement. They took what was left of him back to Ellsworth and buried
him there. He was seventy-seven years old.

Larry Gorman worked for Roderick McDonald for many years, and
from past indications we could be pretty certain that the two men would
not get on well. It would be nice to believe that here was a parsimonious old slave driver who would get his due from the irrepressible
Archpoet, but he was no more stingy than Larry himself, and further,
there are several instances where McDonald only gave Larry what he
had coming to him. For instance, Larry had a fantastic appetite; he
would heap his plate high with no thought for the others. One time when
they were working the quick water above Great Pond somebody gave
McDonald a big basketful of eggs, and he had decided that each man
was to have two. Larry sneaked out a half-dozen and started to break
them into his plate, but McDonald reached out and gave him a sharp
lick on the back of his hand with a ladle; "You damned hog! I said two
apiece," he barked, taking back four of the eggs from Gorman's plate.
Another time he had a ten-quart pail of milk, which he wanted to have
go around, so he decreed that everyone would take his tea half milk
that day. Larry edged up to the pail and stood there quietly until Roderick looked the other way for a minute; then he dumped his tea and
dipped his cup into the milk and started off, but again McDonald was
too quick for him and knocked the cup from his hand. Larry drank his
tea black that day.

The story about Larry Gorman's Christmas present is probably too
good to be true, but it is said that up in the woods shortly after Christmas one year, he got a letter from one of his sisters asking whether he
had gotten the red socks she had sent him. He had not, and he eyed
everyone suspiciously until he saw Roderick wearing a brand-new pair

of bright red socks. He saw a conclusion and jumped to it, demanding that McDonald take those socks off immediately since they were rightly his. Roderick demurred, and they hassled back and forth for a while, until finally Larry said, "You'll sit right down and take those socks off or I'll make a song on you," whereupon McDonald removed the socks.

Whether or not the story is true, it was inevitable that Larry would "song" this man. The story is that around 1890 Larry was laid up sick in camp for a few days, and Roderick approached him with the following proposition: since Larry had nothing better to do for a while, why didn't he make up a poem on Frank Mace, the Aurora storekeeper with whom McDonald had had a falling out. What Larry answered we do not know, but soon there was a new song about Roderick himself going the rounds. For his central incident Larry had taken a time when Mc-Donald had a drive in the East Branch and found that he did not have all the water he would have liked, so he asked the crew at Ledge Falls Dam to give him some more. They refused, on the grounds that if they gave it to him there would not be enough for Hen Rowe's drive when it came into the East from the Middle Branch. That night McDonald took a crew of men up to the Ledge Falls Dam; they not only opened the gate, they took it clean out and hid it way back in the woods. He got a big head of water that helped him get his drive down in record time, but, as might be expected, it hung Rowe's drive up pretty badly. The words I give here were recited to me by Irving G. Frost of Bar Harbor (formerly of Mariaville); the tune is from the late Alden F. Mace of Southwest Harbor.

Roderick McDonald (I)

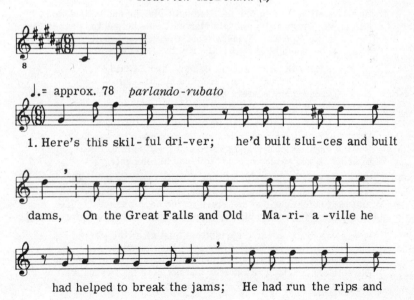

J.= approx. 78   *parlando-rubato*

1. Here's this skil-ful dri-ver;   he'd built slui-ces and built

dams,   On the Great Falls and Old   Ma-ri- a -ville he

had helped to break the jams;   He had run the rips and

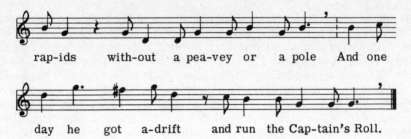

rap-ids   with-out   a pea-vey   or   a pole   And one

day   he   got   a-drift   and run   the Cap-tain's Roll.

Roderick McDonald (I)

Here's this skilful driver; he'd built sluices and built dams,
On the Great Falls and Old Mariaville he had helped to break the jams;
He had run the rips and rapids without a peavey or a pole,
And one day he got adrift and run the Captain's Roll.[6]

Roderick McDonald (II)

1. I met a river-driver eleven years ago
   Down on the Union River where the crystal waters flow.
   His brow with age was wrinkled, and his hair was silvery gray;
   He looked just like a monarch or some man that held great sway.

2. His height was fair to medium, his figure spare and thin.
   His nose was like an eagle's beak, with a goatee on his chin.
   His voice, though still commanding, it had a Scottish brogue;
   He left his home and never got our language in his vogue.

3. He was well skilled in driving, had built sluices and built dams,
   And on the Great Falls and Old Mariaville he helped to break the jams;
   He's run the rips and rapids without a peavey or a pole,
   And one day when he got adrift he run the Captain's Roll.

4. He drove the Alligator, Middle Branch, and Buffalo,
   And on the Little Guagus he'd handled his batteau;
   He logged for many winters on the township twenty-one,
   And he drove his logs and stavewood[7] from the shores of Rocky Pond.

5. His tales, though interesting, they vary from the truth.
   He'll tell you these were feats performed when he was but a youth;
   But the greatest of his wonders to you I will relate:
   In order to get water once he stole and hid the gate.

6. 'Twas up that narrow pathway, he led his little band,
   Over hills and over windfalls with a lantern in his hand;
   And long before the sun had risen or the hour was getting late,
   This crafty driver and his crew they lugged off Ledge Falls gate.

7. It was one morn in early springtime, just after the sun did rise,
   The men on the rear[8] with Rowe was taken by surprise;
   They found their water falling and their logs began to jam,
   But this brave and crafty driver had his rear by Twynham's Dam.[9]

8. Well it 'twas then too late to stop him, for he'd gained that mighty head;
   He'd put his lumber o'er Great Falls and by the Gravel Bed.
   And less than two days after, he'd gone through Jordan's Bridge,
   And this crafty driver and his crew was sneaking home over Waltham Ridge.

9. It's been forty years or nearly since he struck this town;
   He's always done the best he could to keep men's wages down.
   He drove by the cords and thousands[10] and hoarded up his dimes,
   And always hired his drivers cheap by preaching up hard times.

10. For when he sees a stranger, it always was his style
    To approach him very gently with a sweet, soft-soapy smile;
    But you'll find him very different when you get him out of town,
    For then you'll find his countenance wears nothing but a frown.

11. He said when dead and buried, it was their chief intent
    In honor of his memory to erect a monument;
    It will be in polished granite in the pattern of a cone
    To commemorate him for the service he had done.

12. Now we'll have this noble hero in some conspicuous place —
    Rubber boots, an old straw hat, and a worn and haggard face;
    With a cant-dog on his shoulder or a pickpole in his hand,
    He looks like some mighty general while giving off commands.

McDonald did not fire Larry for making up that song, but he didn't like it at all. Joe Tosh said that one day he and Larry were coming downriver in a batteau full of men when Roderick signalled them from the bank to come over and pick him up too. He climbed in and sat on the lazy-seat facing Larry, but Larry was looking down into the bottom of the boat, studying the floorboards. McDonald watched him for a minute, then reached out and gave him a shove: "Get your head up there, you son of a bitch; you're just making up another song on me!"

There are supposed to have been several other songs about McDonald, but I haven't found them. However, another song that Gorman made up has to do with the drivers and their friends who lived along the Union River. I have never found a man who knew the whole of it, but many remembered individual stanzas. In fact, I thought of them as separate poems until several people pointed out to me that they were all part of one long song (one man claimed the original had twenty-eight stanzas). It is reminiscent of "The Scow on Cowden Shore" and like that poem, contains many local allusions, whose meanings have been lost, but enough remains to give us the feeling of the whole. It is a series of quick caricatures: of the bald blacksmith of Great Pond; of the P.I. (Prince Edward Islander) who took out his pal Jimmy Coleman's girl; of another P.I. who, though he was getting old and blind, still wanted to go on the drive and would work on the old logs stuck back in the bushes; and of three of the four Jordan brothers (not Nahum, who will figure in another song). The version I give here is a composite; credit for the individual stanzas will be found in the Appendix:

The Union River Drivers

1. Here's Johnny Archer, that blacksmith of skill,
   Who irons the peaveys and sharpens the drills;
   He's working for Haslam on the big spruce and pine
   And the top of his head like a full moon does shine.

2. There is Bert Haynes, that wonderful guide,
   Who boarded with Asey before Asey died;
   Down at the Steep Landing he must have felt cheap
   When John Laughlin came down there and found him asleep.

3. There's Charlie Sweeney, that big Irish chap —
   I'll tell you the reason he's wearing a cap:
   'Twas up in the dead water he fell through the gap[11]
   And went down to the bottom and there left his old hat.

4. Here's to Mickey Dalton, that noted P.I.
   Wherever he meets you he'll tell you a lie,
   And when the jam makes, he's always on deck,[12]
   And now he's laid up with a kink in his neck.

5. There's Flossie Laughlin that lives on the hill,
   And when she sees Jimmy it gives her a thrill;
   One night while she was walking with Dalton the Mick,
   She laughed up her sleeve and said, "Here comes Jimmy the Stick."

6. Now here's Maynard Glidden, bless his old soul;
   He was once a good man but he's now growing old.
   His eyesight is failing so he can't go on logs
   But he'll climb through the alders and card the old sogs.

7. There's two little Jordans that works in our crew —
   Now isn't it surprising to see what they'll do?
   For when the jam makes, Dana will scream,
   "Let's mount 'em, Urban, and give 'em Old Jeems!"

8. Now there's William Jordan, whose byword's, "By Jeems!"
   He once worked for Frank Frost up on Dead Stream;
   One night while William was taking a snooze,
   Along came a hedge hog and et up his shoes.

9. Here's to Mose Estey, that filthy old tramp;
   Everyone knows he lives in a camp;
   He works all day on the logs with the men,
   And when it comes night, sneaks off to his den.

10. Now here's Henry Folsom, that big honest man;
    He's always eating whenever he can.
    And when the cook hollers, he's first to be seen
    Down at the table with a plate of baked beans.

11. Here's to Hen Folsom, that big honest man;
    He has a neat shop where he makes Injun Tans.
    One day on the logs that Haslam did peel,
    He leaped high in the air and lost his boot heel.

The joke of the last stanza was explained to me as follows: Folsom was a tremendous man who never could have leaped high in the air. But one day while he was working on some slippery peeled hemlock, he lost his balance, and in order to regain it he jammed down so hard on the log that when he tried to pull loose the heel of his boot came off. "Injun Tans," by the way, were low-cut mocassins.

Why Bill Watts should have had a song written about him no one knows. According to Alden Mace, who sang the song for me, Watts had the drive on the East Branch one year, but others remember him as a scaler and cannot recall that he ever had the drive. Whatever the facts may have been, the song is a rather interesting one. The first six stanzas are reportorial: during the winter months, the logs had been landed in four places on the ice at Rocky Pond, and booms had been secured around the landings to keep the logs together when the ice went out. That spring Watts took a green crew up to drive the logs down and discovered that the booms had broken, which meant he had to prepare new ones and spend precious days corralling the logs and getting them over to the outlet in order to sluice them into the river ("sluicing" does not necessarily imply a sluice or even a dam; it may mean simply running logs from a lake into a river). Since he felt he needed experienced drivers to "tend out" at danger spots along the stream, he asked Hen Rowe to send them to him; he could then use his greenhorns on the rear. The last two stanzas are full of the old Gorman vitriol.

Bill Watts

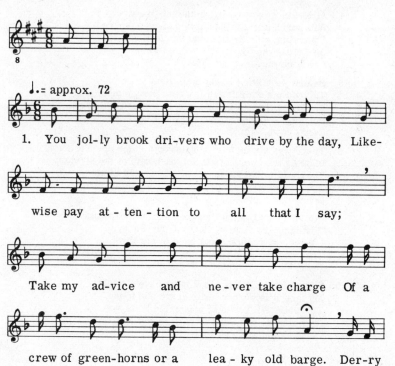

♩.= approx. 72

1. You jol-ly brook dri-vers who drive by the day, Like-

wise pay at - ten - tion to all that I say;

Take my ad-vice and ne - ver take charge Of a

crew of green-horns or a lea - ky old barge. Der-ry

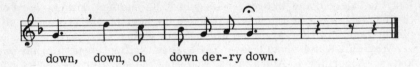

down, down, oh down der-ry down.

Bill Watts

1. You jolly brook drivers who drive by the day,
   Likewise pay attention to all that I say;
   Take my advice and never take charge
   Of a crew of greenhorns or a leaky old barge.
   Derry down, down, oh down derry down.

2. It was upon Tuesday, the first day of May;
   As long as I live I'll remember the day.
   I took my whole crew up to Rocky Pond
   In full expectation the ice would be gone.
   Derry down, etc.

3. When I got there my heart it grew sad;
   The task was enough to drive a man mad.
   All four of the booms they were broken and gone,
   And all of the logs drifted over the pond.
   Derry down, etc.

4. At length we got ready, a rigging prepared,
   With much difficulty got some of them snared;
   Consisting of cedar, peeled hemlock and spruce;
   On Friday the fourth, we began to sluice.
   Derry down, etc.

5. Before we h'isted I sent up to Hen
   To send me down ten of his best peavey men,
   For those that we had were both useless and green,
   But jolly Jim Coffey and Ruel McKeen.
   Derry down, etc.

6. There was six men from Ellsworth came up on a team,
   In haste they were stationed the length of the stream;
   They was well-able drivers, full worthy of hire,
   They could handle a peavey or fight against fire.
   Derry down, etc.

7. For forty-odd years I've been known in this place,
   The name that I go by is Old Dirty Face;
   I never yet washed it but once in my life,
   That was the first time I went courting my wife.
   Derry down, etc.

8. When I get to Ellsworth, I must have a wash;
   My face it is covered with gurry and moss.
   The water I'll bottle to poison the botts —
   Now what do you think of your friend Mr. Watts?
   Derry down, etc.

There were plenty of others whom Gorman satirized in his twenty years on the Union River, but the songs have been forgotten or are extant only by reputation. Up in Great Pond Settlement, where a lot of the people named in "The Union River Drivers" lived, the local girls used to give a dance for the drivers when the logs reached the dam below the pond. Larry attended one of these dances and asked Bessie Williams to dance; she refused, and that made him angry enough to make up a new song called "Ace Williams' Foolish Girl." It was certainly a mistake, because he made bitter enemies of the extensive Williams family. Another time Mack Dyer borrowed a pair of driving boots from Larry and neglected to return them. Larry settled his hash by refurbishing an old song, "The Shan Van Vogh,"[13] and calling it "The Great Pond Tramp," but in the process he almost settled his own, because he enraged not only Mack but also his three brothers, three sisters, and his father-in-law, old "Dad" Clark Dunn. It would have been bad enough to have angered Mack Dyer alone (who, legend has it, could "balance a big side-hill plow on his chin"), but when Larry saw Mack so formidably reinforced, he felt that the time had come to retire. He spent three days and three nights in the woods waiting for things to cool off. Had he been caught, his biographer's job might have been a great deal simpler.

There were a few other people on Union River who could make up verses. Dan Donovan of Ellsworth turned out an occasional piece. He made up one when he was sick and the object of a great many visits. Ralph Cushman recited it as follows:

> I'm Captain Jinks, a man of fame,
> I lately moved from Paddy Lane;
> For better neighbors you'd have to hunt
> Than James Frazier and Laura Lunt.
> There's Mrs. Bowden on the east,
> She's in here twice a day at least;
> Thank God there's no one on the west
> So I can get a little rest.[14]

But the best-known wit and poet besides Larry Gorman was Freeman Archer of Great Pond, who also had a great reputation for composing impromptu verses. He was on the drive for many years, and one year after the drive was in and the boys were all gathered in a tavern, Freeman was called on for a toast. He was stumped for a minute; then he pulled off his hat, and, in a study, stood there looking into it. Suddenly he spoke:

> Here's to this old hat, and what of that?
> It was once so new and shiny.
> What could entice those goddamned lice
> To eat up all the lining?

Once when Archer was on a drive the foreman was keeping the men on the logs from before they could see in the morning until it was almost too dark to see at night. At supper one night, the foreman noticed that

Freeman was wearing a red jacket that had seen better days, so he said, "Freeman, that jacket of yours is getting kind of faded out, isn't it?"

"Yes," snapped back Freeman, "it gets that way working in the moonlight!"

It may have been the very next morning, when the men were rolled out again at three o'clock, that Freeman is said to have reached for his pipe and started puffing on it right away without lighting it. "Huh!" he grunted, "that damn tobacco must have been wet to have went out so quick as that!" Nobody ever got ahead of Freeman when it came to kidding and wisecracks. The men tried to get him to sing one night but he said he couldn't. "I only know two songs," he said, "and I forgot one of them and I can't remember which one it is I forgot." At another time, fed up with codfish and beans and having just been handed another meal of them, he quipped, "That's what I call a meal. We could have had ham and eggs if we'd had any ham but there weren't any eggs."

People who did not know Freeman thought it odd that he had an extra pair of heels nailed on to the ankles of his shoes. The explanation? He had an odd hitch in his walk that caused him to kick himself on the ankle bone, and this simple expedient saved his uppers from wearing through.

The story goes that Freeman occasionally got drunk and beat up his wife. One time his son Amos, a man of some 240 pounds, stepped in as his mother's protector and gave his father a terrible beating. This tickled Freeman so that he made up a little piece about it that began,

> My boy is of a tedious length;
> His muscles fairly ache with strength.
> 'Twas by my neck my boy he took me:
> He kicked, he cuffed, and then he shook me.

His wife finally left him, I was told; and he even made up a sort of good-riddance verse about that:

> She took the kettles and the pots;
> She'd have taken the stove if it hadn't been hot.
> And all that remained there to be seen,
> Was half a box of paris green.

He lived alone for years. One day the people of Great Pond Road discovered that they hadn't seen Freeman driving by with his horse Pete (every horse he ever owned was named Pete) for quite some time. They went up to the house, and, unable to rouse him, forced their way in. They found Freeman on the floor; he had been dead for many days and his cat had eaten half his face away.

Larry Gorman could hardly have been expected not to satirize Freeman Archer; and sure enough, Merle Richardson of Great Pond Road, Aurora, recited this verse for me:

On the road to Bull Hill, there's no church nor mill,
Freeman Archer lives in a brush shanty;
He sells cider and hay for very small pay,
And his table he sets very scanty.

Not as well-known as Archer was Mose Estey, whom Gorman satirized in "The Union River Drivers." Many people remember that
Estey used to make up pieces, but I have found none of them unless
Alden Mace was right when he insisted that it was he, not Gorman, who
made up "The Champion of Moose Hill." Most people credit this piece
to Gorman, but when I tell them of Mace's claim, they usually say that
Mose Estey *could* have written it at any rate. We will never be able
to decide finally, but until I have much more conclusive evidence for
Estey's authorship I will assume that Gorman wrote the song.

The central figure in this ballad is Emery "Muck" Mace, a huge
man, who was eternally interested in stirring up a little excitement.
Once while he was living up on the Great Pond Road with a farmer by
the name of Joe Ritchie, he found an old stove out in the woods. He
broke it up and spread the pieces along the line between Ritchie's and
Freeman Archer's places, but as he went back from the road he veered
over slowly into Ritchie's property. Then he took Ritchie out and
showed him what that no-good poet of a neighbor had done to get himself a slice of Ritchie's land by deflecting the compasses of the sur-
veying crew which was coming to settle the line between the two prop-
erties. It was a pretty thin story, but Ritchie swallowed it, and he and
Freeman all but came to blows over the hoax.

Mace was reputed to be a perfectly fine person until he got "full,"
but then he became a bully and a scrapper. "He wasn't so much a
fighter as he was a chewer," one man told me; he would get a man
down and then start to chew on his ear or his arm. Once in 1889, in a
fight that was ferocious enough to get mentioned in *The Ellsworth
American,* he bit Fred Titus on the cheek and just held on. It looked
murderous to those who were watching; everybody was ready to pry
Mace loose, but Titus would not allow it. "Let the damn bulldog bite,"
he said. A short time after that Titus met Mace out on Silsby's Plain
and "drove him right down into his boots."

The incident celebrated in "The Champion of Moose Hill," occurred
at the old Fred Jordan place at the foot of Moose Hill in Osborn. Jordan had a large ell attached to his house; the downstairs served as a
carriage house and woodshed, and upstairs there was a large room that
was used for dances. On this particular night, Mace arrived at the
dance pretty full, and right away asked Annie Giles to dance with him.
She refused and went out on the floor with Nahum Jordan. Mace swore
that if he couldn't dance he'd be damned if anyone else would either, so
he grabbed for Nahum, but Nahum's daughter, Helen Jordan Giles, came
to the rescue; she hit Mace over the head with a stick. Reports vary
as to just how hard she hit him. Some agree with the ballad in saying
that she knocked him cold; others say she only gave him a couple of

light licks "to give him the idea." At any rate, there was soon a song celebrating the struggle.

The Champion of Moose Hill

♩. = approx. 88 *parlando-rubato*

1. You peo - ple all, both great and small, I pray you lend an ear; My name and oc - cu - pa - tion you pres- ent- ly shall hear. My name it is bold Em -ery Mace, I prac-tice fis -tic skill, Oh, the fa-tal night when I got tight and got knocked out on Moose Hill.

The Champion of Moose Hill

1. You people all, both great and small, I pray you lend an ear;
My name and occupation you presently shall hear.
My name it is bold Emery Mace, I practice fistic skill —
Oh, the fatal night when I got tight and got knocked out on Moose Hill.

2. On that fatal day I chanced to stray to Moose Hill for a spree;
It was the plan of every man to prove my destiny.
I saw it in their faces and I read it on the bill
That if I got tight I'd have to fight that night upon Moose Hill.

3. I let them run and have their fun, I hoed right in with them;
   There was Mrs. Giles, she was all smiles, I saw her wink at Nahum.
   Then Nahum he jumped and grabbed me and tried to hold me still,
   While Mrs. Giles the club she piles upon me at Moose Hill.

4. The first blow that she struck me came square across my head;
   For twenty minutes I lay there — they thought that I was dead
   The women they revived me then, they did try all their skill,
   For they thought that I must surely die that night upon Moose Hill.

5. My brother Fred stood at my head, so mournful he did cry;
   The poor little lad he felt so bad, for he thought that I must die.
   He knew that he alone would be to pay the funeral bill,
   For he knew that Muck had had hard luck and was penniless on Moose Hill.

6. I didn't die, I'll tell you why: my skull was only cracked;
   But little you know the terrible blow that lady gave poor Mack;
   It would have killed a tiger or slain a wild gorill',
   But you know that Muck had better luck than to be murdered on Moose Hill.

[7. Now I fought 'em all, both big and small, the best I didn't care;
   And I never fought 'em with a club, I always fought 'em fair.
   I licked the Amherst champion, Fred Titus I nearly killed;
   But with just one welt I lost the belt to a woman on Moose Hill.]

8. So now I'm done, my race is run, my fighting days are o'er,
   So I'll confess, my mind oppressed, I'll mount the stage no more;
   And from the ring I'll gently spring, and it's sore against my will
   That Helen bold the belt shall hold, the champion of Moose Hill.

On the same night that Alden Mace sang "The Champion of Moose Hill" and "Bill Watts," he also sang "Myles Everett More," or rather he sang as much as he knew of it to me. The story behind the song is that More started calling Larry a "Bluenose" and ignored the poet's warnings to quit. Larry got to work and discovered a blot on More's escutcheon. He heard that years ago More had taken a neighbor's bull, driven it between two young saplings and mutilated it; some say that he not only cut off the tail but castrated the beast. All Mr. Mace could recall were the first four stanzas and the last one, but he said that there was "quite a lot more of it, too."

Myles Everett More

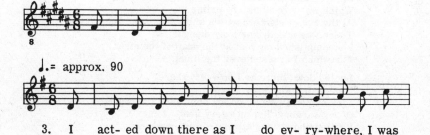

♩.= approx. 90

3. I   act- ed down there as I   do ev- ry-where, I was

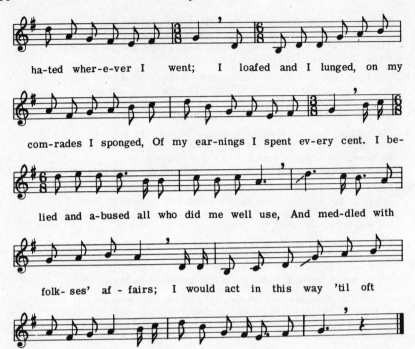

ha-ted wher-e-ver I went; I loafed and I lunged, on my

com-rades I sponged, Of my ear-nings I spent ev-ery cent. I be-

lied and a-bused all who did me well use, And med-dled with

folk- ses' af - fairs; I would act in this way 'til oft

times they would say, "You've a room that's not fi-nished up-stairs!"

Myles Everett More

1. You good citizens all, your attention I'll call;
   I'll speak of my reckless career;
   I'll sing you a song that is truthful and long,
   If you wish to hear it, draw near.
   All about my own self, a degraded poor elf —
   My name I'll not give you in full —
   Though my deeds of disgrace are well known in this place,
   For I once mutilated a bull.

2. It was eight years ago as my neighbors well know;
   Right well I remember the time;
   I played this low trick upon my neighbor Chick,
   Which was a penitentiary crime.
   At the age of eighteen with a knife sharp and keen,
   There was nobody knew my designs,
   I accomplished my feat at the dead of the night,
   For which I crossed over the lines.

3. I acted down there as I do everywhere,
   I was hated wherever I went;
   I loafed and I lunged, on my comrades I sponged,
   Of my earnings I spent every cent.
   I belied and abused all who did me well use,
   And meddled with folkses' affairs;

I would act in this way 'til ofttimes they would say,
"You've a room that's not finished upstairs!"

4. I would them deceive if you would me believe,
Then just you pay attention to me,
Of the wonders I've done on the River St. John
And the waters of Miramichi.
I there undertook to act as head cook
For thirty-two dollars per month;
The nice bread I make, both mince pies and plum cakes,
And hot doughnuts for every lunch.

. . . .

5. Now I'll conclude and no longer intrude;
Of my life I have given full note;
I will admit before that I quit
To stealing a new overcoat.
I'm a wild roving blade and a bootcher [i.e. butcher] by trade,
I'm stout, rugged, hearty, and hale;
I perform a great feat when I kill my own meat
For I always begin at the tail.

Another of Gorman's long poems was called "Ellsworth News of the Day." It took its name from a column in the *Bangor Daily Commercial* and is a parody of the sort of local news items that appeared in that column: a Franklin man's cow was run over by a train; "Doc" A. C. Haggerty "refused to run for mayor"; and "Lots of hansom carriages in John Maloney's shop." I have recovered only one complete stanza:

There is a dame I blush to name —
They say she's getting stout;
She goes to Bangor twice a month
To have a good blowout.

There are a couple of fragments of songs Larry made up when he was working at Hall's sawmill. This mill was run by two brothers, Barlow (who was blind) and Martin. They used to have their disagreements, but they had a way of settling them too:

Old Barlow was blind and his teeth he would grind
When Martin went out on a toot;
But they always made up as together they'd sup
The juice of that forbidden fruit.

There was quite a lot more of this one, Joe Tosh said. It is simply a parody of a well-known song, "The Juice of the Forbidden Fruit," in which each stanza tells of a famous person's experiences with alcohol. Another piece tells of a fight that took place in the mill; I have the first stanza and no more:

The Fight at Hall's Mill

Last Sunday morning Sewell
He drank a bowl of gruel

And called to fight a duel
With Sam Whittaker and his boy Gene;
Johnny Coleman was the trainer,
Mel Joy shut down the planer,
And they called for Buckley Gaynor
To sweep the mill out clean.

There were many other songs that Larry made up in Ellsworth, but they exist only by report. One man recalls that Larry made up a song about "Old Mike Abrams' Five-Saw Dam," while another remembered that he made one that started, "They call me Doctor O'Connell, a man of great knowledge and skill." Harold Archer of Ellsworth Falls said that there was one on Del Avery, Roderick McDonald's cook, that began "They all found fault with Avery because his legs were thin." There was another one, Archer claimed, called "On Lead Mountain's Lofty Brow," that his father pasted in the front of the family Bible. "That one wasn't at all comical," he said. "It was a real poem."

Finally, from up on Prince Edward Island comes the report of another song. I had asked Frank Sweet of St. Eleanor's if he knew any of Larry's songs from Maine. *"No, I never heard any of his songs he ever made up after he went away," he said, "but I did hear that he made a song about a party over there ... and they took him to court over it, but he proved what he had in it and he gained the trial. ... He made it on some woman in the State of Maine and she ... had him up for trial." So far I have been unable to discover any such litigation, but there's the story.

In 1897, Larry Gorman married Julia Lynch of Bangor, and while they lived in Ellsworth for about five more years and some of the songs we have already considered may have been written during this time, this second marriage makes a convenient transition from Ellsworth to Brewer. But first comes an interlude that will take us from the White Mountains to the St. Croix valley.

SIX

The Henrys and the Lambs:
Granite State to Tomah

In 1892, James E. Henry bought a large tract of land in New Hampshire, set up a sawmill and several woods camps, and went into business making a fortune as fast as he possibly could — and as boldly. "Make money," he advised his three sons, "honestly if possible, but make money."[1] The settlement that rose up through his industry became the present-day town of Lincoln, and it wasn't long before he owned the whole of it. All, that is, but a little patch of land belonging to a recluse named Sid, who refused to sell for any price. One day Sid met Mr. Henry on the street. "Good morning, Mr. Henry," he said. "You and I between us own this whole town, don't we?"

That was sass, and Henry was not a man who always took that sort of thing lightly, but in this case there wasn't much he could do about it. Once, before he came to Lincoln, when he was still operating up in Zealand Valley, he had hired Larry Gorman and Larry had given him considerable sass. But he had asked for it.

Knowing Larry Gorman and what he had done to little Jimmy Yeo, Michael McElroy, and Roderick McDonald, anyone could have predicted how he would serve Henry, for "Ave" Henry was a tightfisted, hard-driving lumberman. It is said that he charged his men for every bit of equipment they used. One time a man killed a horse in an accident, for which Henry charged him sixty dollars. Since the man had only about twenty dollars coming to him, his brother asked Henry if he was going to keep *his* pay too. Henry walked up to the brother and grabbed his gold watch: "Yes," he said, "and this too."[2] He had the legendary boss's contempt for the humanity of his men. The story goes that a man died in camp, and, since they did not know where he belonged, they decided to bury him right there. So they sent a man out to dig the grave. Later in the morning the man returned, saying that the soil was just too hard and rocky to dig a grave in. "Oh hell," said Henry, "don't bother with all that. Just sharpen him and drive him in!" A similar story tells of another man who died. "George," he said to his son, "was he a good man?" He was told that the man was one of the best. "Then take him out and bury him next to old Ranger," he said, "because he was one of our best horses."

Henry had an excellent "chance" there in Lincoln Valley, as good as he had had earlier in Zealand Valley. There was very little pine left, but straight and clear spruce was plentiful. "I never cut so many one-to-a-thousand trees[3] in my life," said Peter Jamieson of East Bathurst, New Brunswick, but he added that the work was all up and down hill, hard on the legs for anyone accustomed as he was to the flat land along the Bay Chaleur. Henry didn't have to drive his logs at all, because he had his own sawmill near where the cutting was going on, and over in Zealand Valley he had had his own log railroad, seven miles long. The whole operation was a family affair, too, for his three sons worked right there with him. John managed the office, George was walking boss and took charge of work in the woods, and Charlie ran the sawmill. "All I care about a dollar is to see it tick," said old Henry. And he saw plenty of them tick. What he left behind him in Zealand Valley in 1892 was described thus in the Boston *Transcript*:

> The beautiful Zealand Valley is one vast scene of waste and desolation; immense heaps of sawdust roll down the slopes to choke the stream and, by the destructive acids distilled from their decaying substance, to poison the fish; smoke rises night and day from fires which are maintained to destroy the still accumulating piles of slabs and other mill debris.[4]

Before we come to Larry Gorman's song on the Henrys, let's take a brief look at the credit side of their ledger, something it is easy enough to ignore. John Jamieson claimed that Henry and Co. always used him well, and his brother Peter said it was the best outfit he ever worked for — strict but good. They both claimed that this strictness was excusable: the general quality of the men who came to work for Henry was not high, and he had been losing so much money on stolen equipment that he had to charge the men for it to stop the pilfering. However, if a man turned in a broken ax-handle he would get a new one without any trouble at all. Further, Henry and Co. was not alone in this practice; many men who worked on the Penobscot have told me that they too were charged "for all things broke or lost." But Larry Gorman was not a Penobscot man; he came to New Hampshire from Union River, and there it was not customary to charge for lost or broken tools. In fact, Joe Tosh said that one time he lost his temper at an ax he was using and simply threw it in the woods; then he told the boss what he had done. The boss said he didn't blame Joe at all and gave him a new ax. The next year Joe found the old one where he had thrown it and turned it back in, but the boss told him to keep it since he probably needed one "around the house."

Nor was Henry alone in not paying men for days they did not work. Many Penobscot woodsmen have told me that often they lost their pay when illness or bad weather kept them from going into the woods. Not only that, but they were often charged room and board in camp for such days. Again, though, Larry seems to be using Union River practices as the basis for his comparison, for there the men were always paid straight monthly time. Dan "Captain Jinks" Donovan even made up a little prayer for rain so he could stay in camp:

> Oh Lord of love, look from above
> On us poor men from home;
> And give us a shower within an hour
> So we'll have all day in the bone.

Several men who worked for Henry have told me that there was no truth in the story that he would hold back a man's wages. A man would get every cent he had coming to him, but absolutely no advance. Even here old Mr. Henry was known to make exceptions. Peter Jamieson told me the following story: one time a man who had worked for the company many years came into the office saying that he had received a letter from his wife telling him that the mortgage on their house was being foreclosed. He wanted to go right home and he needed money; was there *anything* the company could do? Young John said he was sorry but rules were rules: no advance. Old Henry, who was sitting in the office at the time, told his son to go ahead and give the man what he needed. "But, Father," said John, "you know as well as I do that advance of any kind is against all our rules. We just can't do it." The old man snorted, "Well, if *we* can't, *I* can!" And he gave the man what he asked for, taking his note for it. "Of course," said Mr. Jamieson, "he was pretty sure of his man there."

Here is Larry's song on the Henrys, as it was sung for me by John A. Jamieson. We can be pretty safe in dating the song between 1884, when Henry's logging railroad went into operation, and 1892, when he moved his whole operation to Lincoln.

The Good Old State of Maine

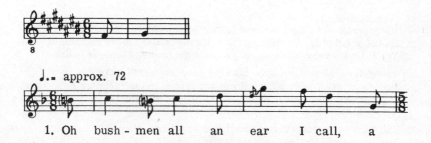

J.= approx. 72

1. Oh bush - men all   an   ear   I call,   a

tale I will re - late, My ex -

pe -ri -ence in the lum - ber-woods all

in this Gra-nite State; Its

snow- clad hills, its wind- ing rills, its

moun- tains, rocks, and plains, You'll

find it ve - ry dif- f'rent, boys, from the

good old State of Maine.

The Good Old State of Maine

1. Oh bushmen all, an ear I call, a tale I will relate,
   My experience in the lumberwoods all in this Granite State;
   Its snowclad hills, its winding rills, its mountains, rocks and plains,
   You'll find it very different, boys, from the good old State of Maine.

2. The difference in the wages, boys, is scarcely worth a dime,
   For every day you do not work you are forced to lose your time;
   To pay your passage to and fro you'll find but little gain,
   You would do as well to stay at home in that good old State of Maine.

3. And here in Zealand Valley you'll find seven feet of snow,
   And work when the thermometer goes thirty-five below;
   It averages three storms a week of snow and sleet or rain,
   You seldom find such weather in that good old State of Maine.

4. They reckon things so neat and fine 'tis hard to save a stamp,
   For every month they do take stock of things around the camp;
   Stoves, pots, kettles, knives, and forks, a spokeshave or a plane,
   Of those they take but small account in that good old State of Maine.

5. Then every night with pen and ink they figure up the cost,
   The crew are held responsible for all things broke or lost;
   An axe, a handle, or a spade, a bunk-hook or a chain —
   The crew are never charged with tools in that good old State of Maine.

6. Those rules and regulations as I've mentioned here before,
   They're in typewritten copies posted up on every door;
   To lose your time and pay your board or work in snow or rain,
   They'd call us fools to stand such rules in that good old State of Maine.[5]

7. The boss he'll then address you in a loud commanding voice,
   Saying, "You know the regulations, boys; therefore you have your choice."
   We know he did not make them, and of him we don't complain,
   For a better boss I never knew in that good old State of Maine.

8. If you don't like their style, my boys, you can go down the line,
   But if you leave them in the lurch they'll figure with you fine;
   They'll cut down your wages, charge you carfare on their train,
   We never heard of such a thing in that good old State of Maine.

9. The aleners [i.e. *aliens*] and foreigners they flock in by the score,
   The diversity of languages would equal Babbler's tower;
   Italians, Russians, Poles, and Finns, a Dutchman or a Dane,
   We never had such drones as those in that good old State of Maine.[6]

10. And for those sub-contractors now I've got a word to say,
    If you work for a jobber here you are apt to lose your pay;
    For there is no lien law in this state, the logs you can't retain,
    While the lumber's holding for your pay in that good old State of Maine.

11. Now for the grub, I'll give it a rub, and that it does deserve,
    The cooks become so lazy they'll allow the men to starve;
    For it's bread and beans, then beans and bread, then bread and beans again,
    Of grub we would sometimes have a change in that good old State of Maine.

12. Our meat and fish is poorly cooked, the bread is sour and old;
    The beans are dry and musty and doughnuts are hard and old;
    To undertake to chew one, that would give your jaws a pain,
    For they're not the kind we used to find in that good old State of Maine.

13. So now my song is concluded and my story's to an end,
    If I have made a statement wrong, I'm willing to amend;
    I like the foreman and the crew, of them I can't complain,
    For a better crew I never knew in that good old State of Maine.

14. So here's adieu to camp and crew, to Henery and Sons;
    Their names are great throughout this state, they're one of her largest guns;
    I wish them all prosperity e'er I return again,
    For I'll mend my ways and spend my days in that good old State of Maine.

Peter Jamieson claimed that Larry had nothing to complain about at all. Both he and his brother John told me the story of Larry's going into the office to get his wages. Old Mr. Henry was there at the moment, "Larry," he said, "I understand you've made a song on us."

"Oh," said Larry diffidently, "I'm always making up songs about something or other."

Mr. Henry pulled out a chair. "Sit down, Larry, and sing it for me, will you?" he said.

"No, sir," said Larry, "all you want to do is keep back my wages on it somehow."

Henry turned to his son. "John," he said, "give Gorman here every cent he has coming to him right now." But Larry still held back. Finally, Henry reached into his own pocket. "Look, Larry, here's five dollars extra. That'll buy you a bottle and whatever else you want. Now will you sing it?"

Larry finally consented and sang the song for him. To everyone's surprise, Henry was delighted. "That's a good song, Larry, and as for that verse about being willing to change anything you've said wrong, there's no need of that. It's just as true as the Bible, that song; you've got us down there O.K., even to the rules and regulations on the door."

There are reports that Larry Gorman worked elsewhere in New Hampshire too. At least two people have told me that they are quite sure he worked around Berlin, but I can discover no more. One man wrote me that Gorman "worked in New Hampshire for many years," but he did not know when or where. The same man told me that "he also worked in lumbering operations in many parts of Maine." If we exclude the Union River and the Penobscot, where else in Maine did Gorman work? I have only found one other place, Tomah Stream. And I have my doubts about that.

The evidence that Larry was ever in the St. Croix-Grand Lake area is slight: the word of one man, Robert MacArthur of Grand Lake Stream. "It was about 1895...," says William Doerflinger, who got his information from Mr. MacArthur, "that Larry found himself, when fall came on, in Milltown, a busy sawmill center on the lower St. Croix, and in need of a job."[7] Accordingly, he got a job with Natty Lamb and went up to Tomah. He was used very poorly and made up a song about it:

Tomah Stream[8]

1. Come all you Mill-town row-dies that drink and have no fear, I'll

have you not to   touch a drop   in

the   fall   of   the   year;   For

if you do,   you'll   sure - lye   rue, - like-

wise   my-self   I've   seen,   Be

care-ful,   do   not   hire   out   to

work   on   To - mah   Stream.

Tomah Stream

1. Come all you Milltown rowdies that drink and have no fear,
   I'll have you not to touch a drop in the fall of the year;
   For if you do, you'll surelye rue, — likewise myself I've seen,
   Be careful, do not hire to work on Tomah Stream.

2. For the last fall that ever was, I was drunk and on a spree.
   I swore that I would hire, and the very first sight I'd see.
   The first it was old Natty Lamb, and up to him I steered.
   I hired to work on Tomah and to drive six little steers.

3. He said the chance for lumbering was the best I ever did see.
   "The spruce they stand upon a ridge, as thick as thick can be.
   The provisions I'll provide for you, and of the very best kind!
   The cook will dish 'er up for you and have yer males on time."

4. But when I got to Squirrel Point, 'twas there I was struck dumb
   To see the load of provision that into the camp must come.
   There was three little loaves of bread as black as the Ace of Spades,
   And about a quarter of a pound of tea and an old bull's shoulder blade.

5. We packed our provisions up and put them on a sled,
   We hitched behind an old gray mare that had a broken leg.
   We all marched up the turnpike behind this fancy team.
   That is the fate of any man who works on Tomah Stream.

6. At length we got to Tomah; 'twas there we made a stop.
   We hitched the old mare to a tree and cast about the lot.
   The way we had to travel, it was a muddy tramp.
   Each man he had to sack a load that night in to the camp.

7. At length the camp it hove in view; it was a sight to see.
   There laid an old dead porcupine, full as large as me.
   A piece of an old hemp carpet, 'twas wore as thin as gauze,
   This was the beddin' that Natty had for to keep out the frost.

8. We rested hard that night, my boys, we shivered with the cold.
   We rose by day in the morning a sight for to behold.
   We kindled up a fire and the frost was cutting keen.
   I cursed the day I hired out to work on Tomah Stream.

9. About ten o'clock in the morning old Natty he appeared.
   We all rushed to the door and grieved him with a cheer.
   He said, "You look quite happy, all in your little abode.
   A pox upon the devil, boys! Why didn't you skid the road?" [9]

I have never found another version of the song, nor have I found anyone else who has even heard of it.

There are several indications that the song is not Gorman's work. First of all, what he was doing in Milltown in 1895 is hard to imagine; at this time he was a married man living in Ellsworth. Of course, MacArthur could have been wrong about the date, but still Milltown seems an unlikely place for an Ellsworth man to go. Second, Larry was not a man who went on sprees. The only other place where he mentions his own drinking is in "The Hoboes of Maine." Third, he was never to my knowledge a man who could work as a teamster. Finally, as several people have pointed out to me — people who know Gorman's songs — it just does not sound like his work. But none of these points is conclusive, and the song may well be his. If it is, I have a hunch it goes back a lot further than 1895. The mention of "six little steers" probably puts it back at least twenty years before that — perhaps more; ox teams were rare in the woods in the late years of the century. Perhaps Larry worked on Tomah before he went to Ellsworth, say in 1880 or a little earlier. Whether or not Larry Gorman wrote the song, it seems not to be the only one that voiced dissatisfaction with the Lambs. H. E. Lamb of Calais, a distant relation of Natty Lamb, recalled another long poem about him which ended as follows:

> I would rather go down to Oak Bay and dig clams
> Than go up to Tomer Stream and work for those damn Lambs.

SEVEN

"Poor and Neglected":
Brewer and the End

Julia Lynch has been described to me as an "attractive, compact little woman," very neat and very much of a lady. She came from a good Bangor family, and her antecedents were just as Irish as Larry's. Both Jeremiah Lynch and his wife Catherine (*née* Hagerty) had come over from County Cork, and Jerry, who drove the street sprinkler on the East Side, had done well enough to own his own house and provide very decently for his large family.

All of this raises a question: how did Julia come to marry someone like Larry Gorman? The obvious answer is that she was forty with no other immediate prospects, but that answer assumes that she would have married anyone who came along, which I doubt. Let's not forget that the Larry Gorman she probably saw when she came down to Ellsworth to visit relatives was a tall, well-built man, far from homely, extremely well dressed, polite, an excellent conversationalist, and a wit. He came from good people too, as we know; he came by his good breeding quite honestly. Larry Gorman was anything but riffraff; he was a rather respectable widower who owned his own home in a good part of town.

They were married in St. John's Catholic Church (her family's church) in Bangor by the Reverend Edward M. McSweeney on September 7, 1897. Julia's sister Delia was maid of honor, and Dr. William P. McNally, a well-known local physician, was best man. The whole thing was done very quietly; there is hardly a mention of it in the Bangor papers.

The couple went back to Ellsworth to live in the old house at 16 Union Street. Julia was an excellent housekeeper and a very orderly person, but she evidently discovered rather quickly that her new husband's old habit rankled; Larry's song-writing was a lifelong problem for her. Some people told me that they thought she had rather taken him in hand and "gotten him off this poetry stuff and made a man out of him." If she got him off it he obviously got right back on it again, because there were still plenty of songs to come, but Julia never liked them. As one man said, "She used to get after him about those songs. Larry'd get going on a line or two and then she'd land on him and shut him up."

Exactly why Larry and Julia left Ellsworth for Brewer I cannot say, but it may well have been her idea. Perhaps she wanted to be closer to her family in Bangor. Possibly Larry felt he could make better money in the Brewer mills than he could in Ellsworth, but I doubt that he wanted to move, because he always referred to Ellsworth as "home" and made several nostalgic trips back there to see friends. Neither can I establish exactly *when* they left Ellsworth, but my guess is 1903, for this is the first year we find Larry listed in the *Bangor-Brewer City Directory*. Mrs. Fannie Hardy Eckstorm notes that in January, 1902, he was still in Ellsworth.[1] In 1904 he paid his first poll tax of $3.00 in ward five (South Brewer). Finally, on August 20, 1904, Larry sold his property in Ellsworth back to Colin McKenzie for $450 (McKenzie was to take over a $300 mortgage too). So now Larry had cut his last official tie with "home."

Brewer was, and still is, for all practical purposes, a part of Bangor, which is to say that it is part of the base of that great funnel, the Penobscot River, the top of which extends from beyond Jackman on the west to the Mattawamkeag River on the east — a drainage basin of over ten thousand square miles including over sixteen hundred streams and close to two hundred lakes and ponds. Hundreds of thousands of trees were cut in this area every year; a million logs were landed and driven down into the booms at Argyle and Pea Cove above Old Town; and often more than two hundred million board feet of lumber were sawn and shipped out from Bangor in a year. Sometimes the river between Bangor and Brewer would be so full of lumber schooners that a boy could, with some ingenuity, cross the river dry-shod. And every day there would be ships, some so heavy-laden as to be almost awash, making their way out with the tide. Thoreau saw it at mid-century:

> There stands the city of Bangor, fifty miles up the Penobscot, at the head of navigation for vessels of the larger class, the principal lumber depot on this continent, with a population of twelve thousand, like a star on the edge of the night, still hewing at the forests of which it is built, already overflowing with the luxuries and refinement of Europe, and sending its vessels to Spain, to England, and to the West Indies for its groceries — and yet only a few axemen have gone "up river" into the howling wilderness which feeds it.[2]

If only "a few axemen" went upriver, all of them who lived through the winter and the spring came down to Bangor when the drive was in the boom, and they headed for Hancock Street, Harlow Street, and lower Exchange Street, where they called for strong drink and loose women.

They found plenty of both, for Bangor was a city especially constructed not only to saw and ship lumber but to fleece the woodsmen who cut and drove it and to get them upriver again before they knew what had hit them. Mention such places as the Franklin House, the Central House, Barney Kelley's Saloon, or Pope McKinnon's Globe Hotel to an old woodsman, or ask him about Fan Jones' place or Aunt Hat's up in Veazie, or ask him what it was like around the "Devil's Half Acre," Haymarket Square, and you are apt to get story after story of the roaring life of the lumberman in town, enough to make the worst of Sodom and Gomorrah sound like what went on behind the water-cooler at the office Christmas party. Maine taught lumbering to the world, the Penobscot taught it to the rest of Maine, and Bangor was the center of it all — a hard-working, hard-drinking boom town that for over a hundred years was one of the most important seaports in the world. It was a glorious day and the night was full of promise and the smell of fresh-sawn pine and the scream of the mills going it around the clock in double shifts. And now? The cold light of dawn, the morning-after. Utterly normal and properly bustling, Bangor has parking meters and plans for tomorrow. Perhaps it is better this way, but whatever Bangor is destined to become in the future, it will never again be the fabled town it was. In that respect it is one with Nineveh and Tyre, not to mention the Cities of the Plain.

Brewer was a part of all this activity, but it was tamer. It was a city less than one-quarter the size of its neighbor, yet it was one of the biggest shipbuilding centers on the river, often building more ships in a year than did Bangor itself. Also, some of the major sawmills were on the Brewer side of the river. South Brewer, where Larry Gorman lived, was, in fact, largely an adjunct of the Eastern Manufacturing Corporation, better known as the "Eastern." The plant was built on the site of Colonel Brewer's original sawmill at the mouth of Sedgeunkedunk Stream, but when Fred Ayer and his friends took over the old Palmer Mill on this spot in 1889, they turned it into the largest bandsaw mill in New England. Then they added a pulp-mill to utilize the wastewood from the sawmill and later a paper mill to utilize the pulp. It was a big establishment, and all around the yard, as close as they could get, were clustered the old frame boarding houses. After all, when a man worked from dawn to dark and only got half an hour for lunch and twenty minutes for supper, he didn't want to spend much time walking.

South Brewer was heavily French, but on DeRusha Lane, close to the yard, there was a whole colony of Prince Edward Islanders: Days, Barrys, Callaghans, and Adamses, and nearby there were others, like the McGillens. Here it was that Larry and Julia Gorman came to live around 1903. They rented a little house and Larry went to work. Larry was right at home on DeRusha Lane. Occasionally there would be parties over at Adams' and everyone would get him to sing. They especially enjoyed the Island songs because they knew all the local references. Clarence Adams, although he was a child at the time, can remember hearing him sing, "The Horse's Confession" and "The Gull Decoy." "Larry'd sing sitting straight up with his arms folded across his chest — not like other woods singers," he said. He also remembers that when his family bought a farm about two miles out of town, the men from DeRusha, Larry among them, would often hike out on a Sunday afternoon to play cards, usually "forty-fives." At night Clarence would have to pile the whole gang of them into a wagon and drive them home again.

It was not long before he was pretty well known in South Brewer. But right from the beginning we get the familiar reports of Larry Gorman's going his own way. He was "different"; some have defined this difference by saying he was "odd," while others say that he was a man that people looked up to — a man of some reputation, one they could point out to others and say, "That's Larry Gorman over there." He was a "lone wolf," one old resident told me. "He did what *he* wanted to do; he never impressed me as the marrying kind at all, and I somehow don't think he and Julia were ever very happy together." Yet from all appearances, they were well suited to each other, for all their being different. They had no children, however, and that set them apart in this neighborhood of big families. "Julia always kept her house a little bit neater, her curtains a little bit stiffer than the rest did," I was told. "You never went to her house for tea and when her sisters would come over from Bangor she'd never have the neighbors in to meet them, nor did she take them around. And when she and Larry went to mass they were always on time, not having any kids to haul along like the others. Julia never could see why the others couldn't be on time too."

Clarence Adams of Brewer recalls seeing the two of them in church at St. Theresa's. Larry would stand there, head and shoulders over everyone else, holding his missal up in front of him. Pretty soon he would pull his glasses down on his nose and start looking around the congregation slowly and methodically, as if to see who was there. Every once in a while he would settle on one person, giving him careful scrutiny. "Our pew was well back from his," said Adams, "so we kids would watch him. We figured that when he fixed on somebody like that he was making up a song on them, and we'd begin to snicker. I got cuffed plenty for snickering at old Mr. Gorman, but sometimes my folks would snicker too!" Wherever Larry was, he was constantly at work on songs. "Even playing cards he'd be humming and looking off into space half the time," one man told me, while another recalled seeing him walking down the street, hands behind his back, looking abstractedly around and humming a piece of a tune. "When Father would see him doing this, he'd say, 'Well, I wonder who's getting the rap now?'" If you stopped him on the street and talked to him, his clear blue eyes seemed to bore holes in you; suddenly they would light up and he would smile, "and you'd know he'd thought of something he could use in a song."

Earl Doucette of Augusta recalls seeing Gorman's songs around South Brewer: "His songs were printed on single sheets, sans music, and sold to friends and on street corners.... When I knew him, Larry Gorman was writing about our town and its people. His forte then seemed to be barbed humor." Word would get around that Gorman had written a new poem, and people would often go to his house to buy copies, which must have just about driven Julia out of her mind! Billy Bell of Brewer described his method as follows:

*He'd write these pieces and he'd learn them; he could say them right off, but the originals he'd throw into this trunk. Then he'd go around amongst the people he knew and he'd say these pieces over and if they liked them he'd write them off one for ten cents. And he usually was able to put a tune to everything, you know, and he'd sing a little bit and put this tune to it, and of course lots of people liked it, but the most of the fellows that ever bought them thought it was just kind of a joke. They'd read it and pass it around and then it'd disappear. His stuff has never lasted around here very long.

Bell is absolutely right. Very little of Gorman's work has lasted in Brewer tradition. I have yet to collect a whole poem or song there except from printed or handwritten copies. In fact, all we have from *tradition* are fragments. For example, Clarence Adams said there was a long piece called "The Winter of Nineteen Five," but all he could remember was

We drove the cattle to the brook
And then the fun began;
We had to chop their noses out
As soon as they were done.
And if some records had been kept
By some that now survive,
I think you'd hear the most severe
Was that of nineteen five.

Arthur Dalton of Rumford, Maine, gave me part of another:

*He was going on a [hunting] trip with a bunch of the big bugs, you see. And the day come ... for some unknown reason before he got there they all left and went. Went hunting without him. And of course that resulted in a song. He made a piece about each one of them, you know, and honest to God, it would make a horse laugh. One of the fellows was so mad he caught him and he told him he'd kill him if he didn't promise that he'd never sing it again. I remember one verse; it said,

The prize was not so very great
That so many need compete:
An old gray gander, thin and pale,
Long and slim, without a tail,
One wing broke and on the ground,
And 'twas won by the banker, Davy Brown.

Sometimes all that remains is the report of a song, like the following from Billy Bell:

*Larry Gorman came here from Ellsworth around 1900. His first job was in a wood-and-coal yard. So they put him to work in the morning loading this great load of coal, a ton or two, and threw a basket onto it and Larry got up on it and they drove to this house where they found it had to go upstairs. So poor Larry was heartbroken; he couldn't imagine lugging a ton or two of coal up a flight of

stairs. He come pretty near quitting right there, but he stayed with it anyway. Those baskets'll hold about a bushel and a half, you know, and you back up to the thing and catch the handle — and lug! So Larry got through with it but he didn't work at that place very long; he left that pretty quick — that was beyond him. So far as I know the first song or piece of poetry he ever wrote [was] about that, and the name of it was "Carrying Coal in a Basket." Of course that was quite a joke.

And so it goes — a sketch of this song and the title of that one, but practically nothing has lasted in tradition.

Why didn't Larry's songs survive better in Brewer? First of all, it seems to me that the songs he made up here were less singable than those he made up elsewhere. He appears to have been thinking more in terms of print than of singing. He was selling printed broadsides of his poems all the time now, and although he would usually sing over a verse or two to give the tune to whoever bought one, and although he always seemed to have a tune in mind as he composed, nevertheless the end result was more verse than song. But there is a second reason, a more important one: in Brewer the local tradition was not strong enough to absorb and carry on new material. It was an urban area, heavily French, and, as might be expected in a mill town where people were constantly moving in and out, there was not that solidarity, that community of interest, that would make people remember songs as topical and personal as Larry's. The people immediately concerned, those who knew the persons and places mentioned, might remember them, but their children did not because they moved away or the people the songs were about moved away. New arrivals brought with them their own local traditions, and for that reason towns like Brewer are good places to look for, say, Prince Edward Island material. But the local tradition of Brewer itself was weak, where it existed at all.

Few enough of the broadsides themselves have lasted, but they are enough to show us the sort of work Larry was doing at the time. John O'Connor of Portland, a nephew of Larry's, found two of them among his papers and sent them to me. So far as I know, they are the only two Larry Gorman broadsides extant. Both are printed on single sheets in double columns, with the title in large capitals at the top; directly under the title in small capitals is printed "By LAWRENCE GORMAN, SOUTH BREWER."

The Workman.

Comrades, sit down and brush off your frown,
    'Til we'll talk of our sad situation,
Of troubles and strife and struggle for life,
    Between labor and trust combination.

A workman we know he is ground very low,
    He is looked on as something inferior,
He is robbed and abused and badly used,
    By those whom they call his superior.

A workman at best is at all times behest,
    No one but convicts have it harder,
And his dear darling wife to cause him more strife,
    Must be into every soap order.

She needs china wares, couch, and wicker chairs,
    Sideboard and mahogany table,
Rugs, scrub-brush and broom, tar soap and perfume,
    Shampoo and bay rum and witch hazel.

She needs wintergreen likewise boraxine,
    Peppermint, olive oil and vanilla,
With cloves and allspice to flavor things nice,
    And satin to face her couch pillow.

Then the grocery bills would give man the chills,
    He'll be cheated in weight and in measure,
He must be discreet to make both ends meet,
    If he is'nt possessed of great treasure.

There is lettuce and greens, sweet corn and string beans,
    Cabbage, carrots and beets and potatoes,
Canned salmon and peas, eggs, butter and cheese,
    Canned peaches and pears and tomatoes.

. Fresh cod and corned hake and porter house steak,
    Sugar, coffee and tea and molasses,
Rolled oats and whole wheat, soused tripe and pigs' feet,
    A tray and a set of wine glasses.

Lard, flour and cornmeal and a quarter of veal,
    Prunes, onions and mustard and pickles,
Smoked shoulder and ham and a small roast of lamb,
    And that's what picks up a man's nickels.

If his wife isn't well her doctor will tell,
    That delaying of cases is risky,
If she looks thin and pale she must have basses ale,
    And a whole case of duffey's malt whiskey.

You see there's no end to the money you'll spend,
    More money than four men can bring in,
And the kids if they like must each have a bike,
    And a five dollar hammock to swing in.

The girls and the boys must all have their toys,
    Carts, waggons, dolls and rocking horses:
While the boys chew and smoke and crack a hard joke,
    And put forth a great volley of curses.

They must have new clothes, new hats, and new shoes,
    To attend the high school graduation,
And they'll all let you see that they must have a V,
    For the fourth of July celebration.

So now I'll conclude, my words may sound rude,
    Whil'st many would call them outrageous,
But people of Maine, you can see very plain,
    Why a working man can't save his wages.

The second poem takes its title from what was once a common synonym for "old times." "After the invention of the screw-auger (which

was first manufactured at Castine, Maine, in 1810," Fannie Hardy
Eckstorm tells us, "the old pod-auger, with a straight flange and cutting
edge, became the symbol of everything antiquated and out of date. Even
a man might be spoken of as an 'old pod-auger.'"[3] Probably Larry also
had in mind a rather popular song by the same title, which took a similar attitude toward the old days.

The Old Pod Auger Days

Come listen to my story,
   'Til I'll talk to you awhile;
It is my joy and glory,
   For to make all people smile,
If you'll only just permit me,
   For to speak a word of praise,
Of the famous men and women,
   Of the Old Pod Auger Days.

You'd find all men more honest then,
   Athletic, brave and strong,
Their faces heavily bearded,
   And their hair they wore it long.
The women were most lovely,
   They had sweet and cunning ways;
I dearly loved the maidens,
   Of the Old Pod Auger Days.

The children that they had those days,
   Were lovely ones I ween,
They varied some in number,
   From eleven to sixteen;
Their parents seemed delighted,
   As they watched their childish plays,
And they always had big families,
   In the Old Pod Auger Days.

They didn't cram their brains so much,
   About this world's affairs,
They were taught their scripture lessons,
   Said their night and morning prayers,
They went to church on Sunday,
   To sing their Makers praise,
There were fewer unbelievers,
   In the Old Pod Auger Days.

The mother trained the daughter,
   And the father trained the son,
He taught him to be useful,
   How to use an axe and gun,
To clear the land and till it well,
   A livelihood to raise;
And we never heard of hobos,
   In the Old Pod Auger Days.

They always had good horses then,
   Horned cattle, sheep and hogs,

With poultry in abundance,
  But no useless poodle dogs;
Nice vegetables of all kinds,
  And apples they would raise,
And they always made good cider,
  In the Old Pod Auger Days.

They always had their venison,
  Deer, caribou and moose,
A turkey for Thanksgiving,
  And for Christmas a fat goose;
Rye, oats and barley, wheat and corn,
  These farmers used to raise,
And they had plenty buckwheat pancakes,
  In the Old Pod Auger Days.

The mother trained the daughters,
  In their pure domestic lives,
To cook and sew to spin and knit,
  And make good farmers' wives;
To shear the sheep and milk the cows,
  And turn them out to graze,
To churn and make their butter,
  In the Old Pod Auger Days.

This modern profanity,
  It does me much apall,
Of those egredious [i.e. *egregious*] egotists,
  Who think they know it all;
We can tell these young agnostics,
  With their automobile sleighs,
That this country was discovered,
  In the Old Pod Auger Days.

Brave mariners discovered it,
  Before such men were born;
Both continents were coasted,
  From Greenland to Cape Horn,
Our mountains, lakes and rivers,
  Our harbours, capes and bays,
Were all mapped out and charted,
  In the Old Pod Auger Days.

Much credit's due to those brave men,
  Who ventured o'er the seas;
The Spanish, French and English,
  The Dutch and Portuguese,
The Russians and the Danes may claim,
  A meagre share of praise,
For their Arctic explorations,
  In the Old Pod Auger Days.

Of poets, wits and humorists,
  I can name you many's the score,
Pope, Burns and Swift and Goldsmith,
  And the far famed Thomas Moore,
The great immortal Shakespere,
  So famous for his plays,

These men have all existed,
    In the Old Pod Auger Days.

Them days the world had not been blessed
    With kindergarten schools,
And neither was it over-run,
    With educated fools;
We found all men more honest then,
    For wealth they had no craze,
There were fewer bank defaulters,
    In the Old Pod Auger Days.

For sculptors and for painters,
    We have no such men you know,
As perigeno, Raphael,
    Or Fra, Angelico;
Their paintings and their sculptures,
    Do still the world amaze,
And still they lived and flourished,
    In the Old Pod Auger Days.

As to modern conveniences,
    We've many to be sure;
When you wake up in the morning,
    There's a paper at your door,
Tells of murders, robberies, suicides,
    Or some disastrous blaze;
We had seldom heard of fire bugs,
    In the Old Pod Auger Days.

I will finish for the present now,
    Lest that someone take offence;
Some things may sound unpleasant,
    To those folks of consequence,
Though for pains and information,
    We get more abuse than praise;
We've a special veneration,
    For the Old Pod Auger Days.

A third poem, "The Hoboes of Maine," was printed in *Minstrelsy of Maine* with the following headnote: "Written by Mr. Lawrence Gorman, of Brewer, Maine; copied from a printed broadside, autographed in lead pencil...."[4] It is a marvellous picture of men who were the victims of an old Bangor racket, not that Bangor had any patent on it. Say a man came down out of the woods with four or five months' hard-earned pay in his pocket. He'd go to one of the old woodsmen's hotels, get cleaned up, and take off on a spree that would last anywhere from two days to a week. Then he'd be broke again, but he was welcome to stay on as long as he had to, running up a bill of fifty or sixty dollars or even more. But when it came time to go on the drive, the hotel-keeper would take him and all the rest of his credit customers down to the depot, give them a quart of whiskey apiece, and put them on the train for Moosehead Lake. At one time they were locked in the cars like cattle; often enough there wouldn't be an unbroken window glass in the entire train by the time it reached Greenville. The men would hike in to camp, stay in bed sick a day or so, and then get to work. When they returned to Bangor again, they went to settle up with the hotel, and then they began the whole business over again. So long as the hotel men knew the boys were going on the drive or into the woods, they knew how much they were good for. And they were in close touch with the hiring offices, so they knew where their boys were all the time. It kept the operators supplied with woodsmen, the hotel-keepers with regular customers, and the woodsmen themselves with cheap whiskey. A few managed to break this circle and escape; some died on the drive, their caulked boots hung to a tree for their only memorial; some found no way out until they arrived at "Strangers' Row," where they were laid on top of the last one in an unmarked grave.

"Here they are to the life," said Mrs. Eckstorm, "with their telescope bags of the nineties, replacing the mealbags of the earlier days, their slickers to shed the spring rain, their calked boots hung on their shoulders, and the 'long-neckers,' or bottles of whiskey, present if not evident. It is a grimy picture of dazed, doped, half-drunk woodsmen being loaded in the early morning on the upriver train at the old yellow depot, to be sent on the drives after a brief carouse on their winter wages."[5]

The Hoboes of Maine[6]

1. All brother Hoboes, I pray come along,
        I hope you will listen and join in my song;
    I would be delighted to have a thing righted,
        Especially now, if there's anything wrong.
    I'm poor and neglected, I'm mean and dejected,
        I never can visit my birthplace again,
    I've joined that great order, since I crossed the border,
        So prominent now, called the Hoboes of Maine.

2. There are many young men crossing over the line,
        Who have not in their hearts a bad thought or design;
    They'll come in great hopes, for they know not the ropes,
        And fear not the allurements of women or wine.
    They leave their dear mothers, their fathers or brothers,
        Their kind, loving sisters they'll ne'er see again;
    As soon as they come here, they'll each find a chum here,
        And fall into line with the Hoboes of Maine.

3. They'll come by the hundreds, those hardy young bloods,
        All neatly attired in their own native goods,
    In search of employment and earthly enjoyment,
        They'll find it no trouble to hire for the woods.
    They'll send them up stream then, to chop and drive team then,
        In hopes that their wages will all be clear gain;
    But by those man traps they are all handicapped,
        And their names are enrolled with the Hoboes of Maine.

4. They'll come down in the spring and they'll hang around some dive;
        When their money is gone they will hire for the drive,

Their eyes with a glaze on, most painful to gaze on,
  Like bears in the winter, more dead than alive;
With calked boots and greaser, a long-neck apiece,
  They are marched to the station and shipped on the train;
I doubt if they wake till they reach Moosehead Lake,
  When they'll take the toe path with the Hoboes of Maine.

5. With boots on one shoulder and coat on one arm,
  Their destiny next is the Roach River Farm;
Their way they will take over mountain and lake,
  As the sceneries around them afford little charm;
They'll look tired and dreary, fatigued and leg weary,
  Each one of his lot will sorely complain,
Their toes and their ankles both blistered and rankled,
  A common complaint with the Hoboes of Maine.

6. With little regard for a room or a bed,
  They'll throw themselves down on a filthy old spread;
They'll lie there till morning, until given warning,
  When each will arise with his eyes crimson red.
They'll rise from their beds then, with awful swelled heads then,
  Prepare to resume their hard journey again,
O'er mountains and ridges and corduroy bridges,
  All cursing the fate of the Hoboes of Maine.

7. That night they will reach the camp where they drive,
  Where they are packed thicker than bees in a hive;
Both tired and half-drunk, they roll into their bunk,
  As you'd think by their groans they would never survive.
They'll curse and they'll swear then, they'll vow and declare then,
  They'll never be seen on Roach River again,
That they'd rather go beg, with one arm and a leg,
  Than be caught on the drive with the Hoboes of Maine.

8. Then the City Police they plot and connive
  To snare those poor dupes coming off of the drive,
They'll hang round the station, in deep consultation,
  In watch of those victims before they arrive.
They'll joyfully hail them, all ready to jail them,
  And welcome them back to their city again;
Each man, as he'll walk up, is booked for the lock-up,
  To lie there and sweat with the Hoboes of Maine.

9. The man who resists them is used very rough,
  He is thrown on the pavement and quickly handcuffed;
You'd think by their twisters, their chains and cell-wristers
  They surely had captured some notable tough;
They'll pound and they'll bruise him and shamefully use him,
  They'll capture his money, his watch and his chain;
Likewise their design to collect a big fine,
  Or to keep out of jail with the Hoboes of Maine.

10. Next morning he's brought to his honor Judge Vose,
  Who sits there prepared to give him a dose,
As the victim acts silly from blows of the billy,
  His cuts and his scars he will scan very close;
He bids them to stand up and hold his right hand up,
  Saying, 'They tell me young man, you've been drinking again;
A fine I must levy, exceedingly heavy,
  Or have you break stone with the Hoboes of Maine.'

11. Now I have served out my thirty long days;
    Last night I slept in a cold alleyway;
I'm totally busted and cannot get trusted,
    Folks would know, if they'd trust me, I never should pay.
I'm shabby and bare now, and never would dare now
    To visit my own native country again:
They'd jeer me and boot me and threaten to shoot me,
    And bid me go back to the Hoboes of Maine.

12. I'll tell of a man who was given to roam
    Being weary of tramping he thought he'd go home;
I mean not to name him, in case I'd defame him,
    But just for a nickname I'll call him Bill Vroam.
He thought he could bluff them, and tried hard to stuff them,
    He claimed he had served in the Cuban campaign;
But as soon as they spied him, they identified him;
    They knew he belonged to the Hoboes of Maine.

13. But the Hoboes of Maine are still in great hope
    That in some future day they will have further scope;
There's too much restriction, too much interdiction —
    In some other states they've tasted the hope.
If those would-be rulers kept out of the coolers,
    They'd soon become powerful and certain to reign
In the lowlands and highlands and Prince Edward Island,
    Quebec, Nova Scotia, New Brunswick and Maine.

The Spanish-American War ("the Cuban campaign") was in 1898, Gorman came to Brewer about 1903, and Judge Thomas W. Vose died in 1907. This dates the poem pretty well, but the question arises: how much did Larry Gorman actually know of the life he talks about here? Knowing what we do of Larry's personality, his circumstances, and his inclinations, we may be sure that he was not one of the hoboes himself. He was not a habitual carouser; in fact, most of the people who knew him are at some pains to point out that, as one man said, "So long as I knew Larry Gorman, I never saw him take a drink." However, he probably did take one from time to time, but to classify himself as one of the hoboes he describes is certainly poetic license.

How well did Larry really know the country upriver from Bangor? The poem indicates that he had some knowledge of it, but anyone who had been there only once with his eyes halfway open (and Larry's were always wide open!) could have seen what the poem describes; that is to say, "The Hoboes of Maine" shows no very close acquaintance with the area. Is there, then, any record besides "The Hoboes of Maine" that Larry had ever worked in Penobscot waters? Plenty of woodsmen have told me oh hell yes he worked up there, but when I press them for particulars, it always turns out that that is what they were *told*. I have never met a man who worked with him up there or who could even name a camp or operation he had been connected with. Further, there are no pay records or rosters that go back that far. On the other hand, one of Larry's grandnieces can remember that her Aunt Julia used to be alone for long periods of time in the winter, and she had always assumed that Uncle Larry was up in the woods. And we have his own statement in a letter that he worked in the woods right up to 1914, though where and for how long at a stretch is not clear.[7] Perhaps the most plausible solution was offered by Clarence Adams, who claimed that Larry was what is called a "camp inspector," that is to say, a man who worked a short while in many different camps. He'd take a job, and before long he'd get sick, fired, or chased out of camp for his songs; then he'd return home for a short while before going back into the woods, sometimes repeating this process three or four times in a winter. This would explain both the general certainty that he had worked on Penobscot waters and the vagueness as to particulars. At any rate, there is absolutely no foundation for Beck's statement that Gorman "was hired to work for the Great Northern Paper Company and his songs became so popular that eventually he came to spend a considerable portion of his time writing songs for the company paper."[8] There is no record, there is no tradition, and there was no company paper until four years after Gorman's death.[9] Larry's role with that company was indeed "unique," as Beck says; it did not exist at all, save as he may have hired on as a driver or woodsman from time to time.

The three preceding pieces are all we have of Larry's songs in printed form. There are reports of many more, though. For instance, Joe MacDougall of Alberton, P.E.I., told Helen Creighton about visiting Larry in Brewer:

*I worked for Getchell's Ice Company and I boarded at my aunt's house in Brewer, Maine, and Larry Gorman and his wife lived on...a little short street in off Main Street, and I used to go over there and see him....Found out a lot of news. He give me an awful lot of ballets — oh I had a whole handful — and I lost them all, all these old ballets of songs....He had them all wrote down. He had them all in print....all the ballets that I got. Oh, I suppose I must have had nearly a hundred ballets, and I lost them....the whole thing.

"The Boys of the Island" does not belong in this chapter chronologically. Mrs. Eckstorm dated it "not later than 1894, and it may have been some years earlier."[10] She is right; it could not have been written after 1888, the last year Bradford Kelley ran his saloon on Water Street just off Bangor's "Devil's Half Acre." And Timothy J. O'Leary gave up river-driving to become a policeman in 1885:

> Brade Kelley will poison a man with bad whiskey,
> For pastime they will banish their lager and ale;
> Then on the corner when he does get frisky,
> They will call for Tim Carey to take him to jail.[11]

That would seem to bracket the song pretty well; still, it may go back even farther than that for all we know. Perhaps it belongs to that time between Larry's leaving Miramichi and the Island and his settling down in Ellsworth, or to a slightly earlier time when he may have shuttled back and forth between Maine and P.E.I. The song is very widely distributed, being known not only in Maine but also on Prince Edward

Island and in Miramichi — further evidence of its early composition.
Nevertheless, it seems logical to take it up here since it is about Bangor.

"The Boys of the Island" is by far the most popular song Larry
Gorman ever wrote, if indeed he did write it. And on this point there
is no agreement. That it seems to be about the Bangor of the eighties,
when Gorman was in Ellsworth, might argue against his authorship; but
that can hardly be called conclusive evidence. Eckstorm and Smyth
make no attribution, but Louise Manny included it in her article "Larry
Gorman — Miramichi Balladist," and Doerflinger attributes the exact
same version to Gorman.[12] Many of my informants who were able to
give me a verse or two said that it was by Larry Gorman, but just as
many said they did not know who made it up. The brothers Fitzgerald
of Waterford, P.E.I., were unqualified in their insistence that Larry
Gorman did *not* write it, attributing it instead to "Beaver Jack" Mac-
Innis, another Island man who went to Maine.[13] The argument cannot
be settled; it is one of those pieces that could easily have become Gorman's by an obvious association, yet it could just as easily have been
written by him. For the present I will leave it in the Gorman canon
until I have a true bill stating otherwise. To come clean, I hope Larry
wrote it, but I have my doubts.

The first version was sung for me by Edmund Doucette of Miminegash, P.E.I., and the second by Arthur Dalton of Rumford, Maine, a boy
from the Island himself. Dalton's tune is essentially the same as Doucette's except that in stanza one only the first half of the tune is used.

The Boys of the Island (I)

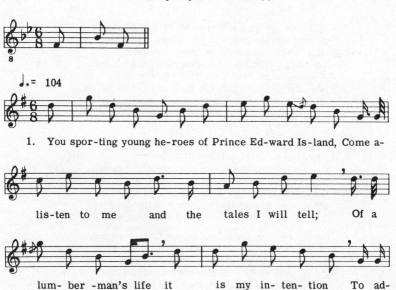

1. You spor-ting young he-roes of Prince Ed-ward Is-land, Come a-

lis-ten to me   and   the   tales I will tell;   Of a

lum- ber -man's life it   is my in-ten- tion   To ad-

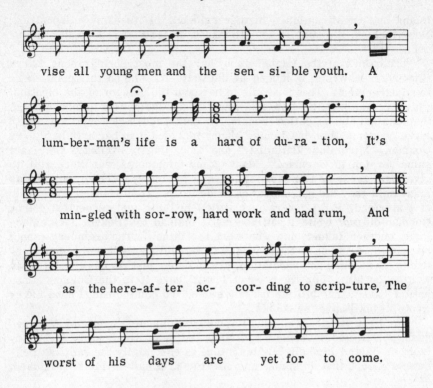

vise all young men and the sen-si-ble youth.   A

lum-ber-man's life is a hard of du-ra-tion,   It's

min-gled with sor-row, hard work and bad rum,   And

as the here-af-ter ac-   cor-ding to scrip-ture, The

worst of his days are   yet for to come.

The Boys of the Island (I)

1. You sporting young heroes of Prince Edward Island,
   Come a-listen to me and the tales I will tell;
   Of a lumberman's life it is my intention
   To advise all young men and the sensible youth.
   A lumberman's life is a hard of duration,
   It's mingled with sorrow, hard work, and bad rum;
   And as the hereafter according to scripture,
   The worst of his days are yet for to come.

2. It's true I'm a native of Prince Edward Island;
   I left my old parents when eighteen years old.
   I started out early all for to do better,
   Return in the spring with two hands full of gold.
   It's true my brave boys I have earned lots of money,
   But the curse of all bushmen fell on me also;
   My money it went like the snow in the June sun,
   And back to the woods every fall I must go.

3. Oh the boys on the Island on the farms are not happy;
   They'll say, "Let's go 'way, boys, we're doing no good."
   Their mind is uneasy, continuously crazy
   To go over to Bangor and work in the woods.
   A new suit of clothes is prepared for the journey,

A long pair of boots made by Sherlock or Clark,
And a long kennebecker all packed up with homespun,
And then this fine young man's all ready to embark.

4. When he gets to Bangor he gets off at the station,
   The bushmen look at him with a very keen eye;
   Just look at the clothes that the youngster is wearing
   And that will soon tell you he is a P.I.
   In Bangor, they poison this youth with bad whiskey,
   God, man, or the devil comes to him also;
   All night he will drink; he'll get drunk and then sober;
   He'll lay in the shade of a mulberry tree.

The Boys of the Island (II)

1. You sporting young fellows of Prince Edward Island
   Come listen to me and I'll tell you the truth;
   From a lumberman's life it is my intention
   To advise all young men and sensible youth.

2. Now the boys on the Island on the farms are not happy,
   They say, "Let us go; we are doing no good!"
   Their minds are uneasy, continually crazy,
   For to get o'er to Bangor and work in the woods.
   So a new suit of clothes is prepared for the journey,
   A new pair of boots made by Sherlock or Clark,
   A new Kennebecker well stuffed with good homespun,
   And then the young Islander, he will embark.

3. He'll go o'er to Bangor and stand at the station —
   The bushmen gaze on 'em all with a keen eye.
   They look at the clothes that young fellow is wearing
   And that will soon tell you he is a P.I.
   Then up in the woods, happy and contented,
   Where God, man, and devil come to them the same,
   For rearing and tearing, cursing, and blaspheming,
   For kicking and fighting is the down-river game.

4. In Bangor they'll poison the youth with bad whiskey
   To the devil they banish all brandy and ale,
   And then on the corner they find the youth tipsy,
   They'll send for Tim Leary and march him to jail.
   They may talk of the laws of the mother of Moses,
   I've seen better laws among heathen chinee,
   Where a man can get drunk and lay down and get sober
   Beneath the deep shade of the mulberry tree.

Several people recall visiting Larry Gorman while he was living in South Brewer. His nephew John O'Connor recalls the first time he visited him; O'Connor himself had just come down from a trip to the Island, and when Larry heard this he started asking one question after another about who was still alive and who was living where. The next day O'Connor saw him over in the mill yard at work, and Larry started right in on him again. "I don't think Uncle Larry thought I was of much account," he said. "I had just finished working up around Berlin once when I went to visit him, and all he was interested in was why I had left. He kept right after me all the time about it. Had I been discharged, and so on. He was the kind I'd never want to have too much to say to; he'd find a flaw somewhere."

Peter MacDonald of Rumford, Maine, recalls a visit. He had left P.E.I. shortly after 1900 and settled in Rumford. It was about 1908, while he was attending the University of Maine Law School, when he went to visit Larry:

Ives: How did you happen to find out he was there [i.e. in Brewer]?

MacDonald: There was a fellow name of Kelley living here at that time who ... lived for some years in South Brewer and knew him there. So he asked me to go see him. And it didn't take any great lot of coaxing for me to go, having heard so much about him, and I actually wanted to see him.

So he went over to South Brewer and found the house. He was let in by a woman (obviously Julia) whom he described as very neatly dressed and probably about forty. Larry was sitting in the front room, a tall, slender man with a grey mustache:

*I told him who I was; 'course he didn't remember me. I told him my father's name and he didn't remember that. Then I told him my grandfather's name and where he lived in Waterford, Prince Edward Island, and then he recognized him immediately.... I'd heard of Gorman since the time I was a young boy, about these poems and songs and graces before and after meals so I was very anxious to get him started on some of those things, you know, so he did. He started on them and he gave me quite a number....

Ives: You mean you just asked him about his poetry and he started to recite it?

MacDonald: Oh yes, he started to recite 'em. There was some I knew that he repeated and some I'd heard that he didn't go over and then he went over a lot that I'd never heard.... Some of them were about people there that I knew about. I got rather a kick out of it.... He'd skip from one thing to another. Well, he knew I was in a hurry, I suppose, and he wanted to get as much in as he could. He'd go along and then he'd ask about a certain place — who was living there now. Then he asked about the Corbett place — places like that, you know; he wanted to know about them. So he'd skip from one to the other and then he'd happen to think of somebody he'd made a song about and he'd go over part of it....

Ives: But you say that he said that he never made a song about your father?

MacDonald: He never made a song about my *grandfather* .... He said, "I never made a song about him because he was always the same."

Larry Gorman never really had a "proper trade" in Brewer. His woods work, however much he did of it, was only occasional. He worked for the railroad a little with the track and fencing crews, he dug ditches, and he worked as a hand in Brooks Brickyard. But most of the time he worked for the Eastern. His personnel card shows him to have worked there only from 1914 to 1917, but many people recall his working there as far back as 1906 piling slabs and edgings in the yard. He worked in several different parts of the mill, but whatever he did he was still poet first, workman second, for the poems kept on coming.

*Darn it all [said Billy Bell of Brewer], he wrote an awful lot of foolish pieces. Now I remember one of his pieces. . . . A fellow was working with us down in the mill . . . name was Newcombe. And he'd been to a raffle and he got a goose. And he brought the goose home and after he had his supper he thought he'd go and put the goose away for the night, so he took the goose out to the henhouse. And he was out there for an hour. By and by Mrs. Newcombe got wondering what was the trouble so she went out; and there was Newcombe. He'd been all the time trying to make the goose set on the roost with the hens. 'Course the minute he'd let the goose go she'd fall right off onto the floor. So when she went out, he had a six-inch board and he was nailing it on top of the roost (it was a short board) to see if the goose would sit on that. Of course when poor old Larry heard about that, he made this great song about "Newcombe's Goose." It was all just silly, you know. . . . All his stuff was just some little thing like that.

"He *would* make up one about old Frank," said George MacLeod of Brewer, laughing. Neither he nor Bell recalled the song itself, though MacLeod did recall one line: "Newcombe's goose come home to roost."

Billy Bell recalled another piece Larry made up, although once again he did not remember the poem itself:

*Another fellow down there bought a little pig. Well, when the pig come — oh! he was tickled to death with it. "The cutest little thing," you know . . . and every day he'd come over and tell us something about this little pig: how it was learning, "Why," he says, "it'll almost do tricks, it's such a cute little thing." And of course Larry made up a foolish piece about "Gaynor's Trained Pig." It was so foolish, you know. Just fun.

Larry seems to have spent a lot of time working in the woodyard at both the sawmill and the pulp-mill. At one time a fellow by the name of Tozier was superintendent of the sawmill and George DeRusha was foreman in the yard. Sometimes the men in the yard would drift off by ones and twos under cover of darkness and go home a bit early, especially when the weather was bad. DeRusha never said much about it, but one day Tozier got wind of what had been going on and bawled DeRusha out. DeRusha now had to tell the men that they would have to stay on until quitting time. Larry, who was in the yard at the time, made a long piece about this "injustice," using for his refrain:

> No matter how hard it rains or blows,
> You can't leave the yard 'til the whistle blows.

Another song about George DeRusha that has nearly been forgotten is "The Man Who Wheeled the Ashes." In this song, Larry chronicled DeRusha's rise from the ranks to yard-foremanly eminence. "*He made up this song," said Larry's grandniece Sister Mary Clare (*née* Callaghan), "and at the end of every verse — if I could only remember the things he'd say; they were very funny — he'd say 'But you'd never think he was the man that used to wheel the ashes, O!'"

After 1910 there was a new yard foreman, John McNamara, who seems to have been every bit as tough and hard-driving a boss as De-Rusha was easy. This was the sort of change that did not augur well for Larry Gorman, never a strong worker and now well over sixty.

The two men did not get along well, as could have been predicted, but there are two separate stories about what actually happened. One of them claims that John Mac tried to hire only Poles; they could under-stand just enough English to get the work done, and they not only had to work hard but kick back a couple of bucks a week to McNamara as well. Larry would not pay, so he was fired. But Billy Bell told a dif-ferent story, when asked about it:

*That was John McNamara, and that never should have been. He went to work for John McNamara in the yard handling pulpwood. And I guess he was too light for the work or something, so McNamara — he didn't exactly let him go but he saw some of the other bosses and told them that Larry wasn't quite man enough for that work and they better change him. Well, they did; they took Larry and put him at another job — something easier, you know.

And he was so mad at John McNamara for that that he wrote this great poem about him, and the name of it was "Nero and the Great John Mac." And the way he had it put together was as though John McNamara had died and went down be-low and one of his great joys was to meet up with Nero. And the great times they had telling each other about how they punished people on Earth and how John Mac was so pleased to meet him. Of course, every verse ended up with "Nero and the great John Mac." First one would tell about how he punished the people on Earth, and then the other; each one would make up a verse. The last line or two:

> And then they each embraced the other
> And hugged until their joints did crack;
> Then they disappeared forever,
> Nero and the great John Mac.

Joe MacDougall of Alberton, P.E.I., told Helen Creighton another little story about Larry and John McNamara:

*We were working one time at the mill [in] South Brewer and Larry was there working. And there was a fellow bringing in the pulp going into the mill and he got a crowd of Polanders [*working for him*]. And we used to always have our dinner outside — take our dinner with us, see — and they was always at Larry sing a song, sing a song, sing a song. He didn't pay much attention to them. So one day . . . we were all setting [there] . . . and the foreman, his name was McNamara, [said *to* Larry *he* wanted *him* to] make a song, sing a song. And he went to work and made one! And it was just the time that the Americans was in war with . . . Mexico . . . and Larry was sitting back and bye and bye he started this [*song*]. It was only just a verse or two. He says — I know the last of it was,

> Down along the border where the Mexicans invade
> They'll call for McNamara with his Polack brigade.

He'd just stand there and make a song about you in a minute! It didn't seem to bother him one bit.

Clarence Adams recalled two more lines of that song:

> Down in Hell when it's a hundred in the shade,
> You'll see the great John Mac and his Polack brigade.

In 1911 or 1912, The Old Colony Trust of Boston became chief stockholder in the Eastern and wanted to develop ways of making the mill more modern. Among other things, they hired a nurse, part of whose job was to see what she could do toward improving working conditions in the mill. She set right to work, and one of her first crusades was for more fresh air; she went all over the plant opening windows, much to everyone's disgust. She also decreed that the men could no longer eat at the machines but would have to go to specified areas. She even tried to get the men to stop chewing tobacco on the job, offering them gum instead. Naturally she took plenty of abuse for her pains, but evidently she was well able to hold her own. "She was a real peeler," one man said, "and took no sass from anyone." Whether or not Larry Gorman hung the name "Sanitary Jane" on her there is no way of telling, but it seems likely. At any rate he made up a poem about her. Some of the men thought she might be amused by it, so they persuaded Larry to pass her a copy. He did, and she was furious about it. Sass was one thing, metrical sass another, it seems.

Billy Bell gives us a nice story of the poet at work, as he heard it from his father, who had worked for the Eastern too. He and some others, Larry Gorman among them, were piling two-by-four joists out in the yard, leaving them stepped back in places so as to form a sort of stairway to allow workmen to get up on top of the pile later on. They were sitting down eating their lunches when along came an old-timer by the name of John Anderson, who surveyed their morning's work and began to tell them how *he* would have done it and they never did it *that* way when *he* worked here and things had *really* gone to the devil, etc., etc. All at once a passing wheelbarrow struck a loose joist and swung one end around, jamming Anderson's head against the pile. He began to scream:

*He let out the awfullest yells. My father happened to be handy and he reached out his foot and he gave this [joist] a kick and he kicked it away from the wheel so it let him loose and down he fell. And he started to rip and swear and take on, and he scratched his ear pretty bad so he struck home. And all this time old Larry he was setting there, and he picked up a piece of planed board and a piece of paper and he was scribbling away. And when he finished it up he had this piece.

And he said when old John was hollering he just sounded like a banked beaver. ...You know, they used to tell about, years ago, if a beaver dam got too many beavers they'd drive some of them out and they'd sit on the bank and holler like the dickens. And old Larry said he sounded just like one of them beavers....

Beaver Jack

1. John Anderson went prowling round,
   Giving orders, we might say;
   By chance got caught within a trap
   And couldn't get away.

2. He called for help, Oh Lord! such cries,
   We thought he'd break his voice;
   Until to his assistance came
   Some men from piling joists.

3. With exertion great they unsealed his fate
   And freed the prisoner's head;
   When on the ground his senses got,
   Then this is what he said:

4. "You g__ d___ fools!" burst from his lips,
   As soon as he could see,
   "George Robinson, you cussed fool,
   You tried to finish me.

5. "You spread your bait and sprang your trap,
   Caught what you call a beaver;
   But thanks to Bell and Angus as well,
   For they were my reliever.

6. "So now I'll tell to all you men,
   I'll give no more directions
   To men who can, for I know they will
   Pile lumber to perfection.

7. "And now, my boys, I'll tell no lies,
   I'm thankful for my life,
   But there's one thing I greatly dread—
   That is, to meet my wife."

8. Then home he went for liniment
   To bathe the parts affected,
   And if I got the story straight,
   He got full well corrected.

9. "Now Beaver Jack, what brought you back?
   You almost lost your ear."
   But Jack applied his liniment
   And did not seem to hear.

10. "Now Sophie, pet, you musn't fret
    Nor get in too hot water;
    For at the mill there're traps they've set
    For beaver, bear, and otter."

And that's all I remember. There's another verse that I don't know.

Not everyone suffered at Larry's hands, however, for occasionally he would come out with a song of praise. For example, he seems to have thought very highly of F. W. Ayer himself. It could be said that Larry hoped to gain something by praising the boss, but he did not curry favor; whatever his faults may have been, Larry Gorman was not a toady. We can be sure he is sincere here, and we can hope that Ayer recognized a compliment when he received one:

It's a Wonder

It's a wonder, a wonder, what one man can do.
A stranger comes along, he's soon put to work,
Be he Russian, Rumanian, Polander, or Turk;
There's no discrimination between Gentile or Jew,
It's really phenomenal what one man can do.

It's a wonder, a wonder, what one man can do.

. . . .

There's Ingall's over yonder and Sergeant's below,
But the mammoth four-bander could swallow the two;
It's really phenomenal what one man can do.

According to my informant, Mr. A. Russell Mace of Aurora, Maine,
there was a lot more to the song, telling how good Ayer was to his men.

However, these occasional panegyrics are all the more striking because there are so few of them. Larry Gorman was a terribly disappointed man. His candle was guttering fast, he knew, and he had almost
nothing to show for all its burning. Nowhere is that disappointment
more evident than in the following poem:

Away to the States to Get Rich

1. Young men of P. I., you can hardly deny
   That you've many times left a good home;
   A life on the farm for you has no charm,
   You all seem determined to roam,
   Your harrows and plows, fine horses and cows
   And your sheep all may die in the ditch;
   Your jobs you will jack and your trunks you will pack
   And away to the States to get rich.

2. All the people they kill in the pulp or saw mill
   For such folks have no terror at all;
   They keep coming here at all times of the year,
   In the winter and summer and fall.
   They'll hire out to hay, two dollars per day,
   To mow or to rake or to pitch;
   When they all get their pay they'll laugh and they'll say,
   "Boys, it won't take us long to get rich."

3. They are now set to work with an Arab or Turk,
   With the Lithuanians, Russians or Poles;
   They keep them round here to make people swear
   And to add mortal sins to their souls.
   It would break a man's back putting cars on the track,
   Then they'll run into some open switch;
   Those poor silly elves are the same as ourselves:
   They have come to the States to get rich.

4. If they're active and stout, it will soon be found out,
   Though some may be awkward and green;
   They are taken inside where their skill is soon tried
   In the wet room upon a machine.
   With a rock-maple staff they are set to cut off,
   When soon in their sides there's a stitch;
   When their shoulders will ache they will see the mistake
   That they made coming here to get rich.

5. They must be content in some leaky old rent
   Away in behind some man's back yard;
   Mid the squealing of hogs and the yelping of dogs,

> There's many who'd think their lot hard.
> When the acid and bleach their vitals will reach,
> With rosin and sulphur and pitch,
> They will sneeze and say 'twas a sorrowful day
> That they came to the States to get rich.

6. For quite a long spell things may work very well,
    'Til the neighbors begin for to growl;
    If your girls and your boys make the least bit of noise,
    They will raise a most terrific howl.
    Some neighbors will beg and keep pulling your leg
    And they'll pester you worse than the itch;
    When you cease to pan out, they'll sulk and they'll pout,
    They would like to live cheap and get rich.

7. It's many a year since I first landed here,
    Being then in my youth and my prime;
    Though sorely belied and much vilified,
    I was never convicted of crime.
    I am broke down in health and possess little wealth,
    In every trade there's a hitch;
    These folks who have wealth must acquire it by stealth —
    It's not by hard work they get rich.

Evidently Larry kept up a fairly active correspondence with people back on the Island and even along the Miramichi. Although I had heard of letters,[14] I never expected to see one. But one day Hazen Holmes of McKinleyville, N.B., was going through some old papers in his grandfather Harper's place when he came upon the following pencilled note; he took it to Louise Manny, who kindly sent it to me. I reproduce it here, *literatim et punctatim:*

7 Hardy St Brewer Me Dec 9th 1915

My Dear Mr Harper I suppose you thought that I did not answer your last letter But when you put a thing off from time to time you will grow careless won't write at all, I will try and answer now in a kind of a way Of cource I have got very little to write about times are all right as far as going to the woods is concerned but that has got to be a thing of the past with me, I saw Henry Hay not long ago he [*written above that:* "me"] had seen your son but he did [*not?*] see you I have just had letter from my sister at [?] things are just about as usual there potatoes are 60 cts per Bushel and scarce at that I guess the potato crop was almost failure there this year they have 80 here and $100 in the first of the season but they are not that high now beans are $450 whole sale so you see it costs something to live now days, I suppose you are still on the logs yet you must be about the only one of the old crowd left I was in the woods with Pat McEvoy last year He went home to take charge in the woods for his Father I hear he came back again but I did not see him I am glad to hear that little Sady has done so well in the West I would be somebody yet, I wonder if red Dick Welch is alive or Jack Salter or any of the McCarthies I suppose my old girl is alive yet Miss Harrigan she must be pretty small and dark if she is alive yet, Well I think I have all I can think of now, remember me to all enquiring friends if you see Con Ragan give him my kindest regards hoping to hear from you soon I remain your old and trusted friend L Gorman I have nothing very new to send you but I may have the next I write

It would be a mistake to draw too many conclusions from one letter, but we can remark that the writing is decent and legible, the spelling almost perfect, and the whole thing is quite coherent in spite of the dearth of punctuation. But what are we to make of that "I would be somebody yet"? Is it too much to see this as the old man wondering what would have happened *if* — ? But only for an instant; then he goes back to asking about old friends.

Jim Lynch of Grey Rapids, N.B., on the Miramichi, came down to Bangor to go into the woods about 1915. His pal, a P. I. named Pete Clary, suggested one evening that they go over to Brewer to see old Larry Gorman, and Jim, who knew the name, agreed. So they took a quart of red-eye apiece and went down to the Eastern plant where Larry was then acting as night-watchman. They told him who they were and what they wanted; Larry was delighted and took them to his little watchman's room, where he began to sing one song after another for them, occasionally fortifying himself with a little of their red-eye. Lynch says the two of them went back often, maybe a couple of dozen times before they went off to the woods. "He was a comical old fellow," he said; "always full of jokes."

What did the men in the mill think of him? I asked Billy Bell this question: "*He was just a joke," he said, "just a kind of a joke. Some fellow'd get hold of a piece of poetry and he'd show it around and they'd laugh about it and say, 'An awful man. You'd better be careful; if you got any news about anybody that's not so good as it might be, don't tell Larry Gorman.'" They were snickering at "the man who makes the songs" now.

*At the last of it [recalled Billy Bell], I was working in the fire room and they put Larry out in the yard just a little ways outside the fire room and his work was to break up old boxes and barrels that bleach came in or rosin. And the team would haul that out there and dump it and he would break it up and load it onto trucks ... that run on tracks, and then they'd haul them into the fire room and we'd burn them there. I used to go out and chat with him a whole lot ... but at the last of it, you know, I think he got muddled, kind of; his head got so full of that darned stuff.... There were lots of times he wouldn't have to be working; he'd have to wait, but he'd have to stay right there in case a load came along. Well, he'd be around, and all at once — we'd look out there and see him, and he'd be standing like this [*demonstration — hands behind back, head down*] you know, as though he was thinking about something, and he'd start slowly to walk across the field. He'd put his head down and he'd walk; probably he'd get away fifty or sixty yards. All at once he'd come to himself and he'd look around and see what he was doing and he'd turn around and hustle back. You know, his mind I kind of think was going bad on him. Well, it wasn't too long after that that poor Larry had to quit working.

George MacLeod remembers an incident of Larry's last year or so on DeRusha Lane;

*He was going to get off the trolley car and he fell, and I went over and picked him up and helped him home. I knew he was banged up, and the old fellow was pretty old then and pretty feeble; it was pitiful to have him work — you know what I mean — as just common labor. But in those days, you know, everything went. There was no insurance, there was nothing; you just worked 'til either you fell down or found some means of staying home. You was no longer able to work, that's all. Nothing. There was nothing.

Sure enough, on February 19, 1917, Larry Gorman was laid off at the Eastern "because of no work in the mechanical department" (that included the woodyard). And under this entry, written in a different hand: "Too old to re-employ."

Let us go back a few years. The Gormans had moved from DeRusha Lane over to 29 Elm Street (known as the old Hodges House) in 1909, but in 1913 they moved back again to DeRusha. In 1915 they left South Brewer and moved up to Hardy Street in Brewer proper, where they took an upstairs apartment in Jeremiah Mahoney's house, number seven. Mahoney was an old friend and the apartment was a nice apartment, much superior to what they had been living in. An old neighbor woman remembered the two of them. He was a very quiet man, she said, who came and went about his business but "never mingled much." She was much surprised to hear that Mr. Gorman made up songs. He was just a quiet old man, ailing much of the time, and toward the last he did not seem to be working at much of anything, so Julia had to hire out as a domestic a couple of days a week to make ends meet. There was a young man who was studying for the priesthood who used to come and stay with them occasionally; Julia called him "Father Tom" (he is now the Most Reverend Thomas K. Gorman, Bishop of Dallas-Fort Worth, Texas).

Larry was not well, and Julia didn't like to leave him alone at night.

*"I can remember spending evenings with him and listening to him singing," said a grandniece (now Sister Mary Clare), "and he'd sing all evening to me... and get up and find different songs he thought I'd like.... When they moved to Brewer... I can remember that Aunt Julia would get in touch with my mother and ask if I could go up and spend the evening with Uncle Lawrence because she was going over to Bangor for something special and he'd be alone. So I'd go up, and I can see him now sitting in front of the stove with the oven open and he'd put his feet in the oven... right in the oven to keep them warm.... The poor old man! He was very thin and he didn't look well to me.... I always thought that he couldn't have felt too well when he worked in that yard.... He looked more than [*his seventy years*]; he looked worn. And I think my heart must have gone out to him.... So we'd sit there and... when he found such an enthusiastic listener he would get up and he'd go to this drawer and that drawer and bring in these poems and these songs and sing them to me.... He didn't seem to have them very well organized; they were just here, there, and everywhere.... He had something written about everybody he met and everything that he saw and everything that happened....

As a boy, the late David Dyment of Spring Hill, P.E.I., lived right across Trout River from the Gormans. So when he and a companion found themselves in Bangor on their way to the woods in the fall of 1916, he decided they ought to look up old Larry Gorman. His friend was willing, "but," he said, "we'll never in the whole world find him when we don't know where he lives here." Dyment was of the same mind, but he thought he would ask around a bit, so he asked the first man he saw if he knew where a fellow named Larry Gorman lived. The man took Dyment and his friend down to the tracks and pointed across the river: "Right upstairs in that house there," he said. The two men took the ferry across to the Brewer side, found the house, and knocked on the door. Larry answered but did not recognize either of them, until Dyment told him who his father was. Then he brightened right up and said he was delighted to see them and wouldn't they come in. The three of them sat around and talked for about an hour and a half. Larry had a lot of his printed poems right there with him, so Dyment bought four and his friend bought two. They asked him to sing, and he was only too willing to do so; Dyment asked especially for "The Horse's Confession," and Larry laughed and said that was his own favorite and that every Christmas Eve, Artemus MacArthur, a young Island boy, used to come over and sing it for him. Dyment and his friend left, saying that they would be sure to come and see him again the next fall, but when they did return, the old man had died.

One of the last songs Larry is supposed to have made was called "The Song of All Songs." Some people have told me that he worked in the name of every song he ever wrote, but if the small sample we have is at all representative, the whole piece was just a rhymed catalog of titles and familiar lines from come-all-ye's and songs, some of which (the last three) were his but most of which were not. The type was common enough, and all Larry did was to add a few of his own songs to the list:

The Song of all Songs

1. Will you come and listen to my story
   And I'll sing you something new,
   Although you think it's a pity
   That I've nothing else to do.

2. You've heard the song of Nelson,
   The Battle of the Nile,
   The Bonny Bunch of Roses,
   And the Rose from Britain's Isle.

3. There's Charming Blue-eyed Mary,
   And The Men from Allendale
   And The Men from Tipperary,
   And The Boatsmen of Vinsdale.

4. How well do I remember
   The Cottage by the Mill,
   And Never Push a Man
   When He's Going Downhill.

5. I am bound to be a soldier
   In the Galliant Siege of Troy,

Old Ireland is my Country
And My name is Pat Molloy.

6. There was Bonnie Annie Laurie,
   The Lady of the Lake,
   The Dying Californian,
   And I'm Dying for Your Sake.

7. Cruel Ida Duncan,
   False Young Willy Cain
   And the Man Who Wheels the Ashes
   In the Good Old State of Maine.

The last poem we know anything about is one called "The Cruel Submarine." It was not a long poem, and it was all about what a terrible thing the German submarine was. Up on P.E.I., one of Larry's nieces recalls going to see her Aunt Ellen, Larry's sister, shortly after they had received word that Larry had died. Ellen handed her a copy of the poem, saying what a pity it was that all of Larry's poetry couldn't have been like that, not insulting anyone.

Larry's last days were about what might have been expected: he was just another seedy old man. One woman told me that she could still see old Mr. Gorman walking up Exchange Street in Bangor: all bent over, out at elbows, threadbare, shuffling along the sidewalk with his shoes so run over that it looked as if he were walking alongside them instead of in them. He would sell his poems and talk to old friends; perhaps he'd sit around Mayo's Livery Stable for a few hours; then later in the afternoon he'd take the ferry, the little *Bon-Ton*, back to Brewer.

The end was not far off, it would seem, and indeed it was not. On Friday, August 31, 1917, Lawrence Gorman died of a heart attack; he was seventy years old. His old friend and best man, Dr. William McNally, came over from Bangor, but all he could do was sign the death certificate. There was a wake at the house on Hardy Street and the funeral was held the following Monday at St. John's Catholic Church in Bangor.

There was one happy circumstance. Young Father Tom had been ordained just that June and had been assisting that summer in one of the parishes in the Diocese of Portland. His Uncle Lawrence died just before he left Maine to go to the Catholic University in Washington, and he came up to Bangor to officiate at the funeral. It was a small affair; *The Bangor Daily Commercial* for that day found room to say this much on page five:

Funeral services of Lawrence Gorman were held at St. John's Catholic Church, Monday morning at 9 o'clock. Rev. Thomas Gorman, a nephew of the deceased, of Los Angeles, Cal., officiated. The bearers were Jeremiah Mahoney, William McGillen, John Callighan, Paul Murphy, John Barry, and Patrick Gallagher. Interment was at Mt. Pleasant.

That was all for "the man who made the songs." But there was still that little black trunk he kept at home and into which he threw a copy of every poem he ever wrote. Billy Bell tells the story of that:

*And so he passed on. And there was somebody, I don't know who it was, that came there and offered her [*Julia*] a hundred dollars for the trunk with the stuff that was in it, and she said no, she wouldn't sell it. She said that Larry had made too many enemies with his poetry while he was living, he wasn't going to make any more after he was dead. And she burnt the whole works.

So that was all for his songs.[15]

Interstate Highway 95 bypasses Bangor and cuts right through the middle of Mount Pleasant Cemetery. Just over the rise on the north side of the road is the Jeremiah Lynch family plot. There are twelve graves, and in one of them is buried Larry Gorman. There is a central shaft with a cross-and-anchor emblem atop it, and on its sides are the names of all those buried here. Halfway down the northeast face is the inscription, "LAWRENCE GORMAN/ 1846-1917." Beneath that, "His wife/ JULIA LYNCH/ 1854-1928." And down at the bottom, *"Requiescant in Pace."*

EIGHT

The Larry Gorman Legend

Gib Morgan wandered through the Pennsylvania oil fields telling wonderful stories about himself and his travels, until the real Gib Morgan became almost completely hidden behind the legend.[1] The legend of Paul Bunyan, it would seem, moved a stage further, completely obscuring the man himself. In the latter case, advertising copywriters and popular authors like James Stevens reworked and manipulated the legends themselves to suit their own particular purposes, further removing Paul Bunyan from whatever flesh and blood he may once have had.[2] The legend of Larry Gorman never reached these proportions; whether he came too late to find a culture hospitable to the growth of a legend or whether he simply did not have the requisites for a true folk-hero, the fact remains that his legend is abortive. Yet there is a legend, and we should look at it.

The figure that we see most often as we talk to people and read secondary sources is one that is not very far from the truth: this Larry Gorman had the ability to compose appropriate satirical songs on the spur of the moment, and he used these songs as his chief weapons in a lifelong war on hypocrisy and sham, particularly when he found these qualities in the great of his world. He was the delight of the men he worked with, but his disgust at stinginess made him the universal despair of the lumber operators. To top it all off, he was a famous fighter. Apotheosis has begun, obviously, but so far we can still recognize that this figure began as Lawrence Gorman from Trout River, P.E.I. How did he become suddenly eight feet tall? The answer is not far to seek: like Paul Bunyan's legend, Larry's was partly created by a writer; like Gib Morgan's, it was partly of his own making.

In April, 1908, Harper & Brothers published *King Spruce*, a novel by Holman Day. The plot is simple: Progress and the New Order in the woods, in the form of young Dwight Wade, are pitted against the status quo, the old, wasteful order, represented by "Stumpage John" Barrett, timber baron, and Pulaski D. Britt, Barrett's upriver man, who exemplifies for Holman Day the "brusque, rough-sneering, culture-despising spirit of the woods." After many rousing adventures and some views of woods life that are not half bad, it looks as if the bad guys are going to win out. But their compounded skulduggeries begin to catch up on them. Somebody dynamites their dam, giving the good guys the water they need and the whole Old Order comes toppling down in ruin. Dwight Wade and the New Order get their drive in the boom in the best Hairbreadth Harry tradition, Pulaski D. Britt is so angry he has a stroke on the spot, "Stumpage John" gets converted, and Dwight Wade marries "Stumpage John's" beautiful daughter. As a novel, it is no great shakes, obviously, but it was very popular in Maine, and, shame to say, it was one of the very few halfway decent books about the lumberwoods.

We are not concerned with the quality of the work — only that it had wide circulation in the Northeast and that one of the characters, albeit a minor one, is Larry Gorman. After an epigraph to Chapter One which purports to be "From song by Larry Gorman, 'Woods Poet,'" we hear no more about him until Chapter Eighteen, over two hundred pages further on. To make a long story short, the crew of Dwight Wade and his partner Rodburd Ide, have met head-on with "Britt's Busters," Colin MacLeod foreman, and a fight is brewing. The chapter opens thus:

Larry Gorman, "the woodsman's poet," whose songs are known and sung in the camps from Holeb to Madawaska, was with Rodburd Ide's incoming crew. His three most notable lyrics are these: "I feed P.I.'s on tarts and pies," "Bushmen all, your ear I call until I shall relate," and "The Old Soubungo Trail."

The first two titles are recognizable as echoes of the real-life Gorman. We can puzzle about the third until we turn the page. Seeing that a fight is imminent, all hands prepare:

It might have been noted that Poet Gorman cut the biggest shillalah of any of them. And while he rounded its end and waited for more formal declaration of hostilities, he lustily sang the solo part of "The Old Soubungo Trail," with a hundred hearty voices to help him on the chorus:

> "I left my Lize behind me,
> Oh, she won't know what to do,
> I left my Lize for the Old Town guys,
> And I left my watch there, too.
> I left my clothes at a boardin'-house,
> I reckon they're for sale,
> And here I go, at a heel-an'-toe,
> On the old Soubungo trail.
> Sou-bung-o! Bungo!
> 'Way up the Bungo trail!"

The opposing bosses, Ide and Wade, Barrett and Britt, are having a violent argument, but so far there is no fight:

Larry Gorman, having peeled a hand-hold on his bludgeon, was moved to sing another verse:

> "I ain't got pipe nor 'backer,
>   Nor I ain't got 'backer box;
> I ain't got a shirt, and my brad-boots hurt,
>   For I ain't a-wearin' socks.
> But a wangan's on Enchanted,
>   Where they've got them things for sale,
> And I don't give a dam what the price it am
>   On the old Soubungo trail.
> Sou-bung-o! Bungo!
>   'Way up the Bungo trail!"

Neither the tone nor the style nor the subject matter is Gorman's. The rollicking phonily-authentic language is pure Holman Day, as is the choral accompaniment; and that bit about how he left his "Lize for the Old Town guys" must have scandalized Julia.

The fight seems about to piffle out, until Pulaski Britt suddenly sees that his best teamster, Tommy Eye, has decided to switch allegiance to Wade's crew. Britt decides he will do nothing of the sort and sends his foreman, Colin MacLeod, to get him. Wade steps in to prevent the foreman's move, but MacLeod advances with an ash sled-stake in his hand. At this moment, "Poet" Gorman, "who had been gradually edging near the spot which he had sagely picked as the probable core of the conflict," steps between them and faces MacLeod:

"Sure, and a gent like him don't fight with clubs," said Gorman. "We've all heard about his lickin' ye once, and man-fashion, too! Now, go get your reputation. Start with me." The redoubtable bard poked his shillalah into MacLeod's breast and drove him suddenly back. At this overture of combat the men for Enchanted came up with a rush. They met the "Busters" face to face and eye to eye.

"We're all axe-tossers together, boys!" cried Gorman. "Ye know me and you've sung my songs, and ye know there's no truer woodsman than me ever chased beans round a tin plate. Now, Britt's men, if ye want to fight to keep a free man a slave when he wants to chuck his job, then come on and fight. But may the good saints put a cramp into the arm of the man that fights against the interests of woodsmen all together!"

This makes them hesitate, because it is said by the great Larry Gorman. Only MacLeod advances, and Larry taunts him some more. MacLeod swings the sled-stake at his head, but "that master of stick-play warded and leaped back nimbly." Everyone is watching now, for they know "that Larry Gorman was vain of two things — his songs and his stick-swinging."

Now comes a lovely scene. The two men begin to fight, and the poet tells his antagonist that he will "sing a bit of song for you to dance by."

The merry insolence of this brought a hoarse hoot of delight from both sides. And pressing upon his foe so actively that the crippled MacLeod was put to his utmost to ward thwacks off his head and shoulders, this sprightly Cyrano of the kingdom of spruce carolled after this fashion:

"Come, all ye good shillaly men,
Come, lis-ten unto me:
Old Watson made a walkin'-cane,
And used a popple-tree.
The knob it were a rouser —
A rouser, so 'twas said —
And when ye sassed old Watson
He would knock ye on the head."

MacLeod got a tap that made his eyes shut like the snap of a patent cigar-cutter.

"Chorus!" exhorted the lyrist. And they bellowed jovially:

"Knick, Knock,
Hickory dock,
And he'd hit ye on the head!"

Larry leaped back, whirled his stick so rapidly that its bright peeled surface seemed to spit sparks, and again got over the boss's indifferent guard with a whack that echoed hollowly.

Gilbert and Sullivan couldn't have done it better.
MacLeod is taking a bad beating, but wait:

But his pride kept him up, and forced him to meet the fresh attack that Gor-man made — an attack in which that master seemed to be fencing mostly to mark the time of his jeering song:

"Old Watson was a good old man,
And taught the Bible class,
But he didn't like the story
Of the jawbone of the ass.
'Why didn't he make a popple-club,'
So Uncle Watson said,
'And scotch the tribe of the Philistereens
By bangin' 'em on the head?'"

The blow that time staggered MacLeod.

"Chorus!" called "Poet" Larry. But...the Honorable Pulaski Britt was be-tween them....He yanked the sled-stake out of the nerveless grasp of the sweat-ing and discomfited MacLeod, and raised it.

"Be careful, Mr. Britt," yelped Gorman. His mien changed from gay insouci-ance to bitter fury. "You've struck me once in my life, and I took it and went on my way, because I was getting your grub and your pay. You strike me to-day, and I'll split your head open like a rotten punkin!"

The two men eye each other a moment. Then, "The tyrant lowered his club and backed away, muttering some wordless recrimination at which the poet curled his lip." Britt damns all his men for cowards, but Larry demurs:

"Oh, but they're not cowards!" cried Larry. In his bushman's soul he real-ized that even now a chance taunt, a random prick of word, might start the fight afresh. "Every man-jack there is known to me of old, and the good, brave boys they are! But your money ain't greasy enough, Mr. Britt, to make good men as them fight to take away a comrade's man-rights."

The "Busters" nodded affirmation and kept on. One man stepped back and hallooed: "Right ye are, Larry Gorman! And when ye try to get your Enchanted logs first through the Hulling Machine next spring, ye'll find that we're the kind of gristle that can't be chawed. . . ."

There was a grin on the man's face, but none the less it was a challenge, and Larry accepted it.

"Sure and we'll be there!" he called, "We'll be there with hair a foot long, pick-pole in one hand, peavy-stick in the other, ready for a game of jackstraws in the white water and a fist-jig on the bank!"

"And will ye write it into a song, Larry Gorman?"

"All into a song it shall go!"

And roaring a good-natured cheer over their shoulders, the "Busters" filed away into the mouth of Pogey Notch.

Obviously Holman Day had heard of Larry Gorman and his songs, but he does not seem to know anything about Larry Gorman, the man. In *King Spruce* he presents a rip-snorting fighter; Larry Gorman was not a fighter at all. Day's Gorman was strictly one of the boys; the real Gorman was not. People who knew the real Larry Gorman have often spoken of this disparity. "*[He was] a nice, agreeable man," said Ralph Cushman, "He wasn't the fighter that Holman Day makes him out to be. 'Course that name sounds good, I suppose." Herbert Rice was a bit more outspoken: "Holman Day didn't know Larry Gorman from a cord of wood!"

Day wrote and published *King Spruce* in Larry's own lifetime. What did Gorman himself think of it? "It may be of interest to you, for your estimate of his character," Bishop Gorman wrote me, "to know that both he and his wife agreed that the Larry Gorman in *King Spruce* was a caricature. He was a simple, mild, hard-working man to whom any type of violence was certainly a stranger." Yet, whether he liked it or not, there is no doubt that the book did a great deal to spread the fame of Larry Gorman over a wider area and to reinforce it in the places where he was already known. It is amazing how many people who knew of him only at second hand have described him to me in terms that derive directly from, or are colored by, Day's caricature. Even Mrs. Eloise Linscott in her book *Folk Songs of Old New England* speaks of him as "one of the most famous of the fighting lumberjacks of Maine."[3] And back on P.E.I. one man even told me, "Larry Gorman wrote the novel *King Spruce*."

Many American folk-heroes' cycles are made up of traditional and fictional tales which they originally told as personal experiences. I began this chapter with a reference to Gib Morgan, whose legend was built in this way. Davy Crockett and Oregon Smith are other notable examples that come to mind, and Bacil Kirtley has recently pointed out that the same thing seems to have happened to a local Maine hero, John Ellis, who "at first owed his local renown to his skill as a raconteur, and doubtless the stories that others later told about him he told first about himself."[4] While there is no great cycle of stories connected with Larry Gorman, we can see the same process at work on a small scale when we consider a group of *cante-fables* that have become associated with him.

We are dealing with one minor type of *cante-fable:* the humorous anecdote with a verse for its clincher, the story and verse being mutually dependent. (This definition is meant to exclude all those examples wherein the prose part simply explains a local allusion in the verse.) So far, I have found eighteen rather clear examples of this simple tale-type, some of them in many variants. They all have Larry Gorman as their protagonist.

There are several examples scattered throughout my narrative of Larry's life,[5] but perhaps the best known *cante-fable* that is told about him is a humorous "grace before meat."[6] I have heard this story told about Gorman at least twenty times, the circumstances varying only slightly according to where I found it. Here is a typical version, sent me by Peter MacDonald, a former resident of the west end of Prince Edward Island, now living in Rumford, Maine: "He went to the home of John McCollister of Miminegash, who had two young daughters who were getting supper...and they were having porridge and just then a team drove in with two young men, so immediately they changed the table set-up and got a different supper for the young men and when they sat down to eat, they asked Gorman to say grace and immediately he replied:

> Oh Lord be praised, I am amazed
> How things can be amended,
> With cake and tea and such glee,
> When porridge was intended.

Several other people told me the same story, identifying it with McCollister and/or the town of Miminegash, some even identifying Gorman's companion. Another slight variation has Gorman seeing the woman of the house whisking away the porridge at his arrival, while still another tells of his watching the substitution being made when the minister arrived. All of these versions come from Prince Edward Island. In Maine the same story is usually told in the following way: "Some officials made an unexpected visit to a camp. The cook made a quick change of menu for dinner. Larry Gorman, aware of the change, on coming to his seat at the table remarked:

> Lord be praised! I am amazed!
> How quick things can be mended!
> Tarts and pies for us P.I.'s
> When codfish was intended."[7]

We even find the same story told about Mike Gorman, who often claimed to be Larry's brother or nephew but was neither. Obviously Larry did not invent this story. What we have here is clearly an example of the localization of a more general tale, so well localized on Prince Edward Island that several people even used the same names.

How many of the other *cante-fables* told about him are more general tales that have been localized I cannot be sure yet. I am quite certain that the following one (told me by the late Herbert Rice, woodsman, of Bangor) is not original with Gorman: back on P.E.I. one of Larry's neighbors stole sheep from one MacMillan; but he could not catch the old ram. Larry was at the neighbor's house for a meal one day, and was asked to say grace. Larry complied:

> Lord bless the meat that we do eat,
> Ham and I together;
> God send him speed that he will need
> To catch MacMillan's wether.

Louise Manny reports the same story localized in Miramichi, as does William Doerflinger, who attributes it to another Miramichi poet, Bill Day, although he acknowledges that some people have attributed it to Gorman.[8] I have never found this same story elsewhere, but a short time ago a man gave me the following verse, which is clearly related to it: John Clark, a Maine tin peddler, while upon his travels, had supper with a family of Robertsons, a pious lot of suspected sheep thieves. As they started the meal, Clark was asked to say grace. He responded with this:

> God bless the sheep meat that we eat,
> Caught by Sam Robertson and his brother;
> God give them grace to run the race
> And try to catch another.

There are several other rhyming graces attributed to Gorman. I have already given the one he made up at McElroy's in Miminegash, P.E.I.:

> Oh Lord above, look down on us
> And see how we are forgotten
> And send us meat that is fit to eat
> Because by Christ, this is rotten.

At another time he came out with the following verse (the story has been lost):

> Oh Lord above, look down with love,
> And pity us poor creatures;
> And give us meat that we may eat
> And take away fish and potatoes.

Another story tells of Larry working for a P.E.I. shipbuilder by the name of Robert Bell. Bell liked everyone to be right on time for meals. One day Larry came in late to lunch; he just slid into his place and started eating, but Bell caught him and, as punishment, demanded he say a grace. Larry complied:

> Oh God above, look down with love,
> Not eyes like Robert Bell;
> And give us meat that we can eat,
> And take these herrings to hell.

The preceding three graces are obviously variations on a theme, the second and fourth lines changing to suit the circumstances.[9]

Wherever Larry Gorman went, he was known as "the man who makes the songs." This epithet is part of a verse one finds often:

> And when they see me coming,
> Their eyes stick out like prongs,
> Saying, "Beware of Larry Gorman!
> He's the man who makes the songs." [10]

The verse is often found alone, but just as often some variation of it is worked into a story like this one (which I have collected three separate times: twice in Lot Seven, P.E.I., and once in Rumford, Maine, from a man who had come from Lot Seven). Once when Larry came out of the woods wearing a winter's growth of beard he went to a boarding house he knew to get a room. The landlady let him in, but she went on at some length to say that one person who would never be permitted to set foot in her boarding house again was that Larry Gorman. Larry agreed with her, saying that all that fellow would do would be to make a nasty song about her. Later on, a friend, who recognized him in spite of the beard, asked him how he had gotten on with the woman. Larry replied,

> She treated me very kindly,
> But her eyes stuck out like prongs,
> Abusing Larry Gorman,
> The man who makes the songs.

Another variation tells of his passing through Blackville, New Brunswick, on his way to the upper Miramichi. As he and his friends passed by a local boarding house all the boarders ran to the windows to look out at him, so Larry sang out,

> As I went by McKenzie's,
> Their eyes stuck out like prongs,
> Saying, "There goes Larry Gorman,
> The man that makes the songs."

A variant of the preceding group is the story that tells of Larry stopping at a farmhouse to ask for a meal. The lady gave him bread (stale) and tea (weak). "But," she said, "I'd never give that Larry Gorman a meal if he came here. He made up a song about my husband once." Larry finished his meal and then said,

She told me that her bread was fine
And that her tea was strong,
Not thinking I was Gorman,
The man who makes the songs.

I picked this story up from the late Herbert Rice of Bangor. William Doerflinger found a version of it in Boiestown, New Brunswick, where the teller *sang* this verse and the preceding one as part of the same story.[11] This makes the only instance I know of in which one of these *cante-fables* was really sung or in which the song part consisted of more than a single stanza.

Louise Manny sent me the following example, which she got from Tom Hunter of Boiestown: "Larry Gorman was given supper by a Mrs. Lynch, whose outstanding characteristic was a mustache. Mrs. Lynch had expressed the hope that Larry would never make a song about her, but he did:

Here's to Mrs. Lynch,
Whose mustache would measure 'bout an inch,
Her supper was good and her tea was strong;
Little she knew I was Gorman, the man who makes the songs."[12]

I collected two other *cante-fables* in Miminegash, P.E.I., both of which were about people in the area. The first was given to me by Gerry Tremblay: on one occasion Larry had dinner at the home of the Sentners, who were distinguished in this fishing village because they were not fishermen but farmers. Larry evidently expected to eat rather well there, but he was served fish instead of the meat he had hoped for. Later on a friend asked him how he had fared, and he replied,

Lord be praised, I am amazed
How Sentners got their riches;
They sold their meat to buy some fish,
The dirty sons of bitches!

Another time Larry went to dinner at the house of James Alfred Rix, Eddie Tremblay told me, and Rix's wife also made the mistake of feeding the poet fish. He looked at his plate and said,

Oh herring, oh herring, what brought you here?
You swam the seas for many a year.
They brought you here for lobster bait
And not for us poor devils to eat.

This, of course, is a variation on the well-known "Sailor's Grace":

Old horse, old horse, what brought you here?
You have been dead for many a year....[13]

The final example of Gorman's *cante-fables* comes from Peter MacDonald, who, as I have said before, visited Larry in Brewer about 1908.[14] During the course of their conversation, Larry asked him about things back on the Island, particularly about people and places he had known; occasionally he would remember a song he had written about some person MacDonald named. Among the stories he told him was the following:

> *And then he told me this one. He asked me if I'd ever been in Charlottetown (that's the capital of Prince Edward Island — beautiful little city! Beautiful city!). And he said he was working there and he used to go down to Mrs. Yeo's to have his laundry done....And he was going through government park carrying his laundry. And this fellow and girl were sitting on a bench in the park and the girl said, "That's Larry Gorman." So he hollered out, "Larry, come back and sing us a song." So he turned right around immediately and walked back, and he said,

> As I was going down to Mrs. Yeo's
> With my shirts and underclothes,
> Heard a voice (not very strong)
> Saying, 'Come back here and sing a song.'
> I turned around all in surprise,
> Saw goose and gander in disguise.

At least one, probably two, and perhaps more of these *cante-fables* are localizations of more generally known tales, yet many of them seem to be original with Gorman. The point is that he probably not only made up the verses but invented the situations, the anecdotes, too. It is possible that some of the incidents are true (the last one, for example, is plausible), but that is not generally likely. Most of the situations are a bit unrealistic; for example, it is hard to imagine anyone being fool enough to ask Larry to say a grace, especially under any circumstance that could be considered even slightly compromising. Almost all of the stories have a certain after-the-fact quality; they are what *should* have happened, what someone *said* happened. And who is more likely to have been the first to tell these tales about Larry Gorman than Larry Gorman himself?

I pointed out in the preceding chapters that many songs Gorman didn't write were probably attributed to him because he sang them at some time or, under certain circumstances, claimed them. Peter MacDonald's narrative above shows us Larry in the act of telling a *cante-fable* on himself, and others have heard him tell them too. He loved to spend an evening singing songs, and best of all he liked to sing his own songs. We have seen that in Brewer when Islanders would drop in to visit him he would talk about people they both knew and recall verses he had written about them. This type of *cante-fable*, anecdotal and endlessly adaptable, with its emphasis on situations wherein the pompous, the pretentious, and the penurious are discomfited by witty, impromptu verse, would certainly add cubits to the stature of "The Man Who Makes the Songs."

The Larry Gorman legend, then, had its beginnings with a song-maker, Lawrence Gorman, and a writer, Holman Day. Incidentally, we know that the story went around that Larry Gorman was chased off Prince Edward Island for writing "The Gull Decoy," and I know of at least one instance of his telling this story on himself. Whether the story is true or not — and I think that it is probably an extension of the facts — its persistence in both Miramichi and Maine would indicate that it at least had Gorman's approval, and, what is more likely, his enthusiastic support, for it showed clearly that "people all, both great and small" had best beware of the terrible Larry Gorman.

NINE

The Ghost of Larry Gorman

When I began my study of Larry Gorman, I made various public appeals for information. These brought me some of my best information and, surprisingly, some of my most enigmatic. Take the following, for example: the late Mr. James Leeman of Bangor called me up after I had made an appeal on television one Sunday. His father and uncle used to run the Central House, one of the old woodsmen's hotels in Bangor, and he remembers that as a boy he saw Larry Gorman come there. He was a tall, husky, "P.I.," about thirty, full of pep, and always ready to sing. In the woods he was a cook. When the other men would see him coming, they would say, "Here comes the song-maker." He would sit in the bar and sing as long as anyone would keep him in drink. He died a pauper and was buried in Strangers' Row.

"When was this?" I asked him.

"About 1915," said Mr. Leeman.

It was clear that the man he remembered was not Larry Gorman, so I wrote the whole thing off as a simple case of mistaken identity. But when I received report after report from people who had worked with Larry Gorman in the twenties and even in the thirties, I began to wonder what was going on. I knew there were certain people whom they could have taken for Larry Gorman, and I usually asked about them specifically. Even so, I was still left with a mystery: a protean figure, never described in quite the same terms, who was known as "the man who makes the songs," who sang some of Larry Gorman's songs and, it would seem, sometimes claimed he was the great Larry Gorman himself. That this was not the real Larry Gorman is clear from the physical descriptions and from the dates. Who, then, was it?

There were several different figures whose presence could account for this seeming apparition, but by far the most logical choice is "Mike" Gorman. Michael Gorman, no relation to Larry, was born in Nelson, New Brunswick, July 24, 1880. In build he was quite different from Larry, being short and stocky, but they both had reddish hair. He came over to the State of Maine in 1901 and worked for various outfits and operations, mostly the Great Northern Paper Company, in the woods of the Penobscot watershed. Lloyd Houghton of Bangor recalls that when he was superintendent of the St. John Pond operation, Mike was at one of his camps. Mike made his home in Greenville; he had a camp (i.e., cabin) down the Bangor and Aroostook track south of Greenville Junction, and he became a familiar figure around town. In 1947 he entered Camp Jefferson, an old men's home run by the state; he died April 4, 1953, at the Willowcrest Home in Pittston.

Clearly, many people have confused Mike and Larry because Mike used to make up songs too. The only one that we are sure he wrote is "The Drive on Cooper Brook," which was printed in *The Northern* for May, 1925, with the following headnote:

This genuine woods song is here printed for the first time. The place and characters are familiar, the "occurrences" were actual ones and took place in 1923, the last year that Cooper Brook was driven. Mike Gorman, its author, is well known for his ability to "make up a song" on any subject that strikes his fancy. He is the nephew of Larry Gorman, in his day a well-known singer....[1]

The poem was reprinted in *Minstrelsy of Maine* two years later. Walter Creegan of Seboomook wrote me the following story:

I once loaned him my copy of Mrs. Eckstorm's book, so that he might see his poem in print, and when he returned it he enclosed a scrap of paper with the following lines:

My camp it is at ... Brook,
Where the water it is sweet;
And take it in open season, boys,
There's plenty of good meat.

I can't for the life of me remember the name of that brook right now — it is a tiny stream — and there was another stanza which included the line, "Where the rabbits they are thick."

The song itself is, as these songs go, pretty good. It is a chronicle song, beginning,

'Twas in the month of April, the truth I'll let you know,
I hired out in Greenville, the drive all for to go.
Joe Sheehan asked me for my name and marked it in a book;
The place he hired me for to go was way up Cooper Brook.

Then it tells of the long hike in from Kokadjo to the head of Cooper Brook and about the drive down through Church and Cooper Ponds, how the boom broke in the latter pond, and how they finally brought the drive in. The final verse should be compared to Larry's song, "The Good Old State of Maine,"[2] which follows the same traditional formula.

Now here's adieu to the camp and crew and the Great Northern Companie;
Their names are great through all the state, as you can plainly see.
I wish you all prosperity till I come home again;
And if I'm alive I'll try to hire for Cooper Brook again!

It is possible that the publication of this song and one of Larry's, "The Winter of Seventy-Three,"[3] in *The Northern* is the basis for Horace Beck's statement that Larry Gorman spent much of his time writing songs for the Great Northern Paper Company.[4] Or what is more likely, that is how Mr. Beck's informant, whoever he was, got that idea.

No one that I have ever met has described Mike as a wonderful singer. "Mike couldn't sing worth a damn," Herbert Rice told me. "Had no voice at all, but he'd sit there all night and sing you all kinds of songs anyway. He'd kind of talk them over to you." A man who ran an employment agency for the Great Northern recalled hearing Mike sing one night. One song was about a meal he had been served at a hotel in Patten, Maine; another was "something about 'the foot of Sawdust Hill,'" and a third discussed "the boys from the Island." These last two songs are easily recognized as pieces either written by or attributed to Larry Gorman. Certainly Mike did not write them, but it would be quite natural that they would be attributed to him in the same way that so many songs were attributed to Larry himself simply because he may have sung them at some time. But did Mike ever try to pass himself off as Larry? So far as I know, he never said he was Larry Gorman, but he did claim to be his nephew and even, at times, his brother. Herby Rice put it this way: Mike did not actually say he was Larry, but the mistake was made sometimes and he did not try to correct it. He did sing Larry's songs and claim them for his own, Herby said, "and those of us who knew better wouldn't say anything about it."

This part of the story is complicated by the fact that Mike had a brother Mose, who used to cook in the woods, but Mose did not make up songs, evidently. Some people claim there were three brothers: Mike, Mosey, and Larry. We can see how easily the identities of the two poets could be confused just in the normal course of things, without anyone's claiming false kinship at all.

Another songmaker who could have helped add to the confusion was John "Beaver Jack" MacInnis. He is said to have "belonged" originally to Waterford, Prince Edward Island, well down toward the North Cape. He came to Maine, lived for many years in Bangor (at the Queen Hotel), and used to work in the woods, mostly as a teamster. Jim Lynch of Grey Rapids, N.B., recalled a tall, well-built man who, he claimed, used to make good songs, although not as good as Larry Gorman's. His forte seems to have been the same as Larry's, though — personal, satirical verses. Lynch said that up on Carry Brook (which flows into Moosehead Lake near Seboomook) MacInnis made a song about George

Fowler, his boss. About a week or ten days before they broke camp, Fowler approached "Beaver Jack" and asked him to sing the song for him, and MacInnis, "who gave a damn for no man alive," complied. That was on a Sunday; on Monday "Beaver Jack" got his time.

From Bangor, MacInnis moved to Rumford, a town already well settled with Islanders. Peter MacDonald, who has had a law office in Rumford for many years, remembered him:

> *We had a fellow name of MacInnis, "Beaver Jack" MacInnis we used to call him. That fellow couldn't read nor write but he could make a song or poem about any darn thing. He'd come up to the office and he'd dictate them to one of the girls and she'd type them for him. Oh, the mill would be having some kind of a time with the union you know; they'd get him to write a poem to put in the paper with their ads. He used to make them right along.

There is a story that "Beaver Jack" once sent Jack Dempsey a poem he had written about him, for which Dempsey sent back a twenty-dollar bill.

Eckstorm and Smyth printed a song called "The Little Barber," written down in 1902, "from the singing of Jack McGuiness, of Bangor, who wrote the song."[5] If this is "Beaver Jack's" work (and it seems likely in spite of the variation in the spelling of the name), and if it is a fair sample of what he could do, we can see how his work could easily be confused with Gorman's. We have been told that Gorman claimed the song on one occasion as his own,[6] and even though I doubt his authorship, he would have been quite capable of making up this lampoon on a cunning woods clerk, and verses like these could be mistaken for his:

> About this jolly barber, he's of a medium size,
> His face is very narrow, a squint in both his eyes;
> His face is very narrow, in his nose there are a crook,
> The Devil ain't a match for him for charging on a book.
>
> These verses are not many, but I think they're very true;
> He never was in a concern, but he always shaved the crew;
> He cut your hair and shaved you, without either shears or comb,
> The Devil ain't a match at all for squint-eyed Johnny Holmes.[7]

I doubt very much that anyone ever mistook Joe Scott for Larry Gorman, but since the two men were in the same area at approximately the same time, some mention should be made of him here. Since I have already written more fully about Scott and his works elsewhere,[8] I will only touch on the similarities and differences between the two men here. Joseph W. Scott was born in Lower Woodstock, New Brunswick, in 1867, and as a young man he wandered over to the Maine woods. In the nineties he seems to have spent most of his time on the upper Androscoggin River in northern New Hampshire and northwestern Maine. He also worked for the Henrys in Lincoln Valley some time after Larry had worked for them. Later on he appears on the Penobscot, mostly on the East Branch. He died in Augusta, Maine, in 1918 and lies buried in the old cemetery in Lower Woodstock, N.B., his old home on the St. John River.

I know of nothing Joe Scott wrote that is at all like the work of Larry Gorman. Of the five pieces that I can attribute to him at present, three are come-all-ye's — long, perfectly traditional ballads making full use of the broadside style and morality: "Ben Deane," "Guy Reed," and "Howard Carey." A fourth, "The Norway Bum," is also in that general tradition, and the fifth is a sentimental song, "The Plain Golden Band," a smooth, music-hall sort of product. All five are still well known in the Northeast, while Joe Scott himself is practically forgotten. Almost the reverse is true of Gorman, whose name and legend are far better known than his songs. Yet in his time Joe Scott was well known as a maker and singer of songs, and it is just possible that some of my informants might have confused the two men in their memories.

I will speak later of several other satirists who might, at one time or other, have been mistaken for Larry Gorman.[9] Then, too, there are scores of unknown men who made up one or two songs. But the task at hand has been to lay the ghost of Larry Gorman that kept appearing. If I have not done so, at least I have succeeded in raising it clear enough to see that it is substantially Mike Gorman with possible assistance from "Beaver Jack" MacInnis and Joe Scott.

TEN

"That Sounds Like Larry Gorman"

Perhaps we can now make a few generalizations about Larry Gorman's songs. Much of what I say here will already be evident to many readers from what has come before, but this chapter can at least serve as a recapitulation.

I. Prosody and Diction

Larry Gorman was "the man who makes the songs," and any consideration of his prosody that neglects the music is likely to be simply irrelevant for two reasons. First of all, what appear to be irregularities in scansion (too many or too few syllables in any particular foot) disappear when the line is sung. This means that a songmaker can be more prodigal with extra syllables than can a poet. Yet in spite of the freedom from syllable counting that he obviously could enjoy, Larry Gorman was an extremely regular and careful versifier. Most of the irregularities in his verse can probably be blamed on the vagaries of tradition, not on Gorman. Second, the maker of traditional song, and that is what Larry was, does not think in terms of metrical scansion but in terms of a tune he wishes his words to fit. And to that assumption we can add another: the stanza forms and meters he uses will be dictated by the stock of tunes at his disposal. New words have continued to appear, but they are almost always set to existing tunes. Let us for the moment, however, look at Larry's songs as simple poetic forms.

The simplest of all traditional forms is the ballad stanza, what the hymnbook calls common meter: a four-line stanza of alternating

iambic tetrameter and iambic trimeter, rhyming *a b c b*. Gorman seldom used it; we find it in "Morris Ellsworth," though a seven-foot
iambic couplet is a much more accurate description of that stanza,
since it avoids the necessity of such arbitrary divisions as the following:

> There's the celebrated rabbit
> From the polar regions came,
> And many other animals
> Too numerous to name.

Adding another foot on to the trimeter lines of the ballad stanza
gives us the hymnbook's "long meter." Although, again, this is not a
form Larry used a great deal, he seems to have felt more sure of himself with it, and one of his best-known pieces, "The Gull Decoy," is
written in it (with the addition of feminine rhymes). However, most of
the versions of this song show the effects of oral tradition and shifting
from one tune to another:

> The other day we got in a tussle,
> 'Twas then his mettle I meant to try,
> But he threw me down and did me guzzle;
> He chewed the thumb of the Gull Decoy.

Substituting the anapest for the iamb in these two basic stanzas will
give us two other forms Larry used and used well. In "Bachelor's
Hall," for example, we have alternating anapestic tetrameter and trimeter, rhyming *a b c b* with internal rhymes in the tetrameter lines:

> I have two iron steads, I have two feather beds,
> Some blankets, some quilts and two pillows;
> I have two hives of bees, I have many fruit trees
> And for ornaments, two weeping willows.

He uses the same form in "The Workman," even keeping the alternating masculine and feminine terminal rhymes consistent throughout.
However, in "The Union River Drivers" he uses straight tetrameter,
predominantly anapestic:

> Here's Johnny Archer, that blacksmith of skill,
> Who irons the peaveys and sharpens the drills;
> He's working for Haslam on the big spruce and pine
> And the top of his head like a full moon does shine.

It is worth noting here that he often begins an anapestic line with an
iamb — again a perfectly traditional pattern.[1] Sometimes he follows
three rhyming anapestic tetrameter lines with a trimeter:

> One morning as Luke he was tasting the juice
> His tongue in his head it hung very loose;
> He gave the old woman some dirty abuse,
> Which didn't go well in the morning.

It is an easy step from this to the so-called double or come-all-ye stanza, one of the most popular forms in the whole broadside tradition. The simplest type is the double seven-foot iambic couplet, and that is the form we find Larry Gorman using more than any other. Take, for example, "The Winter of Seventy-Three":

> He shaved his whiskers all about, except his big mustache;
> He said that when he did go down he meant to cut a dash.
> He took with him ten pounds of gum, girl favor for to gain,
> But all the thanks he'd get for it, they'd say he was too green.

He would often vary this pattern by using internal rhymes, as in "Barren Town":

> In Barren Town of high renown that's where I do belong;
> To speak my mind on womenkind I've now composed a song.
> If you'll agree and come with me, mind what I say is true,
> And these ladies gay we will betray and give them half their due.

Another interesting variation of the double stanza is the one Gorman used in "Myles Everett More," a seven-foot anapestic quatrain with internal rhymes in every line:

> I would them deceive if you would me believe, then just you pay attention to me,
> Of the wonders I've done on the River St. John and the waters of Miramichi.
> I there undertook to act as head cook for thirty-two dollars per month;
> The nice bread I make, both mince pies and plum cakes, and hot doughnuts
>   for every lunch.

The next series of patterns we come to could be called variants of the double stanza with internal rhymes, but they are better described as true eight-line stanzas or double quatrains. "The Scow on Cowden Shore," for example, uses two identical quatrains rhyming *a a a b, c c c b:*

> So now my song is ended
> And I hope no-one is offended
> The like I never intended
> And your pardon I'll implore;
> So you humble, mild, and witty,
> I pray on me take pity,
> And join me humble ditty
> From the scow on Cowden shore.

"Michael McElroy" adds an extra accented syllable to make the triple rhymes masculine:

> He has a wife that's much the same,
> Who glories in the swindling game;
> Were he to rob the blind and lame,
> She'd laugh and shout with joy.

His knavish tricks she does inspire,
She'll counsel with him and conspire,
She'll make the balls for him to fire,
This mistress McElroy.

And "Donahue's Spree" varies this basic pattern by using anapests and feminine rhymes.

Another double quatrain that Larry used has the triple rhyme only in the second half, while the first half has some form of alternating rhyme. "Dame Bruin" is a good sample:

Poor Bruin was now in a terrible stew
Her screams they were loud & alarming.
Oh spare me! Oh spare me! for one year or two
Until I have revenge upon Gorman.
With him I've had dealings, he thus did me wrong
He has hurt my feelings, and has made a song.
But I hope I shall catch him before very long
If you will but spare me, King Satan.

"The Arlington Maid" and "The Horse's Confession" show some of the variations he worked on this pattern.

Perhaps the most out-and-out complex form Gorman ever used is that of "The Hoboes of Maine": eight lines of basic anapestic tetrameter rhyming *a a b a c d e d* with internal rhymes in the third, fifth, and seventh lines. The internal rhymes, by the way, are almost all feminine, and Larry probably labored to have them all so:

There are many young men crossing over the line
Who have not in their hearts a bad thought or design;
They'll come in great hopes, for they know not the ropes,
And fear not the allurements of women or wine.
They leave their dear mothers, their fathers or brothers,
Their kind, loving sisters they'll ne'er see again;
As soon as they come here, they'll each find a chum here,
And fall into line with the Hoboes of Maine.

We find that something less than half of the pieces long enough to allow us to establish a pattern use triple (anapestic) as opposed to duple (iambic) meter. Yet if we consult the music (as we should), we find that a third of the tunes match the triple meter of the words note for syllable, as in "Myles Everett More."[2] At least another third, however, cross-cut the duple meter of the words with a triple meter in the tune, as in "The Good Old State of Maine."[3] The final third are true duple in both words and tune. Now, of those pieces that have no extant tunes, we find that slightly less than half have texts in triple meter, but if we do a bit of conservative extrapolating we can conclude that something like two-thirds of all Gorman's songs were set to triple-meter tunes.

Larry Gorman was a skillful rhymer. He delighted in setting himself difficult tasks — internal rhymes, feminine rhymes, triplets, repeated rhymes running through entire songs, and the like — and he brought them off well. Some of the imperfections can probably be blamed on the vagaries of tradition, but even if we grant (as we must) that there are some make-do rhymes in his printed poems, Larry's knack for rhyme is obvious. He does not often wrench normal word order or employ trite tags to get himself off a hook. In fact, when we find a song with botched or extremely trite rhyming, we can be pretty certain it is not one of Larry Gorman's.

We have now arrived the hard way at some conclusions we could safely have jumped to: Gorman worked with two basic Anglo-American and Irish-American stanza forms, the single and double stanza, and their variations, dividing his efforts about equally between them (though he hardly ever used the straight ballad stanza). He showed a clear preference for triple time, and in his single-stanza forms he used it almost exclusively (if my extrapolations make any sense). And he delighted in complex rhyme schemes. I have never seen a purely literary form in his bag of tricks; all can be found in oral tradition, and a reading of any large collection of Irish ballads and songs (Manus O'Conor's *Irish Com-all-Ye's*,[4] for example) will, I am convinced, make it clear where Larry found most of his models, though almost all occur frequently in Scotch and North Country English songs too.

Larry's language deserves some attention. First, he used very little of the traditional broadside diction. He may begin his song with some sort of exhortation like "You good citizens all, your attention I'll call," and later on we may find "just you pay attention to me," but for the most part there are very few of the rather stale clichés of broadside poetry. Compared to that of John Calhoun or Joe Scott, Gorman's diction is startlingly fresh. Second, he never tries to be high-flown or "poetic" in his songs. Larry would never have attempted to soar on wobbly wing the way John J. Friend of Bangor (one of his contemporaries and "competitors") did when he wrote of "The Bangor Fire" thus:

> I'm standing on Exchange Street,
>   To view this awful scene
> The Stearns block is toppling down,
>   Great heavens what can it mean!
> And just across, the Morse-Oliver
>   Is falling o'er our head
> And gazing there with anxious fear,
>   Upon the aged dead.

And finally, Holman Day to the contrary notwithstanding, Larry Gorman never consciously employed bad grammar or phony dialect. There are lapses, true, but he always tried to be correct and (at the very least) honest in this direction. His vocabulary was a good one, especially good for someone who had very little formal education. *"What used to amaze a lot of people," Arthur Dalton told me, "was the language that Larry Gorman would use. He had only a country-school education, but where he'd get some of the words he'd use they never could figure out. The priests or somebody would look them up and they'd always find out that Larry Gorman was right too."

II. Tunes

What follows will be largely an explanation of why there isn't much that can be said about Gorman's tunes. A set of words, once launched on the stream of oral tradition will, if it lasts at all, retain its structure remarkably well. To labor the obvious for a moment, there is a necessary connection between the words of which a song is made and that song's identity; hence, generalities about a poet's technique based on evidence drawn from oral tradition can be reasonably accurate. But there can be no such certainty when we deal with the tunes. Since a set of words can be sung to different tunes and still be the "same song," there is obviously no necessary connection between tune and identity. In fact, it is possible that we have already learned as much about the *kinds* of tunes Gorman had in mind from our study of the words as we will from studying the extant tunes.

Early in the preceding section, I said that the creator of traditional song works in terms of a *given* tune and that his prosody will be dictated by the tunes at his disposal. That is, he creates new words to old tunes. Since this seems to be a pretty general assumption,[5] all that is necessary now is to trace Larry's tunes to their traditional originals and the point will be made that he was no exception to this practice. There are, however, three scholarly lions in the path. First, before we can make any valid statements about Larry's creative process, shouldn't we know the *specific* tunes he had in mind when he wrote? All we have are the tunes to which these songs were *sung*, and I have collected one of them to at least three different tunes. Second, we have extant tunes for only a handful of the songs. Third, I am a bit embarrassed to report that I have been able to find traditional parallels for less than half of the extant tunes. We cannot get around these lions, but they need not scare us out of our academic wits. First, there is some hope that the extant tunes *are* the ones Larry intended, especially when we find the same song sung many times to the same tune. Second, those songs for which we have no tunes use the same stanzaic and metrical patterns as those for which we do. If we find any common patterns in the extant tunes, then there is no reason to believe that the "lost" tunes wouldn't follow them too. Obviously what we have here are interlocking probabilities, not a set of final proofs, but even so, we can draw at least one careful conclusion.

Herbert Halpert raised the point that the tunes to which local songs were written can be used as some sort of index to the vitality of a folksong tradition in a particular area.[6] If a man wanted to write a song, did he turn to folk tradition for his tune or did he turn to popular songs? Keeping in mind the scholarly lions I spoke of, I think it is pretty clear that Larry Gorman took most of his tunes from folk tradition. Not only are most of the tunes I have been able to identify clearly traditional, but many of the others show evidence of traditional provenience. For example, half of the tunes have the flatted seventh, though for many of them "ambivalent seventh" would be more accurate.[7] Several show "gapped" scales; "The Gull Decoy I" is pentatonic, for example, and "Barren Town" is hexatonic. I grant that this evidence is not at all conclusive but if we add to it what we have already learned from the prosody, and what we will learn from the models and devices Larry used, his dependence on folk tradition is reasonably clear. To be sure, he used other sources; "Hail Fishermen Assemble" is supposed to have parodied a popular song and "The Baptists" appropriately parodied a hymn, but these seem to be exceptions. I do not think that the discovery of more tunes or tune analogues will show Gorman to be heavily dependent on popular songs.

Did he write his own tunes? As I have already said, this was not the common practice for creators of traditional songs. Therefore the burden of proof would be on me to show that Larry was exceptional, and there is absolutely no positive evidence that he was. I can see no reason for believing that he ever created a single tune.

All of which brings up an interesting theoretical point: how much stress did Larry (or any other creator of traditional song) place on specific tunes for specific songs? We know that in folk tradition generally the identity of a song is in its words, and while fairly stable tune-text relationships are frequently established, the tune is, in philosophic parlance, accident rather than essence in that it can be changed without making the song a "new" song. To what extent does a folk poet accept this as a fact of his artistic life and to what extent does he find it a source of constant frustration? Specifically, would Larry Gorman have been annoyed to hear "The Gull Decoy" sung to several different tunes (none of which may have been the one he had in mind)? Or would he have considered it unimportant so long as the words were not botched? With the exception of an occasional piece where the tune is a strong element in the parody (as it was in "The Baptists" and may have been in "The Champion of Moose Hill"), I do not believe Larry thought of a tune as any more than a simple vehicle for his words. Witness that in the three pieces we have from printed broadsides, "The Old Pod Auger Days," "The Workman," and "The Hoboes of Maine," Larry did not even think the tune important enough to mention. Once more, then, we can say that the important thing is not the specific tunes Larry had in mind but the kinds of tunes, the general sources from which he drew.

III. Subjects, Models, Devices

What sort of subject was Larry Gorman apt to write about? Most of his songs deal with personalities, that is to say, with people Larry knew or had worked with. Many of these songs describe only one person, but we have two good examples of songs that discuss many people: "The Scow on Cowden Shore" and "The Union River Drivers." We have reports of other songs like them, such as the one about all the men who worked in Yeo's shipyard, and it seems to me to be one type of song Larry handled very well. The songs Larry wrote about parties should also be included here, because the party really became a convenient frame into which he could fit his individual portraits. Just in passing, it is interesting to see how many of Larry's songs deal with courtship in some way, especially those songs that come from his bachelor days on the Island and in Miramichi. Twice he pilloried men who sought to persuade girls to marry them by impressing them with the number of their worldly possessions. He makes fun of the man who is too quick about remarrying or finding another woman. And the jilted lover is lampooned in "Mary Mahoney" and "Young Billy Crane."

Women in general are discussed in "Barren Town" and "The Workman," which brings us to our next classification: general social commentary. It is here that Gorman does some of his best work, as when he takes up the problem of the young man coming to Bangor to work in the woods in "The Boys of the Island" and "The Hoboes of Maine." And he could have fun displaying his erudition in a piece like "The Old Pod Auger Days."

Even from this extremely generalized discussion of his subjects, one thing should be abundantly clear: Larry Gorman was in no sense a ballad-writer. He was not interested in telling a story at all, save as that story might serve as a device for revealing the character of his subject. Some of his pieces can be called ballads — "Mary Mahoney" and "Young Billy Crane," for example — but very few of them contain sustained, plotted narrative. Pieces like "The Winter of Seventy-Three" or "Billy Watts" are narratives, granted, but very loose ones; they are not narratives as much as they are chronicles. At any rate, it is more proper to speak of Larry Gorman as a songmaker and, more specifically, a satirist.

What sort of models did Larry have? Obviously he had the entire folksong tradition to draw on, and we know that this tradition was a vigorous one not only in the lumberwoods but all through the Maine-Maritimes area. More specifically, as Laws has pointed out, the British broadsides (that is to say the come-all-ye's) were especially common in the Maritimes, as were Irish ballads.[8] Anyone who has collected songs in this area can second this observation. Further, we know that the Gormans were singers. Many people have said that Larry's mother was a good singer; others have remarked that James Gorman, Larry's older brother, was a wonderful singer even in his old age, and I have heard James's son Charles sing (at age eighty-five) and can vouch for quality there. Therefore it would not be surprising to find that Larry Gorman's songs were heavily influenced by the come-all-ye. Yet, Larry wrote only a few pieces that follow the narrative pattern of the come-all-ye ballad. Of this small number, three ("Tomah Stream," "Mary Mahoney," and "Young Billy Crane") have been questioned as not being Gorman's at all, and further, "Young Billy Crane" is more a parody of the come-all-ye style than a serious example of it. This information supports what many people have told me: that Larry did not like and would not use the come-all-ye formula. If the few exceptions to this stricture are truly Gorman's, they are all the more exceptional for it.

On the other hand, we can see one group of Irish songs that provided Larry with models: the wedding and party songs. Take, for example, "Larry Magee's Wedding":

> The guests of both sexes all ate very hearty,
> All crammed themselves up to the very windpipe;
> When an accident happened to Molly McCarty,
> She half-choked herself with a large piece of tripe —
> If you were to see Riley sail into the mutton,
> While all of the ladies did titter with glee;
> He fasted two days, the dirty old glutton,
> To make room for the supper of Larry Magee.

Compare this to Larry's songs, "Yeo's Party":

> There was Sarah Jane Yeo with her face all aglow
> And her sister just eighteen year old;
> They say they are dashes, the both of them mashes
> (I can't say for sure, it's just as I'm told).
>
> When supper was over, like sheep in good clover,
> Our stomachs being full to the collar and tie,
> And now we have parted and home we have started
> To leave Mrs. Yeo and her family goodbye.

The party song, describing in racy meter the goings-on at a lively spree, was a perfect model for what Larry wanted to do: get in a dig at everybody.[9]

The methods Larry used to organize his songs are about what might be expected. There is an occasional straight personal narrative, as in "The Winter of Seventy-Three," or straight story-telling, as in "Mary Mahoney" or the party songs I have already talked about. Sometimes, though not often, he invented a situation, as in "Dame Bruin" or "Nero and the Great John Mac." But by far his favorite method was the monologue, in which he allowed the person he was lampooning to tell his own story. Sometimes he combines the monologue with another device that I have always felt to be one of his favorites, the list or catalog. In "Bachelor's Hall," for example, over fifty items — from barns to chamber pots — are listed. "The Shan Van Vogh" is made up of two separate lists played against each other: what the old woman wants to buy and what she promises to pay with. In the arrangements of these lists, we can often see Gorman at his most ingenious; at least we can be sure he was having great fun. While this sort of listing is not a common traditional device, Helen Flanders and Marguerite Olney have published an amazingly close parallel to "Bachelor's Hall" (even to the feminine rhymes) from Rhode Island. It is called "Making My Will":

> A greasy hat, my old tom cat,
> A yard and a half of linen,
> A woolen fleece, a pot of grease,
> In order for your spinning.
> A small-tooth comb, an ashen broom,
> A candle stick and hatchet,
> A coverlet striped down with red,
> A bag of rags to patch it.[10]

And Margaret MacArthur of Marlboro, Vermont, sings a marvelous twelve-stanza song dating from 1787 called "The Marlboro Medley," which details the wares to be had "When Marlboro Merchants set out for Pedling." Here is the seventh stanza:

> Here comes the Turnips & fine Bobbin-laces,
> Braided-bark mittens (Your hands to case),
> A rare invention, every one says, —
>   Saddle-tree-wood, & Birch-barrel-bottles,
> Shoe-make spools & Iron-wood shuttles,
> Besom's & Oven-lids, (handy when baking),
> Boxes for flour & Tray's to make Cake in,
> And Wickopy stay-tape to lace up the Stays —

One technique that Gorman seems to have enjoyed using is parody. For instance, "The Baptists" is written to the tune of a hymn he is supposed to have heard these believers singing; that trick of putting shocking words to a familiar tune is one that was old when John Gay used it in *The Beggar's Opera*. Several other examples of his use of parody deserve special mention. The first is "The Champion of Moose Hill." For this lampoon of "Muck" Mace, Larry chose to use as his model a piece known as "The Champion of Court Hill," the first stanza of which follows:

> Come lovers all both great and small, I pray you lend an ear.
> My grief I have discovered and to you I will declare
> How a young man did me trepan with all his awful skill.
> I'm wounded quite by Willie White, the champion of Court Hill.[12]

Compare this with the first stanza of "The Champion of Moose Hill":

> You people all, both great and small, I pray you lend an ear;
> My name and occupation you presently shall hear.
> My name it is bold Emery Mace, I practice fistic skill —
> Oh, the fatal night when I got tight and got knocked out on Moose Hill.

His audience would certainly have recognized the model in its burlesque, and I have heard both songs sung to what is clearly the same tune.[13] Another place where Larry has used parody is in "Roderick

McDonald." When Mr. Alden Mace sang me the tune to that song, he
mentioned that that was also the tune to "McCauley's Leap." He then
went on and recited the whole piece for me, the story of which follows.
An old Indian warrior tells the story of his people. He tells how the
white men built a fort at Wheeling and how his people attacked it to
drive them away. They almost succeeded, but up rode Sam McCauley
and his rangers and beat them back again. But McCauley himself got
shut off from his troop, and the Indians, intending to torture him to
death for revenge, drove him to the edge of a great cliff. However,
McCauley leaped from the cliff, spoiled their fun, and lived to fight another day. "*That was a true song," said Mr. Mace. "That was back
in the Indian days. There was an account of it in the history books
when I was going to school." True or not, the introduction to this little
saga of frontier derring-do was in the front of Larry Gorman's mind
as he wrote "Roderick McDonald." The lines I give here are from
Alden Mace's recitation:

> 'Twas on the old Missouri five and twenty years ago,
> I met an Indian warrior, time had dyed his locks to snow.
> He had been among our people, he could speak our language well;
> He learned our ways and learned our actions — many tales of us could tell.
>
> He had climbed the Alleghenys over, old Virginia through and through;
> O'er the lakes up to the northwest he had paddled his canoe.
> He had fought a hundred battles, sometimes lost and sometimes won,
> In a land now owned by white men far toward the setting sun.
>
> He had met with noble spirits, bravest men among the brave,
> Men of every cast and nation, will smile upon their grave.
> The bravest man among them was a man whose face was pale;
> 'Twas of this the timeworn warrior sat him down to tell the tale. [14]

The parody is not exact, but it is plenty close enough to have allowed
his audience to make the connection and thereby reinforce the mock-
heroic tone Gorman desired:

> I met a river-driver eleven years ago
> Down on the Union River where the crystal waters flow.
> His brow with age was wrinkled, and his hair was silvery gray;
> He looked just like a monarch or some man that held great sway.
>
> . . . .
> His voice, though still commanding, it had a Scottish brogue;
> He left his home and never got our language in his vogue.
>
> He drove the Alligator, Middle Branch, and Buffalo,
> And on the Little Guagus he had handled his batteau;
> . . . .
>
> . . . .
> But the greatest of his wonders to you I will relate:
> In order to get water once he stole and hid the gate.

"The Shan Van Vogh" is a third example of Gorman's use of parody.
In the original song, the Shan Van Vogh is Ireland herself, telling of
the coming of the French to help set her free:

"And will Ireland then be free?" says the Shan Van Vogh;
"Will Ireland then be free?" says the Shan Van Vogh;
"Yes! Ireland will be free, from the center to the sea,
Then hurrah for liberty!" says the Shan Van Vogh.[15]

Larry's changing this patriotic rouser to a song about an old woman ordering her groceries is pure anticlimax. I have read several parodies of this song, by the way, in Irish collections. In fact, I have before me now a printed broadside (or, more properly, a slip ballad) of Irish origin called "The Battle of Ballycohy." The first three stanzas follow:

Did you hear of Billy Scully Says the Shan Van Voch
And the boys of Bal*l*ycohy say etc
That day we sho'd them fun we made the tyrant run
With their dubbled barrell*e*d gun says &d

Oh Scully you'er a rogue says &c
Turning t*e*nnants from their home says &c
They had always paid their *r*ent but the tyrant not content
To notice them he went says &c

It is the tyrant Scully says
He had steel upon his belly says &c
He got plenty o the lead he got wounded in the head
What a pitty he's n*o*t dead sáys &c.

The "Shan Van Vogh" was evidently a vehicle for satire on both sides of the ocean.[16]

"Dame Bruin"[17] is a clear parody of a little-known ballad about Napoleon, and while I have no proof positive, if "One Night Sad and Languid" is not Irish then I'm Lady Gregory. I quote it in full as it was sent me by E. G. Huntington of Vineyard Haven, Massachusetts, who found it in a collection made by a sailor named William Histed on board the whaler *Cortes* in 1847:

One night sad and languid I went to my bed
And had scarcely reclined on my pillow
When a vision surprising came into my head
And methought I was crossing the billow
I thought as my vessel sped over the deep
I beheld that rude rock that grows craggy and steep
Where the willow is now seen to weep
O'er the grave of the once famed Napoleon

Methought as my vessel drew near to the land
I beheld clad in green his bold figure
With the trumpet of fame he had clasped in his hand
On his brow there shone valor and rigor
He says noble stranger have you ventured to me
From the land of your fathers who boast they are free
If so then a tale I will tell to thee
'Tis concerning that once famed Napoleon

You remember that day so immortal he cried
When we crossed o'er the Alps famed in story
With the legions of France whose sons were my pride
As I marched them to honor and glory
On the fields of Marien lo I tyrany hurled
Where the banners of France were to me first unfurle
As a standard of liberty all over the world
And a signal of fame cried Napoleon

Like a hero I've born both the heat and the cold
I have marched to the trumpet and cymbal
But by dark deeds of treachery I now have been sold
Though monarchs before me have trembled
Ye princes and rulers whose stations ye bemean
Like scorpions ye spit forth venom and spleen
But liberty all over the world shall be seen
As I woke from my dream cried Napoleon

All of this brings up an interesting question: how did Larry make
these songs up? Everything that I have talked about in this chapter indicates a careful, rather fastidious craftsman; how does this view
square with the idea that Larry made his songs up on the spur of the
moment? The answer is simple: it doesn't. Some of his pieces may
have been spontaneous, but for the most part that alleged ability to
make up a song on the spot is part of the legend that has grown up
around this man. The few pictures we have of Larry at work show us a
man thinking it over; mumbling to himself in his room at Fitzgerald's
until Mrs. Fitzgerald thought her husband had hired a crazy man; pacing the floor at O'Brien's, occasionally writing something down at a
desk; pausing in his wall-building with Dalton long enough to write
something down in a notebook. On the other hand, we can be sure that
his songs came to him quite easily. The stories about Larry attending
a party and not dancing but just sitting there taking everything in are
probably accurate enough; he was always gathering material. As one
man put it, "Larry Gorman was very nosy; he'd talk to you for fifteen
minutes and at the end of that time he'd know all about you right back
to your grandfather." Probably his pieces would be out within a day or
so of the event they referred to, but, of course, this is only a guess.
The main point is that while these songs were probably not impromptu,
they appeared quickly enough to make them appear so when one looks
back on them from the perspective of fifty or more years.

ELEVEN

The Satirical Song Tradition

The story of Larry Gorman's life has now been told — at least as much of it as I have been able to piece together. Further, I have printed all of his songs I could find and offered some analysis of them. But so far, we have only seen his work for what it is in itself. Before we can judge it intelligently, we should see it in relation to the work of others who were trying to do the same thing. Was there, then, anything we can call a satirical song tradition within which Gorman was working and against which we can measure his achievement?

First, perhaps we should have a working definition of satirical song, something better than "songs like Larry Gorman's." At the risk of being too general, I will take my lead from Frederick Lumley, who called satire "an unanalyzable mixture of humor and criticism" in which "both elements are spread out so thinly in opposite directions as to reach vanishing points."[1] When a song criticizes some person, concept, or institution in such a way as to make us laugh, I will call that song satirical. The critical element may be so slight as to fade off into simple joshing, as it so often does in lumbercamp monicker songs, or the laughter may arise only as a shock reaction to some piece of twenty-three carat invective like "Michael McElroy"; so long as we can detect both elements, we have satire. A further distinction should be made between generalized and particularized or local satire. We will not be much concerned with the generalized satires, which take for their subjects women, lawyers, doctors, Swedes, bosses, and so on, but since Gorman wrote several of them, we should at least point out that they form a separate *genre*. Our interest is in the particularized satires: songs written about specific local events, people, and situations, songs with a reasonably reliable local pedigree.

167

I will further limit the definition to include only songs that can be identified as satire by their style and content. That leaves out any separate consideration of intentions, and sometimes the intent may be all the satire. What, for example, could appear to be a more standard romantic piece than "Jack Haggerty"? Yet, according to Geraldine Chickering, it was made up purely to embarrass someone who isn't even mentioned in the song.[2] Robert Pike has shown a similar origin for a song called "Bright Eyed Etta Lee."[3] Of course, what the author intended may be quite beside the point, while what the *singer* intends may be all important. A generalized satire about Baptists can be pretty pointed if it is sung when there is only one in the room. At an even further remove from content, the satire may be entirely in a parodied singing style, and a tragic ballad thus sung may be viciously funny to those in the know. On the other hand, as I shall mention again later, something made up as a stinging satire may become in time just another song. These matters have theoretical importance. On the current expedition, however, I plan to stay on the terra firma of express content, but I can at least report the presence of surrounding fens which, when properly explored, may turn out to be the more fertile land after all.

Folk tradition can be thought of as having three aspects: the creative, the prescriptive, and the conservative. For the first, the question is, was there a tradition of making up songs? For the second, once a man decided to make up a song, did his culture provide him with a stock of formulae upon which he was not only able but expected to draw? For the third, once a song had been created, how far might it spread and how long might it last in oral tradition? For instance, during the nineteenth and early twentieth centuries there was a ballad-making tradition in the lumbercamps of the Northeast and Middle West, as the number and variety of ballads on woods work and river-driving attest. Obviously, there was a creative tradition, then. It is equally obvious that once a man decided to make up a song, say about a comrade killed on the drive, there was a prescriptive tradition that told him how to go about it. He could draw, that is, on a large stock of commonplace lines, stanzas, plot situations, structures, moral attitudes, and tunes. Historically, we can show that this stock is a development within the British- and Irish-American broadside (or come-all-ye) tradition. Thus, when John Calhoun decided he wanted to make up a song on the death of Samuel Allen, he had only to adapt what he was furnished by the tradition to the immediate situation in order to create a thoroughly satisfactory ballad. Finally, the fact that the ballad he created has been sung along the Miramichi for as long as eighty years demonstrates the existence of a conservative tradition.[4]

The three aspects can exist in different combinations of strengths, not only in different areas but also for different *genres* within any given area. For satirical songs the creative aspect is the most important. There is not enough material available yet to allow us to make more than hazy generalizations about the prescriptive tradition in satire, although the very fact that it is not always easy or even possible to tell from purely stylistic evidence which songs are Gorman's and which are not is some sort of evidence for the existence of traditional formulae. The third aspect, the conservative, can be assumed, since most of the songs we are dealing with come from oral tradition, though because of their topical nature they tend to remain local and seldom live beyond a generation or two. It is the tradition of *making* these songs that will concern us, for, given the limited conservative tradition, unless these songs are constantly being made and remade there would be no tradition at all.

Collectors may not have included large numbers of these local satirical songs in their published works (presumably having been on the track of larger and more rewarding game), but a quick survey of collections from both sides of the ocean will reveal at least enough to show that making them *was* a traditional practice. To begin with, there are numerous examples from the British Isles, enough certainly to show that satirical songmaking was nothing peculiarly American but part of the general British bequest. In Ireland we find songs like "The Hackler from Grouse Hall":

> The busy tool of Castle rule he travels night and day,
> He'll seize a goat just by the throat for want of better prey;
> The nasty skunk he'll swear you're drunk tho' you took none at all,
> There is no peace about the place since he came to Grouse Hall.[5]

Among the Lowland Scots there is a remarkable tradition of ploughman songs:

> Come, all ye jolly ploughman lads,
>   I pray you, have a care,
> Beware o' going to Swaggers,
>   For he'll be in Porter Fair.[6]

And from the north of England comes "Robin Spraggon's Auld Grey Mare":

> The Miller of Ogle bred me, as I have heard them say,
> And gallantly he fed me with the best of corn and hay;
> For meal and malt I wanted not when in his custody,
> But now I'm Robin Spraggon's auld grey mare, ae how he's guided me.[7]

The satirical-song tradition is found all over Canada and the United States. From Alabama comes word of "Uncle Bill" Gross, one of whose songs, "The Clerks of Parch's Cove," tells of a group of drunks who sold out a merchant's entire stock while he was away one day:

> There was old Waffle-eye, so drunk he couldn't go,
> He gave away the candy and ate the indigo.
> He stood behind the counter as loud as he could holler,
> And auctioned off the coffee at nine pounds to the dollar.[8]

North Carolina boasts an eighteenth-century folk satirist, one Rednap Howell, bard of the "Regulator" movement, who is alleged to have composed some forty pieces and was outlawed for his pains.[9] George Korson, working among the coal miners in Pennsylvania and West Virginia, has been able to document a rich and varied songmaking tradition, and satirical songs form no small part of it:

> One morning of late as I chanced for to stray,
> To the Falls of Swatara I straight took my way.
> But ere I reached them what was my dismay
> To meet with Jim Lloyd, the boss, sir.
>
> Cursing and swearing and damning the mines,
> Likewise the poor miners to the flames he consigns.
> But little he thought one would make a few lines
> To bridle his tongue like a horse, sir.[10]

Many of the songs were made by well-known local poets like Con Carbon, Poet Mulhall, and William Keating, and it is interesting to find Korson emphasizing the part played by the Irish in mine-patch songmaking.[11] Some of the satires, by the way, were obviously intended and used as weapons in the miners' labor struggles, but a good portion of them seems to have been written and sung just for entertainment.

Lumbering is another occupation that shows a strong satirical songmaking tradition. One of the earliest, and still one of the best, collections of lumberwoods songs, Franz Rickaby's *Ballads and Songs of the Shantyboy* (Cambridge, Mass., 1926), gives several examples of satire. Then too, his Introduction — pure gold all the way, may I add — goes into some detail on one W. N. Allen, author of that classic of woods song, "The Banks of the Little Eau Pleine." Allen, whose career parallels Gorman's in many ways, wrote a lot of scandalizing songs. "Several of my poems are sarcastic descriptions of characters and failings of our respectable (?) citizens," Allen wrote to Rickaby, "and I have been threatened with libel suits and shot-guns on several occasions."[12] Several stanzas of a scurrilous song about "a hump-backed blow-hard: his name is S. D. Knowles" are quoted; they are quite similar in tone and form to Larry Gorman's "Roderick McDonald." It is too bad there is no more of Billy Allen's satire extant, because what we do have reveals a man of considerable talent. We should also note in passing that Allen was of Irish extraction, and Rickaby points out that "in the logging camp the hegemony in song belonged to the Irish."[13]

Other collectors have made it clear that satires of one kind or another formed no small part of lumbercamp tradition.[14] Maine had at least its share, and we have already met three Maine satirists besides Gorman: Freeman Archer, Mose Estey, and "Beaver Jack" MacInnis.[15] I will mention only one more, Ephraim Braley, the alleged author of "Canada-I-O":

> After we had suffered there some eight or ten long weeks
> We arrived at headquarters, up among the lakes;
> We thought we'd find a paradise, at least they told us so,
> God grant there may be no worse hell than Canada I O!

According to Mrs. Annie Marston, who sent the piece to Mrs. Eckstorm, Braley made the song about 1853; he was "a good singer with a comic and highly satiric turn, who made up many songs about local people and events."[16] If we move from the woods to the sea, there was Amos Hanson of Orland, who was, according to Orland Town Clerk Ernest Sugden, "quite a character around town — always making up verses." He recalled one on a rabid Republican who made it a point always to be first man at the polls:

> My name's Billy Oakes, and I cast the first vote
> For this glorious administration;
> For if the Democrats gain, it will be a shame,
> And we'll all go to Hell and damnation.[17]

Minstrelsy of Maine contains a number of local satires, both from the woods and the shore, many by authors well known locally for their gifts.[18]

Helen Creighton's excellent collecting work in Nova Scotia has made the traditions there extremely clear, and here again we find the scandalizing song.[19] The songs of Prince Edward Island, on the other hand, have not been well collected yet, but enough has been done to show that the Island's traditions are much the same as those found elsewhere in the Maritimes. We have already met Luke Hughes, Gorman's brother-in-law, and Larry Doyle of St. Peters, both of whom wrote satires, and around Campbellton there was a poet named Dan Riley. Further research will certainly uncover more. And we can conclude this part of our tour of the Atlantic provinces by simply referring the reader to the several examples of local Newfoundland satire in *Ballads and Sea Songs from Newfoundland*.[20]

This brief survey has demonstrated how widespread is the satirical songmaking tradition. If we now focus on a locale where Gorman lived and worked, and make a more intensive investigation there for other satirists and their songs, we will have a much clearer standard against which to measure Larry's product. I chose the Miramichi River valley in New Brunswick because there had already been a great deal of collecting done there by Louise Manny, James Wilson, and William Doerflinger, and the combination of the Miramichi Folksong Festivals and Louise Manny's Sunday folksong programs on the local radio station had pretty well galvanized the interest of the whole region (one in which there is still a lot of traditional singing) on the subject of old songs. I will not deny that this galvanism creates some special problems of its own for the student of folksong traditions; but I tried to be aware of them as I went along and, where necessary, to make the proper allowances.[21]

There were many people along this beautiful river who had reputations for making up scandalizing songs. Up around Boiestown there was John Calhoun of Parker's Ridge, who could make up satires as well as come-all-ye's like "Rocky Brook" and "Peter Emberly." Supposedly he made up a lot of songs which "slammed people pretty bad,"

and when (according to Nick Underhill) he was offered a rather large
sum of money for the big school tablets full of his songs, he said, "No,
they're not for publication. I'm going to take them with me." And
when the person who offered the money went to look for those tablets
after Calhoun died in 1939, sure enough, they were gone. His best
known satire is "The Messenger Horse," nineteen double stanzas long.
The horse tells of his hard life, which allows Calhoun to get off a few
cracks at other people's horses and horse handling. It is pretty gentle
stuff, though.[22] John's brother George seems to have limited his work
to satire, as did Abraham Munn (pronounced Moon) of Pleasant Ridge
(present day Holtville), whose masterpiece is a travesty of the legend
of "The Dungarvon Whooper."[23] And all of Davey Hunter's surviving
songs are satirical. His best-known piece is "The Rose Ann Song,"
made up to torment a Holtville woman and her son. "*She had this boy
Freeman," one man told me, "...and she just stayed there and worked
whatever she could get a day's work, and these men that brought the
lunch were portashers [portagers] and...whatever lunch they'd have
left over on the road they'd give it to her."

The Rose Ann Song[24]

1. 'Twas on a Saturday's morning
   In eighteen ninety-four,
   I started up the county line
   As I'd often done before.

2. My brother he was along with me,
   And being somewhat lame,
   Says, "Now we'll súrely get a drive
   For here comes Ken McBean."

3. McBean and Fairley's pacer,
   And like the wind did fly,
   And in another moment
   He quickly passed us by.

4. He drove to Alley Cameron's,
   With his daughter Sade,
   And when he passed us by again,
   "Good evening, boys," he said.

5. At length we reached John Hovey's field
   And crossed it with a run,
   Until we reached that little hill,
   'Twas where the fun begun.

6. "You are a lazy fellow,"
   I heard a woman say,
   "You are a lazy fellow,
   You've done nothing this long day."

7. "The wood I've sacked so on my back
   'Til my poor heart does ache;
   Now don't you give me any lip
   Or your mouth I will break."

8. 'Twas then up spoke bold Freeman,
   Saying, "You have challenged me;
   You'd better stack your dry goods
   If you're going to quarrel with me!"

9. No sooner had he spoke the words
   Than to the floor he come,
   You'd thought a bullet had pierced him
   From the muzzle of a gun.

10. "Lay there," she says, "and take it all,
    You brought it all on thee;
    Your cursed scandalizing tongue
    Just keep it off of me.

11. "Yes, your cursed scandalizing tongue
    It would provoke the Lord;
    You twit me of Tom Hunter,
    Likewise Beniah Norr'd.

12. "I grant they are two honest men —
    It's that you can't deny —
    If it wasn't for the lunch they bring
    I'm sure that we would die.

13. "Next you twit me of that Robert Ross,
    A man whom I despise;
    And if you do it any more
    It's you I'll paralyze."

14. 'Twas then up spoke bold Freeman,
    Saying, "You'll see me no more;
    Tomorrow morning early
    I'll step out from your door.

15. "Yes, I'll give to you this warning,
    So take it all in time:
    With my bundle packed upon my back
    I'll quit the county line."

A few miles below Blackville on the south shore of the river is Grey Rapids, and, as several people have said, "Everybody sings at The Rapids." Not only that, but a lot of people around there made up songs, too, and by far the best-known of them all was Frank O'Hara, who also "could make a fair drop of moonshine." One of his best songs, "Joe Brook," tells of a winter in the woods. It is essentially a monicker song with a good share of mild joshing, but O'Hara is not joshing the scalers. Wilmot MacDonald, a really great traditional singer, who was in camp about five miles away that winter, tells the story thus: "*Tryon Coughlan he was ... [on a] brook running into Burnt Hill, see, like what they call the North Branch ... they call it Joe Brook.... When he yarded those logs and put them on the brow there, you know, in the woods, — well, the scalers come in for to scale his logs. Well, they give him an awful hard scaling. Logs that shouldn't of took any more than twenty-two for the thousand, they took thirty of them,[25] ... which put him in the hole bad.... Oh, we had some awful mean scalers, paid by the company to do so!" Here is Wilmot's singing of the song:

Joe Brook[26]

♩. = approx. 69

1. It was Fri-day in Oc-to-ber,

nine-teen and twen-ty four, I

left dear old Grey Ra-pids with a half a

do-zen more; I took the train for

Deers-dale, a place I did not know,

For to work up in the lum-ber-woods,

with Cough-a-lan did go.

Joe Brook

1. It was Friday in October, nineteen and twenty-four,
 I left dear old Grey Rapids with a half a dozen more;
 I took the train for Deersdale, a place I did not know,
 For to work up in the lumberwoods, with Cough-a-lan did go.

2. It was on a Saturday morning, the day broke with a chill,
   We started o'er that rocky road to a place they called Burnt Hill,
   And the small birds in that country they whistled loud and shrill.

3. Now 'twas on a Sunday morning, and bitter was our lot,
   We started out for Coughlan's camp, that drear and lonely spot;
   And soon we covered five miles or more, when sad was our outlook,
   When I saw that ragged cabin on the stream they call Joe Brook.

4. Now we had men from every country, from Frenchmen down to Swedes,
   Yes, men from every country, and men of every breed;
   The brush it lay upon the ground, where every place you'd look,
   It would fill your heart with misery 'round that stream they call Joe Brook.

5. Tom Sullivan was our leader, he'd lead us all in prayer;
   He'd cast his eyes up to the skies and bitterly he'd swear.
   He'd rake all the apostles from Jacob down to John —
   It would fill your heart with misery to hear that man go on.

6. Now we had a young timekeeper, MacDonald was his name,
   A man of education and from Grey Rapids came;
   Tryon Coughlan was our foreman, a man both tall and proud,
   And just before the break of day he would turn out his crowd.

7. But we had not worked there very long till the scalers they came in;
   They sure cut down our lumber for they always cut her thin.
   Took thirty-four the thousand, that made our foreman look,
   When I saw his broad chin quiver on the stream they call Joe Brook.

8. But they are a man among this crowd, his name I will not say,
   Who always treated all the boys that ever came his way;
   He always treated all the boys, to everyone proved true;
   He was the man to watch the camp while boiling of home brew.

But perhaps the most fascinating of all the local satirists was Joe
Smith, "The Roving Joe." He came from around Renous, and his deeds
are still legend, though he died a comparatively young man in 1909.
His full story will have to wait to be told, but one of his songs should
be included here, not only because it is an excellent sample of local
satire but also because it refers to Israel Brown, whom Larry Gorman
scandalized so unmercifully.[27] The subjects lived near Joe, a few
miles above Pineville.

Charming Laura Brown

♩. = approx. 80 *parlando-rubato*

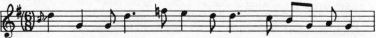

1. Oh In- dian-town of sad re-nown where Paul's dwelt on

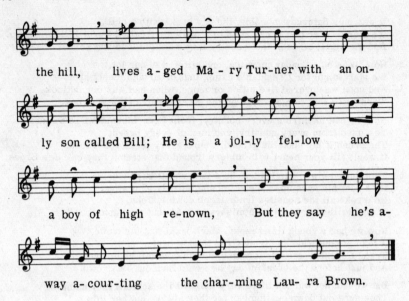

the hill,   lives a-ged Ma-ry Tur-ner with   an on-

ly son called Bill; He is   a jol-ly   fel-low   and

a boy of   high   re-nown,   But they say   he's a-

way a-cour-ting   the char-ming Lau-ra Brown.

Charming Laura Brown [28]

1. Oh Indiantown of sad renown where Paul's dwelt on the hill,
   Lives aged Mary Turner with an only son called Bill;
   He is a jolly fellow and a boy of high renown,
   But they say he's away a-courting the charming Laura Brown.

2. She sleeps in every morning, and at noon she will get up;
   Then a-growling and a-grumbling she will break a china cup.
   They give her education and they done the best they could,
   But she being wild and wayward and she done but little good.

3. Now William's gone a-courting, the neighbors they do say;
   He used to drive a red horse but now he drives a grey.
   "I'll go down to Father Murdoch's to the place of high renown;
   I will marry but I will not tarry with the charming Laura Brown."

4. She is cross-eyed and she's lazy and is always on the road,
   And lives in on the [lina] road all in a small abode;
   There with her brother Israel, and she never comes to town,
   But young William Turner he cuts a swell for his charming Laura Brown.

5. They have joined their hands in wedlock bands, I am about to say,
   And live up on Dungarvon about six miles away.
   They have one son called Johnny who is noted as a clown,
   And would romp all day all in the hay like charming Laura Brown.

6. So now my friends I will attend and my pencil lay away;
   I have wrote these simple verses I made up the other day.
   Renous River and Dungarvon, those two rivers does combine,
   Stands the home of William Turner sheltered by a bunch of pine.

There are several *cante-fables* about Joe Smith too. Take for example, the following, told me by Al Keating of Strathadam:

*Joe one time he went to sleep in a barn way up in Renous someplace, and there was a rooster way up on the collar beam. He dirtied down on Joe's face, see, in the night . . . so in the morning [when] daylight come he says,

> Little bird of little wit,
> Who taught you on my head to shit?
> But since you've been so jeezly mean,
> I'm going to sweep you from the collar beam.

And he killed the rooster.

The "Nor'west" Miramichi had its poets too, not the least of them being Jared MacLean of Strathadam, whose song, "Lizzie's Canoe" can still make temperatures rise around Northwest Bridge.[29] And "Barlow Bill" McKay of Millstream made up many songs too. The most famous of them is "Peelhead," a song made on a local lumberman, the last stanza of which follows:

> Now Mr. Isaac Peelhead, I hope you may do well;
> I hope that you'll get logs enough all for to pay your men,
> And not like it was last summer when you said they'd be good times,
> And some of your men you owe six months and more you do owe nine.[30]

Heading across and downriver, we come to Weldfield, just off the Richibucto road, and "Michael Dignam's Spree" (of uncertain authorship) tells of a wonderful party that took place there. One stanza will set the tone:

> Her boyfriend lives at the Rapids, as near as I can tell;
> He's one of the biggest liars, and that you all know well.
> He always wears a broad-brimmed hat for fear his skin might spoil;
> He ought've had more better [sense] than flirting with a child.[31]

Then there was Martin Sullivan, the cow doctor from Kouchibouguac. He made up several satires and is reputed to be the author of "Jeremiah of Bartibogue," which closely parallels Larry Gorman's "The Gull Decoy." Since Gorman's song was well-known along the Miramichi, Sullivan may well have used it for a model. Here is one stanza:

> In the town of Chatham I was much admired,
> Because I wear such excellent clothes;
> And the only thing that affects my beauty
> Is a spot of crimson upon my nose.[32]

One final example of the satirical songs of this region comes from George Duplessis, who lives down in Eel River Bridge. Everyone in his large family has music in him, and someone is always singing, playing the violin, or strumming a guitar in his house. In 1947, George and one son went to work in the woods for a Bay du Vin farmer; after they had worked for him for three weeks, the man refused to pay them, and George made up the following song about him. It is, so far as I know, the only satire he ever wrote:

The Bay Du Vin Farmer [33]

1. Well there was a jol-ly far- mer who lived up Bay du Vin; He was the mean-est man I know, the worst I ev- er seen To me right fol the dad-dy, with me right fol the day.

The Bay Du Vin Farmer

1. Well there was a jolly farmer who lived up Bay du Vin;
   He was the meanest man I know, the worst I ever seen.
       To me right fol the daddy, with me right fol the day.

2. He hired two woodsmen one day, two men from Eel River,
   And all he fed the men was with — with onions and liver.
       To me right etc.

3. He put us cutting furnace wood at a place where there was none,
   And if we had kept cutting there we'd soon been on the bum.
       To me right etc.

4. He put us cutting pit props; the chance seemed very good,
   And if you don't believe me, I'll show you where it stood.
       To me right etc.

5. We worked for him for three weeks, we thought we were doing big,
   And when we came to settle up he give us a little pig.
   To me right etc.

6. And now my song will soon be ended, I hope you'll understand;
   And if you're looking for a place to work, don't be his hired man.
   To me right etc.

7. That man that made this song up is an old woodsman you see;
   He's not afraid to tell his name, his name is Duplessie.
   To me right etc.

And now we are in a better position to judge Larry Gorman's work.

TWELVE

Conclusion

Larry Gorman was not unique by virtue of the fact that he was a satirist. The making of satirical songs was a widespread traditional practice. Obviously (and George Duplessis is a good example), many people tried their hand at it, but it had its specialists too. In any community there was apt to be a satirist, well known locally, who was responsible for many such songs and from whom they were, with some apprehension, expected ("He was always making 'em up."). Larry was doing nothing unexpected or unusual when he scandalized a neighbor in song; others in his culture could and did do the same sort of thing. Then why all the shouting, if there was nothing special about him? There is ample reason; there *was* something special about him. But while we are trying to distinguish Larry from the lump, we should also try to see him as part of it.

Can we generalize about the function of satirical song? To some extent we can. Only occasionally do we find a Woody Guthrie or an Aunt Molly Jackson who forged songs meant to be used as weapons in the battle for social justice. In Maine and the Maritimes such songs are almost unknown. Even among woodsmen there seems to have been almost no thought of songs being used in this way, all of which makes for an interesting comparison with coal miners, among whom such songs were rather common. It may be because in the Northeast we are working with a song tradition among groups which have been notoriously unorganized: farmers, fishermen, and woodsmen. It may be that conditions there were never so appalling, injustice never so screaming, as among the miners or the migrant workers, though inequalities and exploitation certainly existed. To be sure, there is an occasional note of protest in some of Larry Gorman's songs (or songs attributed

180

to him), in "The Hoboes of Maine" or "The Boys of the Island," for example, or in "Prince Edward Isle, Adieu." And Jared MacLean struck at abuses in his songs too. But the fact remains that the protest song is not an important *genre* in the Northeast.

How about such songs as "The Good Old State of Maine," "Roderick McDonald," or "Michael McElroy"? Are they not a form of protest that may have been extremely effective? It has been said that employers feared, or had reason to fear, Gorman, because if he "songed" them, characterizing them as hard-driving skinflints, they might find it hard to get men. Eckstorm and Smyth felt that woods poets in general were men of influence in this way and that what Larry's song on the Henrys had done "in the way of keeping good men from going to New Hampshire to work is hard to estimate." They go on: "Like 'Canaday-I-O' it was a warning to all who heard it, and the information it conveyed was sure to be remembered. The good employer and the bad employer, celebrated in song, each had reason to respect the power of the woods poet; for he sent men to them or held them back from applying for work."[1] Doerflinger suggests the same sort of thing.[2] Again, we must be careful not to generalize from the little evidence we have. As Eckstorm and Smyth say, it is extremely hard to estimate the effect of a song. Occasionally a song might discourage men from hiring with a particular operator. Professor Thelma James of Wayne State University (Detroit) remembers her mother telling about the loggers around her home town in Michigan singing a little song which spoke of the bad meat, weevily bread, and spoiled beans one outfit served its men, and the song served there as a very clear and effective warning. And Herbert Halpert found a man in the Jersey Pines country who made up a song on his employer that went like this:

> There's a man called Bob Mulligan lives on old Fisher's place;
> And if you want your money, old Bob you've got to chase.
> It's come then all you laboring men and I pray be warned by me,
> Don't ever work for Mulligan if you want to get your pay.

Halpert continues: "The singer added triumphantly, on my phonograph recording, 'He paid me. When I sung that to him, he paid me. And my brother Warren was working with me, and Fred Mathews, and he *paid them*.' Here we find a local song used to exert social pressure, which reminds us of the magical pressure attributed to the curses of the Irish poets."[3] And A. L. Lloyd speaks of ploughman songs serving as direct warnings at English fairs.[4] These things are as they may be, but so far I have never found a woodsman who admitted to steering clear of any operation because of anything Larry Gorman or any other woods poet said about it in a song. Herbert Rice of Bangor and John and Peter Jamieson of East Bathurst, New Brunswick, had all heard the song about the Henrys, and yet they went to New Hampshire to work for them anyhow. Roderick McDonald of Ellsworth never had any trouble getting a crew although Larry had "songed" him several times. McDonald evidently considered the songs a nuisance but not sufficient grounds for either firing or refusing to rehire Larry. So while it would be nice to be able to say that Larry Gorman had been a strong social force working to better the woodsman's lot, it is more likely that he disturbed the labor market very little.

The main reason why Larry was not more effective in this direction is that he cried wolf too often. As he told old Henry (if that little story is true), he was "always making up songs about something or other." If all the men Larry Gorman "songed" had found it difficult to get up crews, it is hard to see how there would have been a tree cut, a log yarded or landed, or a drive brought into the boom from Lincoln, New Hampshire, to Chatham, New Brunswick. Eventually, his song-making just became a kind of joke, as we have seen from accounts of his last years in Brewer. At any rate, I am sure that his habit of ex-coriating a man for reasons often sufficient only to Larry Gorman was too well known to allow him to be taken as a lumberwoods Dun and Bradstreet.

Yet if these satires were not weapons, we can think of them as safety valves, as ways of blowing off steam. We have an excellent ex-ample of this sort of thing in George Duplessis' song on the Bay du Vin farmer who did him out of wages.[5] When I asked him who the man was he did not want to tell me because it might get back to him, although he was glad enough to sing the song for me. In spite of what the song says, it was not so much a warning as a way for George to work off his anger, not so much revenge as therapy. It is hard to tell how many songs may have been written in this way and for this reason, but I sus-pect a good many. Then too the singing of such songs may have given a lot of people an outlet for their dissatisfactions and resentments, al-though this is all but impossible to prove. In other words, the lumber operators may have had some reason to be grateful to the satirists.

This is not to say that people did not get annoyed or angry at being "songed." We know that Roderick McDonald did not like the song Larry Gorman made on him, and Davey Hunter's "Rose Ann Song" did not please its victim either. People got annoyed at Joe Smith too, but since Joe was one of the roughest and strongest men in Miramichi, their rage was impotent. And, of course, there are the numerous stories of Larry Gorman's being run out of town or into the woods for songs he had made up. The following story, sent me by an old Prince Edward Island resident now living in Montreal, shows the same reaction at one remove: "I always remember a story Dad told us of how he was once helping a farmer in Lot Seven in with his hay. By the way, he had eyes on the farmer's daughter and was a stranger. He was humming 'The Gull Decoy' innocently, when the man who was pitching the hay on the load threw aside his fork and invited my father to come down and do battle. He was the 'Gull Decoy.'"[6] All this is what we would expect to find, but quite as often we find that Silas Curtis of Blackville was right. I had asked him if people got annoyed at these songs: "Sometimes, sure they did," he said, "but often as not they'd go to a lot of trouble to learn the thing too and actually be kind of proud of it."

Yet it is interesting to notice how many of the songs in this book were sung for me by people who were not directly involved with them, either as creators or as victims. Some did not even know who the people named in the song were or where they were from, but usually the singer knew something about these matters. The point is that more often than not the songs were sung purely for entertainment, and once a song lived beyond its immediate situation it was thought of essentially as "another good song" that just happened to be about "someone who lived around here." If it traveled much further, it simply became another song. This is what happened to many of the Scotch ploughman songs, and it is my guess that the American song "The Little Brown Bulls" was a local satire that finally lost all touch with its origin. And we can see that something like that happened to "The Gull Decoy" along the Miramichi, where, at the same time, it could at least draw sustenance from its being known as one of Larry Gorman's songs. To sum up for the moment, then, we cannot assume any direct relationship between community sentiment and the sentiments expressed in a local song. Such correspondence must be demonstrated for each individual song, not taken for granted.

Since these songmakers were the equivalents of poets in their culture, studying them should cast some light on how that sort of person functioned in his society and what position he occupied. Eckstorm and Smyth have put it this way: "In the lumbercamp and on board ship, the man who is both poet and singer can reach all the highest honors. His literary occupation does not suggest effeminacy to the men he lives among. As in the olden, the golden, days of the bards, the poet is the best man there." [7] There is nothing in our picture of Larry Gorman that would support their statement. He was anything but the best man there; while he was clearly a member of an in-group, a part of the community, he was just as clearly a man apart from his fellows. Wherever we see him, we see a man going his own way, not mingling much with the neighbors. Even when he went visiting, as he used to in Ellsworth, his efforts were not particularly appreciated. On the other hand, Joe Smith, Frank O'Hara, John and George Calhoun, Abe Munn, and Davey Hunter do not seem to have occupied a similar position at all but were "one of the boys." Larry Gorman's life should certainly stand as a warning against the making of romantic generalizations about the status of the lumbercamp bard, but we will wind up just as far from the truth if we try to generalize from his singular career. Stripped of its excesses, what Eckstorm and Smyth are saying is that the poet could still be one of the "real guys" and that his craft might even stand in his favor. But the simple fact that a man was a poet would not win him acceptance. Joe Smith was accepted because he was a strong man and a marvellous companion; it is almost incidental that he was a poet. Frank O'Hara was "a swell guy," and he made good home-brew whiskey; he was, by the way, a poet. Larry Gorman, on the other hand, never won real acceptance, not only in spite of his skill in songmaking but partly because of his too great devotion to that craft.

No one was really safe from his wit; if he found something funny about a person, Larry would make up a song about him, whether that person was friend or foe. Further, he had a quick temper and was easily annoyed. Louise Manny is right: "...the jilted lover, the pompous employer, the dishonest inn keeper, the miser, the silly girl, the vain young man..." often enough found themselves "neatly impaled on Larry's wit,"[8] but they were not alone. Arthur Dalton's father always expected to find some day that Larry had made a song about him, although they worked side by side for years and were good friends. The man was simply not to be trusted. "He could be a perfect gentleman to your face," said Joe Tosh, "but he'd as soon write a song about you as not."

Clearly, then, Larry Gorman often considered a song as a weapon, a brickbat. If he felt that a person had insulted him or "made little of him," he was only too likely to make a song. Joe Tosh gives a good example from Ellsworth: down on Paddy Lane, Larry had gone one evening to the wake of a friend. When he went in, he knelt down by the coffin to say a prayer. The room was small and Larry's long shanks stuck out so far that one man tripped over his foot. A woman began to giggle; Larry turned and caught her at it, and the next day there was a song about her that began,

> I'm poor old Fran, I need a man,
> Oh yes, I need him badly;
> Oft times I've tried to be a bride
> But always missed it sadly.

"Dame Bruin" is a case in point too: the girl threw dirt on Larry, and he hit back with a scurrilous song. Myles Everett More called him a "bluenose" once too often, John McNamara fired him, and "The Great Pond Tramp" forgot to return Larry's driving boots: all were victims of his satire. He even considered it something of a courteous gesture *not* to make up a song about a person. Jim O'Brien treated him well and he refused to "song" him at his brother Michael's request, saying that he'd never "song" anyone who used him as well as Jim O'Brien had. (Interestingly enough, he turned the joke back on Michael, making a song about him — a trick he was to pull again when Roderick McDonald asked him to make a song on Frank Mace.) And when, in Brewer, Larry told Peter MacDonald that he had never made up a song about MacDonald's grandfather "because he was always the same," he obviously meant it as a compliment. Gorman was a blue-eyed calamity waiting to strike, and he seems to have struck whenever he could find occasion. Often enough, people were scared to death of him, and certainly he was not the kind to inspire confidence. He was nosy, and everyone knew why; he would go to a gathering just to "take her all in," and everyone knew what he was doing; he was not an outsider looking in, he was an insider looking on — a watcher to be carefully watched. Joe Tosh summed it up: "Larry just wasn't the kind of guy you'd choose for a pal."

There is reason enough, then, in Larry's constancy to his crooked muse for his not being "the best man there." Yet there is more, and Joe Tosh's statement can be taken as our first straw in the wind. Men were not enthusiastic about him; among them he was apt to be withdrawn and taciturn. Up in Miminegash, for example, they claim that often after supper when the other hands at McElroy's would be sitting around together, Larry would be down on the beach by himself. On the other hand, among women he seems to have been outgoing and garrulous, but they didn't seem to care much for him either. As an Ellsworth woman told me, commenting on his gossipy ways, "...that just wasn't like what the other men would do." His mother was an intelligent, active woman; Larry was devoted to her, and she came to visit him often and long, especially before he was married but even afterwards right up to her death in 1907. He only came to marry at all some years after he had left the Island for good, and by that time he was forty-five years old. There are further hints in his songs. It was my wife who first commented, one night after she had read through a group of his songs, "Isn't it funny? So many of these songs are written about women's things — things a woman could be concerned with." True enough, songs like "Bachelor's Hall," "The Shan Van Vogh," "Michael O'Brien," and "The Workman," are nothing but lists of household items and groceries. These straws indicate not a gale nor, perhaps, even a strong wind; but may they not show an unpleasant little draft?

People may not have approved of Larry's songmaking, and they may not even have liked him as a person; the fact remains that among the woodsmen, river-drivers, and sawmill hands of Maine and the Maritimes he was famous. Remember that when David Dyment landed in Bangor from the Island he only had to ask once where Larry lived,[9] and it is surprising even today how many people still "twig" to his name. It remains for me to try and account for that fame.

First of all, Larry Gorman has had good publicity. Holman Day's *King Spruce* may have been a poor novel, but it was popular, and there is no doubt that it helped to get Gorman's name around at least in Maine. Then in 1927, just ten years after his death, Eckstorm and Smyth published several of his songs in *Minstrelsy of Maine*, which may be more symptom than cause, but the book probably did its bit to swell Gorman's fame. Louise Manny's radio program certainly helped to put new life into his legend along the Miramichi. Lots of people I talked to there knew of him but knew only what they had heard "over Miss Manning's program," and countless people told me to get in touch with her because "she plays his songs over the radio and knows all about him."

The fact that Larry was, as I have already pointed out, his own best press agent helped too:

> And when they see me coming,
> Their eyes stick out like prongs,
> Saying, "Here comes Larry Gorman,
> He's the man who makes the songs."

That little verse in its many variations did wonders for Gorman in carrying his name everywhere. Sometimes all a person knows is the epithet, "the man who makes the songs." I asked eighty-seven-year-old Arthur Carr of Boiestown if he had ever known Gorman. "It's just like a dream, it's so dim, but I remember Father talking to someone out by the gate and then when he came back to the house Mother asked who that was he'd been talking to. 'Why that was Larry Gorman, "the man who makes the songs,"' he said." It's the sort of answer I've had from a lot of people: "All I know is he was 'the man who makes the songs.'" Then there was that first stanza to "The Scow on Cowden Shore":

> My name is Larry Gorman, to all hands I mean no harm;
> You need not be alarmed for you've heard of me before;
> I can make a song or sing 'un, I can fix it neat and bring it,
> And the title that I'll give it is "The Scow on Cowden Shore."

Every little bit of publicity helped.

Another thing that certainly helped to spread his reputation is that, while most of the other woods poets we have discussed confined their efforts to one locale, Larry spent his life in three places, or rather four: the West End of Prince Edward Island, the Miramichi, and Ellsworth and Brewer in Maine; and he wrote a lot of songs in each place. Others traveled but always returned to their homes, it seems. Thus Joe Smith is known chiefly in Blackville and Renous, John Calhoun around Boiestown, and Freeman Archer along Union River in Maine. Larry did not just spend a few months or a winter in these places; he actually lived there, worked there, and wrote there. This fact alone might have created an illusion of fame for the eager folklorist.

Larry's notoriety was no illusion, though, and while all of the things I have just mentioned may have added to his fame, they can in no way adequately account for it. The fact is that of all the men who made up satirical songs he was by far the best. Doerflinger is, as we have seen, correct in saying, "Both Maine and New Brunswick were infested, in logging days, with poets and singers whose barbed verses stuck to their victims like burrs to a dog." He is also correct when he adds (in just the right tone), "Larry Gorman, of course, was in a class by himself."[10] His cleverness with parody, his skill in handling rhyme and meter, and the sharp edge of his wit kept him well ahead of the rest. Others occasionally turned out a satirical song that could claim rank with Gorman's, but he turned out "corkers" consistently. And many of them were remembered! No other satirist, no other folk-poet of any kind, for that matter, got one-quarter the stuff into local tradition that Larry Gorman did. People used to keep scrapbooks of his songs, and those people who have told me that their parents knew dozens of his songs by heart were probably exaggerating only a little bit. As one man told me, "There just wasn't anybody else could touch him." We can alter that statement, perhaps: touch him they could, but stay with him they could not. He was the master of the trade.

And well might he have been the master, because he worked full time at what other men did in off hours. John Calhoun and Joe Smith are supposed to have been "always at it" too, but neither appears to have been as devoted to his craft as Larry was. Nothing else he did in his life mattered to him as much as his poetry. To think of Larry Gorman as anything but a poet, then, is to miss the whole point of his character, for that is not only the way his contemporaries saw him, it is the way he saw himself. He was not a woodsman and river-driver who wrote poems; he was a poet who worked in the woods and drove logs on the river. He never seems to have held a skilled job, usually being no more than a swamper in the woods, an awkward hand on the drive, and a sort of odd-job laborer around a mill. Perhaps he was a poor workman because he never had more than half his mind on his job; perhaps he turned to his songs because he was such a poor work-man. The fact is that his songs were his constant preoccupation — at work, in the evenings, playing cards, even in church. The tradition of satire was available to him; he did not invent it. What he did do was to take it more seriously than it had been taken before, to put it at the center of his life, to realize new possibilities within that tradition, and to carry it further than anyone else did. "He just went too far with that damn poetry stuff," I have been told. Too far or not, he went as far as he could.

Larry Gorman was an artist, then. However we may feel about the quality or value of his art, there is no other satisfactory way to de-scribe him. He had lived in Prince Edward Island, New Brunswick, Maine, and New Hampshire; he had worked as farmer, fisherman, woodsman, river-driver, and mill-hand. Wherever he went and what-ever he did, he kept his eyes and ears open, watching and listening to people around him; and out of all this raw material he created funny, biting, satirical songs. His view was not broad nor his insight very deep, yet his focus was often sharp and he has left us some amusing pictures, for all their foreshortening, of a time and life that are gone.

Whatever judgment we may pass on his songs, the people around him listened and laughed. Then they learned them, sang them, and passed them on so that their friends and children might laugh too. And people have been laughing ever since. I have sung Larry's songs and told stories about him, and heard them sung and told, in kitchens and front parlors from Miminegash, Prince Edward Island, to Rumford, Maine. And everyone laughed and shook their heads and said that sounded just like him and he certainly was a rascal and did I know any more. There have been many such pleasant evenings for me, and Larry Gorman was the founder of the feast in each case, the man who drew us together as he had often drawn others together before. Which brings us to Alex Phillips' little story and the end of the road.

Epilogue [1]

Alex Phillips had just been paid off, and he and his companion were walking through the Montana night toward the nearest railhead, a distance of some miles. They had come west on a "harvest excursion," and, after finishing their work in Alberta, they had decided to cross the border to see if they couldn't find more work. They had, and now they were through and beginning their long trip back to their homes on the west end of Prince Edward Island, a good two months' wages carefully sewn into the linings of their jackets. It soon became evident that they were not going to make the railhead that night, so they started looking for a place to sleep. There was a big barn ahead which offered shelter, but as they approached, they heard voices from the loft. Worried about being robbed, they prepared to continue their walking again.

"Wait a minute," said Phillips. "Listen."

His companion listened and heard it too. "Singing," he said. "It's coming from the loft."

Phillips walked up to the door and cocked his ear toward the loft. Then he smiled, "I'm damned," he said, "but that sounds like one of Larry Gorman's songs they're singing. Hey!" he shouted up the ladder, "Are you fellows from Prince Edward Island?"

A head appeared over the hay at the top of the ladder. "No, we're from Maine. You fellows from there?"

"Yes, we are," said Phillips.

"Well, if you know any of Larry Gorman's songs, come on up and join us."

So the two of them went up and spent that night among friends.

188

Appendix

*A Complete Alphabetical Listing of All the Songs
Written by or Generally Attributed to Larry Gorman*

The information in each entry is broken down as follows: A. Source of the version or versions given in the text or, if all I have is a report of the song, where and when it was reported; B. Other versions of the same song I have collected; C. Versions in print or in other collections; D. Miscellaneous notes in addition to those given in the text. All items given an ATL (Archives Tape Library) number are on deposit in the Indiana University Archives of Folk and Primitive Music, 014 Maxwell Hall, Bloomington, Indiana.

ACE WILLIAMS' FOOLISH GIRL (Ellsworth)
    A. Reported only, by William Waldron, Tyne Valley, P.E.I., 6/57.
    B. None.
    C. None.
    D. None.

A.P.A., THE (Brewer)
    A. Not included in the text.
    B. Reported only, by Clarence Adams, Brewer, Me., 4/58. All he could recall was "For forty rod, I swear by God / You could smell the A.P.A."
    C. None.
    D. None.

ARLINGTON MAID, THE (P.E.I.)
    A. Tune and stanzas 2, 3, and 4: Mrs. John Coughlin, Ellerslie, P.E.I., 6/22/57 (ATL 2155.6); stanza 1: Kenneth Lecky, Charlottetown, P.E.I., 7/5/57. The order of stanzas is my conjecture.
    B. None.
    C. None.
    D. For stanza form, compare to "The Horse's Confession" and "Dame Bruin."

AWAY TO THE STATES TO GET RICH (Brewer)
    A. From a handwritten copy given me by William Bell, Brewer, Maine, 10/18/58, 7 sts. w/o tune.
    B. None.
    C. None.
    D. None.

BACHELOR'S HALL (P.E.I.)
   A. Mrs. Cyrene McClellan, Grand River, P.E.I., 6/22/57, 16 sts. w/tune. (ATL 2156.1). Notice that stanzas 5 and 15 are identical.
   B. James Pendergast, Charlottetown, P.E.I., 6/15/57, 7 sts. w/tune (ATL 2154.8); Mrs. John Coughlin, Ellerslie, P.E.I., 6/22/57, 3 sts. w/o tune; Alexander Crossman, Lewiston, Me., 2/1/57, 1 st. w/o tune; Mrs. Louisa Carter, Bath, Me., 12/12/56 (letter), 3 sts. w/o tune; Mrs. E. G. Ellis, Tyne Valley, P.E.I., 3 sts. w/o tune, in a letter published in *The* (Charlottetown) *Guardian* (no date, but probably 1951).
   C. None.
   D. For other songs with the same title but different sentiments, see Emelyn Gardner and Geraldine Chickering, *Ballads and Songs of Southern Michigan* (Ann Arbor, Mich., 1939), pp. 441-42; Henry Fuson, *Ballads of the Kentucky Highlands* (London, 1931), p. 133; Cecil Sharp, *English Folk-Songs from the Southern Appalachians* (London, 1932), II, 205; Sigmund Spaeth, *Weep Some More, My Lady* (New York, 1927), pp. 199-200.

BAPTISTS, THE (P.E.I.)
   A. Charles Gorman, Burton, P.E.I., 8/18/58, 2 sts. and chorus, w/tune (ATL 2163.6). Sts. 3, 4, 5 dictated to me by Charles Gorman at various times. St. 6 recited for me by Frank O'Holleran, Bloomfield Station, P.E.I., 8/18/58. The order of stanzas is my conjecture.
   B. Harry Thompson, Glengarry, P.E.I., 6/25/57, 1 st. and chorus; Arthur Dalton, Rumford, Me., 1/31/57, 1 st. w/tune (ATL 2148.4); Mrs. Lawrence Murphy, Campbellton, P.E.I., 6/28/57, chorus only (ATL 2157.3).
   C. None.
   D. The parodied hymn is a fairly common device. For instance, see Carl Sandburg, *The American Songbag* (New York, 1927), p. 222, for Joe Hill's parody of "The Sweet Bye and Bye."

BARREN TOWN (Miramichi)
   A. Everett Price, Blackville, N.B., 6/9/57, 5 sts. w/tune (ATL 2151.2).
   B. John Holland, Glenwood, N.B., 6 sts. w/tune. Sung at the First Miramichi Folksong Festival, Newcastle, N.B., 9/5/58 (ATL 2176.1); Paul Kingston, Wayerton, N.B., at the Second Miramichi Folksong Festival, 8/19/59 (ATL 2193.2).
   C. William Doerflinger, *Shantymen and Shantyboys* (New York, 1951), pp. 261-62, 8 sts. w/tune. From the singing of Jared MacLean, Strathadam, N.B., and collected from him by Louise Manny. Words first published in Manny, "Larry Gorman — Miramichi Balladist," *The Maritime Advocate and Busy East*, 40 (October, 1949), No. 3, pp. 10-11.
   D. All the tunes are nearly identical.

BEAVER JACK (Brewer)
   A. William Bell, Brewer, Me., 8/58, 10 sts. w/o tune (ATL 2138.6).
   B. None.
   C. None.
   D. None.

BILL WATTS (Ellsworth)
   A. Alden F. Mace, Southwest Harbor, Me., 2/22/57, 8 sts. w/tune (ATL 2144.5).
   B. Fragments recalled by Anton Jordan, Osborn Plantation, Me., 5/11/57.
   C. None.
   D. For a full discussion of this tune, see Bertrand H. Bronson, *The Traditional Tunes of the Child Ballads* (Princeton, N.J., 1959), I, pp. 354-61. See "The

Little Brown Bulls," in Franz Rickaby, *Ballads and Songs of the Shanty-Boy* (Cambridge, Mass., 1926), p. 65; "Blue Mountain Lake," in Helen Flanders and others, *The New Green Mountain Songster: Traditional Folk Songs of Vermont* (New Haven, Conn., 1939), p. 176; "Red Iron Ore," in Sandburg, p. 176. See also Robert A. Kaiser, "Lumberman's Ballad, 'Shannel's Mill,'" *New York Folklore Quarterly*, XI (1955), pp. 133-35.

BOYS OF THE ISLAND, THE (Brewer?)
  A. (I) Edmund Doucette, Ebbsfleet, P.E.I., 8/16/58, 4 sts. w/tune (ATL 2162.5); (II) Arthur Dalton, Rumford, Me., 1/31/57, 3-1/2 sts. w/tune (ATL 2148.2 and 2148.7).
  B. At least twenty people have sung, recited, or sent me fragments of one or two stanzas, or even one or two lines, from all over Maine, New Brunswick, and Prince Edward Island (not to mention one each from Alberta and British Columbia).
  C. Fannie Hardy Eckstorm and Mary Winslow Smyth, *Minstrelsy of Maine* (Boston and New York, 1927), pp. 118-20, 10 sts. w/o tune, and 2 sts. w/o tune; Manny, "Larry Gorman," pp. 12-13, 6 sts. w/o tune; Doerflinger, pp. 218-19, 6 sts. w/tune (same version as that given in Manny).
  D. The tunes to all the versions are related, though Jared MacLean's tune (see Doerflinger) has a different contour. For a close parallel to Doucette's tune, hear Ellen Stekert's recording of "The Black Cook," in *Songs of a New York Lumberjack* (Folkways Records, FA-2354). See also "The Squid-Jigging Ground," in Gerald S. Doyle, *Old-Time Songs and Poetry from Newfoundland* (2nd ed.; St. John's, Newfoundland, 1940), p. 66. See James Wilson, *Ballad Tunes of the Miramichi* (Master's thesis, New York University, 1961), pp. 19-20, for tune analogues with "The Wedding of Darby McShawn" and "Larry O'Gaff."

BULLY OF LOT ELEVEN, THE (P.E.I.)
  A. Ellsworth Gillis, Ellerslie, P.E.I., 3 sts. w/o tune, 1957.
  B. Bishop Thomas K. Gorman, Dallas, Tex., 1 st. w/o tune, letter, 1/57.
  C. None.
  D. Gillis' text was sent to me set down as a block of prose. The stanza form is my conjecture based on the rhymes.

CARRYING COAL IN A BASKET (Brewer)
  A. Reported only, by William Bell, Brewer, Me., 12/56.
  B. None.
  C. None.
  D. None.

CHAMPION OF MOOSE HILL, THE (Ellsworth)
  A. Alden F. Mace, Southwest Harbor, Me., 2/22/57, 7 sts. w/tune (ATL 2144.3). Stanza 7 is from Ralph Cushman.
  B. Ralph Cushman, Ellsworth, Me., 10/56, 6-1/2 sts. w/o tune; Anton Jordan, Osborn Plantation, Me., 5/11/57, 3-1/2 sts. w/o tune; several other people recalled fragments, and practically everyone had heard of it.
  C. Eckstorm and Smyth, pp. 126-28; version collected by Richard M. Dorson from Pompey Grant, Columbia Falls, Me., 7/12/56, 8 sts. w/tune.
  D. Pompey Grant's tune is almost the same as Mace's, except that it does not keep the flatted seventh; it is essentially major, rather than mixolydian. Compare this tune to those of "The Winter of Seventy-Three" and "Mary Mahoney." See also "The Avondale Mine Disaster" in Korson, *Minstrels of the Mine Patch*, p. 189.

CRUEL SUBMARINE, THE (Brewer)
  A. Reported only, by Mrs. Susan Cannon, St. Eleanor's, P.E.I., 7/2/57.
  B. None.
  C. None.
  D. None.

DAME BRUIN (P.E.I.)
  A. Manuscript copy given me by Mrs. Harold Doyle, Campbellton, P.E.I., 6/18/57, from her late husband's collection. 8 sts. w/o tune.
  B. Frank O'Holleran, Bloomfield Station, P.E.I., 8/18/58, 7 sts. w/o tune (ATL 2163.7); Harry Thompson, Glengarry, P.E.I., 6/25/57, 1 st. w/o tune; Charles Gorman, Burton, P.E.I., 6/24/57, 1 st. w/o tune.
  C. None.
  D. No one knew the tune, though all claimed there was one. See page 165 above for the song Gorman was parodying. The song was in Northeastern tradition; I have a fragment of it from Edward MacDonald, Hampden, Me., who learned it more than fifty years ago from his father in Harcourt, N.B. For a similar stanza form from the north of England, see Stokoe, pp. 82-83; for an Irish form, see "The Green Linnet," in Manus O'Conor, *Irish Com-all-Ye's* (New York, 1901), p. 10. See also Gorman's "The Horse's Confession."

DEL AVERY (Ellsworth)
  A. Harold N. Archer, Ellsworth Falls, Me., recalled two lines, 1958.
  B. None.
  C. None.
  D. None.

DEVIL'S BACK, THE (Miramichi)
  A. Reported only, by Harry Thompson, Glengarry, P.E.I., 6/25/57. There is a version of the quatrain, "Their eyes stick out like prongs" in Louise Manny's manuscript collection that begins "As I went over the Devil's Back." I do not think that this is the song referred to by Mr. Thompson.
  B. None.
  C. None.
  D. None.

DOCTOR O'CONNELL (Ellsworth)
  A. Not included in text.
  B. Reported only, by Ralph Cushman, 9/56.
  C. None.
  D. None.

DONAHUE'S SPREE (Miramichi)
  A. Mr. Irvine van Horn, Bloomfield Ridge, N.B., 8/15/63. Recorded and transcribed by James R. Wilson, 10 sts. w/tune.
  B. Hugh U. Crawford of Blackville, N.B., gave me a typed copy of six fragmentary stanzas, which was given him by Clarence Lynch of Chatham, whose mother was Mrs. Sidonia Lynch, daughter of Israel Brown. Additional lines are from Dorothea Cox, Tommy Whelan, and Mrs. Lynch again, through Louise Manny. I also have two and a half stanzas from Howard McKay, Hayesville, N.B., 7/20/61.
  C. None.
  D. For an interesting parallel, see O'Conor, p. 45, "Barney Brallaghan."

DYMENT'S AUCTION (P.E.I.)
 A. David Dyment, Spring Hill, P.E.I., 7/57, 2 sts. w/o tune.
 B. None.
 C. None.
 D. None.

ELLSWORTH NEWS OF THE DAY (Ellsworth)
 A. A. Russell Mace, Aurora, Me., 5/11/57. Fragment.
 B. None.
 C. None.
 D. None.

FIGHT AT HALL'S MILL, THE (Ellsworth)
 A. Mrs. Herbert Young, Ellsworth, Me., 7/30/57, 1 st. w/tune (ATL 2158.2).
 B. None.
 C. None.
 D. None.

FREEMAN ARCHER (Ellsworth)
 A. Merle S. Richardson, Aurora, Me., 5/11/57, 1 st. w/o tune.
 B. William Silsby, Ellsworth, Me., 1/29/59, 1 st. w/o tune.
 C. None.
 D. None.

GAYNOR'S TRAINED PIG (Brewer)
 A. Reported only, by William Bell, Brewer, Me., 12/56.
 B. None.
 C. None.
 D. None.

GOOD OLD STATE OF MAINE, THE (New Hampshire)
 A. John A. Jamieson, East Bathurst, N.B., 6/12/57, 14 sts. w/tune (ATL 2152.2).
 B. James Brown, South Branch, Kent County, N.B., 9/3/58, 11 sts. w/tune (sung at First Miramichi Folksong Festival, Newcastle, N.B.); Mr. Brown learned his version in Lily Bay, Me., around 1900 (ATL 2167.2). Several other people recalled fragments.
 C. Eckstorm and Smyth, pp. 111-12, 10 sts. w/o tune; newspaper clipping, probably from a Bangor paper, date uncertain, sent in by Mrs. Jasper Wilbur, Eastbrook, Me., 12 sts. w/o tune; Helen Creighton has also collected this song in Nova Scotia.
 D. Mr. Brown's tune is very close to Mr. Jamieson's, but sung with a more emphatic rhythm. His singing of it at the 1959 Miramichi Folksong Festival is available on the Folkways record, *Folksongs of the Miramichi* (FM 4053). For a close parallel to the first phrase of this tune, see Norman Cazden (ed.), *The Abelard Folk Song Book* (New York, 1958), pp. 4-5. According to Sandy and Caroline Paton, another set of this tune can be found in Margaret Barry's singing of "The Turfman from Ardee" on her record, *Songs of an Irish Tinker Lady* (Riverside RLP 12-602).

GREAT JOHN MAC AND HIS POLACK BRIGADE, THE (Brewer)
  A. Joe MacDougall, Alberton, P.E.I., 7/62 (collected by Helen Creighton);
Clarence Adams, Brewer, Me., 8/58.
  B. None.
  C. None.
  D. None.

GREAT POND TRAMP, THE (Ellsworth)
  A. Harold N. Archer, Ellsworth Falls, Me., recalled one line; Joe McIntosh,
Ellsworth, recalled half a stanza.
  B. None.
  C. None.
  D. An adaptation of "The Shan Van Vogh."

GULL DECOY, THE (P.E.I.)
  A. (I) J. Spurgeon Allaby, Passekeag, N.B., 6/7/57, 15-1/2 sts. w/tune (ATL
2149.1); (II) James Pendergast, Charlottetown, P.E.I., 6/15/57, 3 sts. w/tune
(ATL 2155.2); (III) Steve Murphy, Alberton, P.E.I., 6/29/57, 7 sts. w/tune (ATL
2157.4).
  B. Charles Gorman, Burton, P.E.I., 2 sts. w/o tune; Frank O'Holleran,
Bloomfield Station, P.E.I., 8/18/58, 13 sts. w/o tune (ATL 2164.1); William Bell,
Brewer, Me., 12/13/56, 4 sts. w/o tune.
  C. Beaverbrook Collection (as sung by John B. Stymiest, Tabusintac, N.B.,
10 sts. w/tune); Doerflinger, pp. 255-56 (as sung by Herbert Hinchey, Boiestown,
N.B., 3 sts. w/tune).
  D. For analogues for tune II (Pendergast), see Wilson, p. 23. Tune III re-
sembles a tune Edmund Doucette of Miminegash, P.E.I., used for "Peggy Gordon."
Charles Gorman used a similar tune for "The Bells of Shandon." See also the
version of "Young Beichan" (Child 53) sung by Thomas Moran of Leitrim, Ireland,
on the record *The Folk Songs of Britain*, Volume IV, edited by Alan Lomax and
Peter Kennedy (Caedmon TC-1145).

HAIL FISHERMEN ASSEMBLE (P.E.I.)
  A. Harry Thompson, Glengarry, P.E.I., 6/25/57, 1 st. w/o tune.
  B. None.
  C. None.
  D. None.

HAPPYTOWN WEDDING, THE (Brewer)
  A. Not included in the text.
  B. Fragment only: "There was old Mr. Robertson, old Mr. Strang, / And
William the Roarer, the tail of the gang." Recalled by Earle Doucette, Augusta,
Me., 7/57, and Clarence Adams, Brewer, Me., 8/58.
  C. None.
  D. None.

HEAD OF GRAND RIVER, THE (P.E.I.)
  A. Mrs. George Harris, Summerside, P.E.I., 9/22/56, letter, 2 sts. w/o tune.
  B. Also recalled by Mrs. John Coughlin, Ellerslie, P.E.I. (ATL 2155.9);
James Pendergast, Charlottetown, P.E.I. Both sang their fragments to a similar
tune.
  C. None.
  D. None.

HOBOES OF MAINE, THE (Brewer)

A. Eckstorm and Smyth, pp. 140-44. From a broadside loaned them by Franz H. Blanchard, 1924, 13 sts. w/o tune.

B. None.

C. None.

D. For parallels for the stanza form, see the Irish song "Nell Flaherty's Drake," in O'Conor, p. 14.

HORSE'S CONFESSION, THE (P.E.I.)

A. James Pendergast, Charlottetown, P.E.I., 12/20/61 (letter), 17 sts. w/o tune.

B. James Pendergast, 6/15/57, 3 sts. w/tune (ATL 2155.1); Mrs. Cyrene McClellan, Grand River, P.E.I., 6/22/57, 5 sts. w/o tune (ATL 2156.2); Ellsworth Gillis, Ellerslie, P.E.I., 6/22/57, 8 sts. (manuscript); Thomas Gorman, Charlottetown, P.E.I., 6/15/57, 2 sts. w/o tune; Mrs. John Coughlin, Ellerslie, P.E.I., 6/22/57, 2 sts. w/o tune; Arthur Dalton, Rumford, Me., 1/31/57 (ATL 2148.3). Widely recognized by others.

C. None.

D. Pendergast's tune will only fit every other stanza of his words. I am convinced that the basic stanza is a double one rhyming *abcbdddb*, and that we have only half the tune. Compare this conjectured stanza form with "Dame Bruin." For other songs which use the device of the horse telling its troubles, see above pp. 169 and 172. See also Sharp, II, 220.

I'M A POOR AND BLIGHTED OLD MAIDEN (P.E.I.)

A. Harry Thompson, Glengarry, P.E.I., 6/25/57, 2 sts. w/o tune. Said to be the beginning of a much longer song.

B. None.

C. None.

D. None.

"I'M POOR OLD FAN" (Ellsworth)

A. Joe McIntosh, Ellsworth, Me., 7/58, 1 st. w/o tune.

B. Mrs. Herbert Young, Ellsworth, Me., 7/30/57, 1 st. w/o tune.

C. None.

D. Said to be the beginning of a much longer song.

IN EIGHTEEN HUNDRED AND SEVENTY-NINE (Miramichi)

A. Everett Price, Blackville, N.B., 6/9/57, 2 sts. and chorus w/tune (ATL 2151.3).

B. None.

C. None.

D. See Doerflinger, pp. 266-68 for an interesting parallel.

IT'S A WONDER (Brewer)

A. A. Russell Mace, Aurora, Me., 5/11/57, 2 sts. w/o tune.

B. Several other people in the Ellsworth-Brewer areas recognized a line or two of the song.

C. None.

D. None.

LUKE AND HIS RAMBLES (P.E.I.)

A. Harry Thompson, Glengarry, P.E.I., 6/25/57, 2 sts. w/o tune; Mrs. George Harris, Summerside, P.E.I., 10/2/56 (letter), 1 st. w/o tune.

B. Mrs. Susan Cannon, St. Eleanor's, P.E.I., 7/2/57, 1 st. w/o tune; Charles Gorman, Burton, P.E.I., 7/24/57, 1 st. w/o tune.

C. None.

D. This song may not be by Gorman but by his brother-in-law, Luke Hughes. For the song that probably served as a model, see Greig CLXXVI ("Arthur McBride") or John Ord, *The Bothy Songs and Ballads* (Paisley, Scotland, 1930), p. 306 ("The Recruiting Sergeant"). See also ibid., pp. 110, 231, 260.

MAN WHO WHEELS THE ASHES, THE (Brewer)

A. Reported only, by Sister Mary Clare. It is also mentioned in the last stanza of "The Song of All Songs."

B. None.

C. None.

D. None.

MC ELROY (P.E.I.)

A. This fragment is a composite: lines 1 and 2 from Harry Thompson, Glengarry, P.E.I., 6/25/57; lines 3, 4, and 5 from Peter MacDonald, Rumford, Me., 1/30/57.

B. None.

C. None.

D. I once had the whole stanza from someone but have lost it.

MARY MAHONEY (Miramichi)

A. Thomas W. Coughlan, South Nelson Road, N.B., collected by Louise Manny for the Beaverbrook Collection, 8-1/2 sts. w/tune.

B. None.

C. Sung by Nick Underhill, Northwest Bridge, N.B., at the Fifth Miramichi Folksong Festival, Newcastle, N.B., 8/15/62. Louise Manny had given him a transcript of Coughlan's words. Nick put a different tune to it, although Coughlan's tune was one he already knew, and he also made several changes in the words, notable among them the change of "or-i-eyed" to "galvanized."

D. See note D under "The Winter of Seventy-Three," and Wilson, p. 29, for tune analogues. See also the notes to "Champion of Moose Hill."

MICHAEL MC ELROY (P.E.I.)

A. Mrs. Lawrence Murphy, Campbellton, P.E.I., 6/28/57, 3-1/2 sts. w/o tune (ATL 2157.3).

B. Recalled also by Harry O'Brien, Alberton, P.E.I., 6/19/57. For parallel stanza forms, see Ord, pp. 32, 121, 179, 268.

C. None.

D. There are supposed to have been ten or twelve more stanzas.

MICHAEL O'BRIEN (P.E.I.)

A. Edmund Doucette, Ebbsfleet, P.E.I., 6/26/57, 6 sts. w/tune (ATL 2156.7).

B. Harry O'Brien, Alberton, P.E.I., 6/19/57, 1 st. w/o tune. Also recognized by Charles Gorman, Burton, P.E.I., 8/58, Frank O'Holleran, Bloomfield Station, P.E.I., 8/58, and W. B. McClellan, Alma, P.E.I., 6/57.

C. None.

D. None.

MICHAEL RILEY (P.E.I.)

A. James Pendergast, Charlottetown, P.E.I., 6/16/57, 3-1/2 sts. w/tune (ATL 2155.3); stanza 5 from Frank O'Holleran, Bloomfield Station, P.E.I., 8/18/58.

B. None.

C. None.

D. O'Holleran gave me this stanza as part of "Mick Riley." The shift in person and tone made me certain that it was actually an interpolation.

MICK RILEY (P.E.I.)

A. Frank O'Holleran, Bloomfield Station, P.E.I., 8/18/58, 4-1/2 sts. w/o tune (ATL 2164.2).

B. Harry Thompson, Glengarry, P.E.I., 6/25/57, 1 st. w/o tune.

C. None.

D. None.

MONAGHAN (P.E.I.)

A. Not included in the text.

B. A scurrilous quatrain on Gorman's brother-in-law. Recalled by several people on P.E.I.

C. None.

D. None.

MONAGHAN'S RAFFLE (P.E.I.)

A. Not included in the text.

B. Reported only. Another song about his brother-in-law.

C. None.

D. None.

MORRIS ELLSWORTH (Miramichi)

A. J. Spurgeon Allaby, Passekeag, N.B., 6/7/57, 14 sts. w/tune (ATL 2149.2).

B. E. A. Mullin, Newcastle, N.B., 1/18/57, (letter), 11 sts. w/o tune; William Brennan, Barnaby River, N.B., 17 sts. w/o tune (from manuscript collection of Louise Manny); version transcribed by D. G. Smith, editor of the *Miramichi Advance* and printed in his paper, August 30, 1888, 14 sts. w/o tune (also from Louise Manny's manuscript collection).

C. Manny, "Larry Gorman," pp. 7-8.

D. Mr. Allaby's tune is almost identical to the tune of "The Oxen Song" in Linscott, p. 263. Mrs. Linscott attributed the song to Gorman. The same tune was used by Davey Hunter for his "Rose Ann Song," see above, p. 172. A version of this song, confused with "Peter Emberly," also turned up along the St. John River. See Emily Mae Earle, *Footprints in New Brunswick* (Perth, N.B., 1959), pp. 159-60. Mrs. Earle's granddaughter, Susan Litz, sang the tune for me; it is essentially the same tune printed here. The song turns up in Minnesota; see Rickaby, p. 228 ("The Maine-ite in Pennsylvania"). Rickaby's singer learned the song in 1879.

MYLES EVERETT MORE (Ellsworth)

A. Alden F. Mace, Southwest Harbor, Me., 2/22/57, 5 sts. w/tune (ATL 2144.4).

B. Several other people along Union River recalled having heard the song.

C. None.

D. For a parallel in stanza form and tune, see "Jack Hinks" in Doyle, p. 9.

NERO AND THE GREAT JOHN MAC (Brewer)

A. Fragment only, William Bell, Brewer, Me., 12/56.

B. None.

C. None.

D. None.

NEWCOMBE'S GOOSE (Brewer)
   A. Reported only, by William Bell and George C. MacLeod, both of Brewer, Me., 1956.
   B. None.
   C. None.
   D. None.

NOW I LAY ME (P.E.I.)
   A. Not included in the text.
   B. Peter MacDonald, Rumford, Me., 1/30/57. Written about a hunchback:

> Now I lay me down to sleep,
> All bundled down in a little heap;
> If I should die before I wake
> It would puzzle the Devil to make me straight.

   C. None.
   D. Very possibly not by Gorman at all but simply attributed to him.

OLD BARLOW WAS BLIND (Ellsworth)
   A. Joe McIntosh, Ellsworth, Me., 7/28/58, 1 st. w/o tune.
   B. Irving G. Frost, Bar Harbor, Me., 2/9/57; Donald Stuart, Ellsworth, Me., 7/18/57.
   C. None.
   D. For versions of "The Juice of the Forbidden Fruit," see Vance Randolph, *Ozark Folksongs* (Columbia, Mo., 1946-50), III, 130-33.

OLD MIKE ABRAMS FIVE SAW DAM (Ellsworth)
   A. Reported only, by Leon Brown, Ellsworth Falls, Me., 2/23/57.
   B. None.
   C. None.
   D. None.

O'LEARY ROAD, THE (P.E.I.)
   A. Not included in the text.
   B. G. R. Rowe, Brandon, Manitoba, recalls reading this poem in a Summerside, P.E.I., paper about 1910. All he recalled was the opening line: "It's been forty years or more since I trod this road before." Letter to the author, 5/6/59.
   C. None.
   D. None.

OLD POD AUGER DAYS, THE (Brewer)
   A. Broadside sent me by John O'Connor, Portland, Me., 9/56, 16 sts. w/o tune.
   B. None.
   C. None.
   D. Another song bearing the same title was well known in the Northeast. See Linscott, pp. 251-53; Flanders, *Garland,* p. 34; version from Hudson, Me., sung by Mrs. L. W. Robbins (ATL 2139.10).

OLD PROWLER, THE (Miramichi)
   A. Silas Curtis, Blackville, N.B., 7/14/61, 4 sts. w/o tune; Everett Price, Blackville, N.B., 7/11/61, 2 half stanzas (lines 1 and 2 of st. 4, and st. 7); Arthur Carr, Boiestown, N.B., 7/19/61, 1 st. w/o tune (st. 6). Tune and 1 st. from Mrs.

Alan MacDonald, Black River Bridge, N.B., 7/13/61. The order of the stanzas is my conjecture.

B. None.

C. None.

D. Lines 3 and 4 of st. 1 are often mistakenly included in "Donahue's Spree."

ON LEAD MOUNTAIN'S LOFTY BROW (Ellsworth)

A. Reported only, by Harold N. Archer, Ellsworth Falls, Me., 1958.

B. None.

C. None.

D. None.

PACK OF HOUNDS, THE (P.E.I.)

A. G. R. Rowe, Brandon, Manitoba, 4-1/2 sts. w/o tune. Letter to the author 5/6/59.

B. Charles Gorman, Burton, P.E.I., 8/17/58, 1 st. w/o tune.

C. None.

D. This is probably by Larry's brother-in-law, Luke Hughes.

PRINCE EDWARD ISLE, ADIEU (P.E.I.)

A. J. A. Gillies, printed in The (Charlottetown) Guardian, 11/13/50, 12 sts. w/o tune; tune from Mrs. Frank Sweet, St. Eleanor's, P.E.I., 6/25/57, (ATL 2156.9).

B. Mrs. John Coughlin, Ellerslie, P.E.I., 6/22/57, 1 st. w/tune (ATL 2155.7); William Bell, Brewer, Me., 12/56, 3 sts. w/tune (ATL 2136.1); Ellsworth Gillis, Ellerslie, P.E.I., c.10 sts. w/o tune (manuscript). Joe MacDougall, Alberton, P.E.I., 7/62, 5 sts. w/tune (sent to me by Helen Creighton).

C. Doerflinger, pp. 256-57.

D. None.

THE PRIZE WAS NOT SO VERY GREAT (Brewer?)

A. Arthur Dalton, Rumford, Me., 1/31/57. Fragment only.

B. None.

C. None.

D. None.

RODERICK MC DONALD (Ellsworth)

A. Irving G. Frost, Bar Harbor, Me., 2/9/57, 12 sts. w/tune; tune from Alden F. Mace, Southwest Harbor, Me., 2/22/57 (ATL 2144.6).

B. Merle S. Richardson, Aurora, Me., 5/12/57, 3 sts. w/o tune; A. Russell Mace, Aurora, Me., 5/11/57, fragment w/tune; Joe McIntosh, Ellsworth, Me., 2/23/57, fragment.

C. None.

D. Mace's recitation of "McCauley's Leap," on which this song is based, is available (ATL 2145.1).

SANITARY JANE (Brewer)

A. Reported only, by George MacLeod, Brewer, Me., 1956.

B. Clarence Adams, Brewer, Me., also recalled having heard this song.

C. None.

D. None.

SCOW ON COWDEN SHORE, THE (Miramichi)

A. Fred McMahon, Chatham, N.B., 14 sts. w/tune. As collected by Louise Manny for the Beaverbrook Collection.

B. Leroy P. Carson, Island Falls, Me., 7/15/58 (letter), 6 sts. w/o tune, as learned from a friend in Blackville, N.B.; William Moore, East Bathurst, N.B., 10/6/57, (letter), 5 sts. w/o tune; George Barry, Blackville, N.B., 1/28/57 (letter), 3 sts. w/o tune; Everett Price, Blackville, N.B., 6/9/57, 2 sts. w/tune (ATL 2151.4); Billy Price, McNamee, N.B., 7/11/61, 11 sts. w/o tune; Sandy Calhoun, Parker's Ridge, N.B., 7/19/61, 6 sts. w/o tune.

C. Doerflinger, pp. 234-36 (3 versions: 1 st. w/tune; 8 sts. w/o tune; 2 sts. w/tune); Beaverbrook Collection (as sung by Willie MacDonald, Black River Bridge, N.B.).

D. Doerflinger's tunes differ markedly from McMahon's and Price's. See Wilson, p. 39, for a tune analogue. For parallels for the stanza form, see Greig, XCVII ("Ye Girls of Equal Station"); Lucy Broadwood, *English Traditional Songs and Carols* (London, 1908), pp. 100-01 ("Travel the Country Round"); O'Conor, p. 10 ("The Bride of Fallow").

SHAN VAN VOGH, THE (P.E.I.)

A. Words: Edmund Doucette, Ebbsfleet, P.E.I., manuscript copy, 20 sts. w/o tune. Tune: Mrs. Lawrence Murphy, Campbellton, P.E.I., 6/28/57 (ATL 2157.2).

B. Mrs. Harold Doyle, Campbellton, P.E.I., manuscript from her late husband's collection, 20 sts. w/o tune; Bishop Thomas K. Gorman, Dallas, Tex., 1 st. w/o tune (letter); John O'Connor, Portland, Me., 10/25/56, 1 st. w/o tune; Arthur Dalton, Rumford, Me., 1/31/57, 1 st. w/tune (ATL 2148.1).

C. None.

D. See O'Conor, p. 32. Of many versions of the "Shan Van Vogh" that I have seen in print, none has had the tune we find Gorman using. In Doucette's text, I have changed "Voche" to "Vogh" and made some minor punctuation changes.

SONG OF ALL SONGS, THE (Brewer?)

A. Stanzas 1-5 from A. Russell Mace, Aurora, Me., 5/11/57; stanzas 6-7 from Frank O'Holleran, Bloomfield Station, P.E.I., 8/18/58.

B. None.

C. None.

D. There is no reason to believe that anything but the last stanza is Gorman's work, and even that contains the title of a song, "Cruel Ida Duncan," of which I have no other record. For other songs of this type, see Randolph, III, 282-85.

SPREE AT SUMMER HILL, THE (P.E.I.)

A. Mrs. Frank Sweet, St. Eleanor's, P.E.I., 3 sts. w/o tune.

B. None.

C. None.

D. None.

STEELSHANK (Brewer)

A. Not included in the text.

B. Reported only. A poem Larry wrote on someone he had worked for in Brewer. The man wore a steel brace on his leg.

C. None.

D. None.

THAT REPTILE MC ELROY (P.E.I.)

A. Alexander Crossman, Lewiston, Me., 2/1/57, 1 st. w/o tune.

B. James Pendergast, Charlottetown, P.E.I., 2/1/57 (letter), 1 st. w/o tune; fragments from at least five others.

C. None.

D. None.

THERE'S THAT WHISTLING CODY (P.E.I.)

A. Not included in the text.

B. W. B. McClellan, Alma, P.E.I., 6/57. In response to a request for a song, Larry songed the present company:

> There's that Whistling Cody,
> And likewise Fiddling Ben,
> There's Sleepy George and Slippery Jack—
> They're all four upright men.

C. None.

D. None.

TOMAH STREAM (Maine)

A. Doerflinger, pp. 216-17.

B. None.

C. None.

D. None.

UNFORTUNATE COOK, THE (Maine?)

A. Not included in the text.

B. None.

C. Mentioned in Manny, "Larry Gorman," p. 8: "There was an unfortunate cook in Maine who never kept a job again after Larry had made fun of his bread and pies. Whenever the cook arrived at a camp, the men all began to sing the biting verses, and the cook, unable to stand it, would move on." So far I have not found this song.

D. None.

UNION RIVER DRIVERS, THE (Ellsworth)

A. Irving G. Frost, Bar Harbor, Me., 2/9/57, stanzas 1-5, 7, 8, 10; Harold N. Archer, Ellsworth Falls, Me., 11/29/57, stanzas 9 and 11; for stanza 6, lines 1-3 are from Frost, and line 4 from Archer.

B. Other people recalled the following stanzas: Harold Archer, sts. 1, 4; Harold Kenniston, Ellsworth, Me., 2/23/57, sts. 1, 6, 7; Anton Jordan, Osborn Plantation, Me., 5/11/57, sts. 6, 7; Merle S. Richardson, Aurora, Me., 5/12/57, st. 7.

C. None.

D. The order of stanzas is my conjecture. I have also supplied the title.

WINTER OF NINETEEN FIVE, THE (Brewer)

A. Clarence Adams, Brewer, Me., 4/58, fragment w/o tune.

B. None.

C. None.

D. None.

WINTER OF SEVENTY-THREE, THE (Miramichi)

A. Nick Underhill, Northwest Bridge, N.B., 7/8/61, 13-1/2 sts. w/tune. He sang me this version to correct mistakes he said he had made in his singing of it at the First Miramichi Folksong Festival, 9/3/58. The new version differs in only a few small word changes. The 1958 version is available for comparison (ATL 2167.1).

B. John A. Jamieson, East Bathurst, N.B., 6/12/57, 10 sts. w/tune (ATL 2152.2); Peter Jamieson, East Bathurst, N.B., 1/31/57 (letter), 10 sts. w/o tune; Wilmot MacDonald, Glenwood, N.B., 6/11/57, 5-1/2 sts. w/tune (ATL 2151.6); David Dyment, Spring Hill, P.E.I., 6/20/57, 2 sts. w/o tune.

C. Doerflinger, 5 sts. w/tune, pp. 214-15; Manny, "Larry Gorman," pp. 6-7, 11-1/2 sts. w/o tune (a composite of two versions from the Beaverbrook Collection); Eckstorm and Smyth, pp. 114-16, 20 sts. w/o tune (also published in *The Northern* for July, 1923, under the title "Lumberman's Song").

D. John Jamieson's tune is almost identical to that of "Mary Mahoney." Wilmot MacDonald's tune is the same one he uses for "Joe Brook" above, p. 174. See Wilson, p. 16, for tune analogues. See also notes above for "Champion of Moose Hill."

WORKMAN, THE (Brewer)

A. Broadside sent me by John O'Connor, Portland, Me., 9/56, 14 sts. w/o tune.

B. None.

C. None.

D. None.

YEO'S PARTY (P.E.I.)

A. Fragments only. Stanzas 1 and 2 from Mrs. George Harris, Summerside, P.E.I. (letter); stanzas 3-6 from Mrs. John Coughlin, Ellerslie, P.E.I., 6/22/57 (ATL 2155.8).

B. Others recall hearing it.

C. None.

D. None.

YEO'S SHIPYARD (P.E.I.)

A. Reported only. Said to be a series of individual sketches of the crew.

B. None.

C. None.

D. None.

YOU CAN'T LEAVE THE YARD TILL THE WHISTLE BLOWS (Brewer)

A. Refrain only. From Clarence Adams, Brewer, Me., 8/58.

B. None.

C. None.

D. None.

YOUNG BILLY CRANE (Miramichi)

A. Doerflinger, p. 259-60.

B. None.

C. None.

D. For a note on the difficulties Professor Samuel P. Bayard encountered in transcribing this and other tunes from the singing of Herbert Hinchey of Boiestown, N.B., see Doerflinger, p. 326.

AS I WAS GOING DOWN TO MRS. YEO'S (P.E.I.)
   A. Peter MacDonald, Rumford, Me., 1/30/57.
   B. None.
   C. None.
   D. None.

DAVIS' CAMP (Ellsworth)
   A. None.
   B. None.
   C. None.
   D. See my article, "Larry Gorman and the Cante Fable," in the *New England Quarterly*, XXXII (June, 1959), p. 234.

EYES STICK OUT LIKE PRONGS (general)
   A. (I) Manny, "Larry Gorman," p. 9; (II) Thomas Doyle, Burton, P.E.I., 6/28/57; (III) George Barry, Blackville, N.B., 6/10/57.
   B. There are many other versions, among them, those from Harry Thompson, Glengarry, P.E.I.; Arthur Dalton, Rumford, Me.; Herbert Rice, Bangor, Me.
   C. Doerflinger, p. 258.
   D. None.

FISH AND POTATOES (P.E.I.)
   A. Mrs. John Murphy, McNeill's Mills, P.E.I., 11/56, (letter).
   B. None.
   C. None.
   D. None.

HERE'S TO YOU MR. PLESTID (P.E.I.)
   A. Mrs. Cyrene McClellan, Grand River, P.E.I., 6/22/57.
   B. None.
   C. None.
   D. None.

HERE'S YOUNG HUTCH (Miramichi)
   A. Manny, "Larry Gorman," pp. 8-9.
   B. None.
   C. None.
   D. None.

HOW SENTNERS GOT THEIR RICHES (P.E.I.)
   A. Gerald Tremblay, Ebbsfleet, P.E.I., 8/16/58.
   B. None.
   C. None.
   D. None.

LORD BE PRAISED, I AM AMAZED (general)
   A. Peter MacDonald, Rumford, Me., 1/30/57; (II) *The Northern*, April, 1926, p. 5.

B. Extremely widespread.
C. See note 6, Chapter VIII, p. 209 for other versions.
D. None.

MACMILLAN'S WETHER (general)
A. Herbert Rice, Bangor, Me., 11/56.
B. None.
C. Doerflinger, p. 258; Manny, "Larry Gorman," p. 12.
D. None.

MR. TEAZLE DIED OF LATE (Miramichi)
A. Silas Curtis, Blackville, N.B., 7/14/61.
B. None.
C. None.
D. None.

OH HERRING, OH HERRING (P.E.I.)
A. Edward Tremblay, Ebbsfleet, P.E.I., 8/16/58.
B. None.
C. None.
D. None.

ROBERT BELL (P.E.I.)
A. Mrs. Susan Cannon, St. Eleanor's, P.E.I., 7/2/57.
B. Frank O'Holleran, Bloomfield Station, P.E.I., 8/18/58.
C. None.
D. None.

SHE TOLD ME THAT HER BREAD WAS FINE (general)
A. Herbert Rice, Bangor, Me., 11/56.
B. None.
C. Doerflinger, p. 258.
D. None.

A STRANGER TO THE PASTURE CAME (P.E.I.)
A. Arthur Dalton, Rumford, Me., 1/31/57.
B. None.
C. None.
D. None.

THIS IS ROTTEN (P.E.I.)
A. Peter MacDonald, Rumford, Me., 12/27/56 (letter).
B. None.
C. None.
D. None.

'TIS TO THE VIRGIN (P.E.I.)
A. Harry Thompson, Glengarry, P.E.I., 6/25/57.
B. Frank O'Holleran, Bloomfield Station, P.E.I., 8/18/58; Charles Gorman, Burton, P.E.I., 8/17/58.
C. None.
D. I give a slightly different version of the story in my article, "Larry Gorman and the Cante Fable," p. 228.

Notes

PREFACE
    1. *Anglo-American Folksong Scholarship Since 1898* (New Brunswick, N.J., 1959), p. 291.

PROLOGUE
    1. The event described here is entirely fictional, as are all the characters except, of course, Larry Gorman.

INTRODUCTION: "My Name Is Larry Gorman"
    1. For an excellent history and analysis of the doctrine of communal composition, see Wilgus, pp. 3-122.
    2. On "Black-Eyed Susan," see G. Malcom Laws, Jr., *American Balladry from British Broadsides* (Philadelphia, 1957), p. 239. On "Young Charlotte," see Phillips Barry, "Fair Charlotte," *BFSSNE*, No. 12 (1937), 26.
    3. William Makepeace Thackeray, "Sterne and Goldsmith," in *The Works of Thackeray*, Vol. XXVI (New York, 1904), p. 381. See also, Leslie Shepard, *The Broadside Ballad* (London, 1962), esp. p. 87; and Albert B. Friedman, *The Ballad Revival* (Chicago, 1961), pp. 35-63.

CHAPTER I: "That Garden in the Seas"
    1. James Phinney Baxter, *A Memoir of Jacques Cartier* (New York, 1906), pp. 100-101.
    2. See Preston Ellis, *History of the Ellis Family and the Descendants of William Ellis of Bideford, Prince Edward Island* (n.p., 1950).
    3. Much of the material in this and the following paragraph was generously furnished me by Mrs. Nina Ross of Tyne Valley, P.E.I., now living in British Columbia. Mrs. Ross has been collecting material for a history of Tyne Valley.
    4. *The Island Argus* (Charlottetown, P.E.I.), March 3, 1874.

CHAPTER II: "Trout River"
    1. William Main Doerflinger, *Shantymen and Shantyboys* (New York, 1951), p. 253.
    2. See below p. 165 f. for more complete information on this song.
    3. Letter from McInnis to Louise Manny, March 19, 1951.
    4. White sand was used as a sweeping and scrubbing agent. It was rather hard to come by on this island of red sand.

CHAPTER III: "Along Lot Seven Shore"

1. As sung by John B. Stymiest of Tabusintac, N.B., for the Beaverbrook Collection. Collected by Louise Manny.

2. Repeat the second half of the tune for these two lines.

3. I would like to thank D. K. Wilgus for tracking down this tune for me.

4. For a full discussion of this and other mock graces, see below, p. 143 ff.

5. *Streal:* "An untidy dirty person, esp. a slovenly untidy girl or woman; a slut." (Joseph Wright, *English Dialect Dictionary.*) The line as it stands in the manuscript makes less sense than do the versions recited for me by Frank O'Holleran and Harry Thompson: "Monaghan's streals, himself [i.e. Monaghan], and old Dunn."

6. The word here is obliterated by a double fold in the paper. It is "storm" in O'Holleran's version.

CHAPTER IV: "And Came to Miramichi"

1. Robert Cooney, *A Compendious History of the Northern Part of the Province of New Brunswick and the District of the Gaspé in Lower Canada* (Chatham, N.B., 1896), p. 49.

2. Cooney, pp. 66 f. For the ballad, see Phillips Barry, *The Maine Woods Songster* (Cambridge, Mass., 1939), pp. 46-47. There are numerous variants in the Archives of Folk and Primitive Music, Indiana University, Bloomington, Indiana.

3. For further information on this aspect of Miramichi history, see Louise Manny, *Ships of Miramichi* (New Brunswick Museum Historical Studies, No. 10 [St. John, N.B., 1960]).

4. Repeat the tune for lines 3 and 4 here, and twice in stanza 8.

5. A kennebecker was a carpet bag.

6. A portage team toted supplies in from the settlement to the lumbercamp. Depending on the season, the supplies were hauled either in a wagon or a sled.

7. The length of the road from the woods (i.e. the yard) to the landing was measured by how many trips a two-sled team could make in a day. A three or four turn road would be rather long, but a ten turn road would be very short. The more turns, the harder the work for the crews on the yard, the sleds, and the landing. As Nick said, "On a road like that the sleigh bells would never be out of your ears!"

8. Manny, "Larry Gorman—Miramichi Balladist," *The Maritime Advocate and Busy East,* Vol. XL (October, 1949), No. 3, pp. 8-9.

9. For a similar verse from Maine, see *BFSSNE,* No. 3, p. 19. Tom MacLeod of Baring, Maine, recited the following verse for me on June 5, 1957. A local wit is supposed to have made it for his own tombstone:

> Old Bob Christie he died late;
> Now he lies at Heaven's gate;
> But up came the Devil with a bottle of whiskey
> And down into Hell went old Bob Christie.

10. Manny, "Larry Gorman," p. 7.

11. *Miramichi Advance,* August 30, 1888 (from Louise Manny's files). The stanzas from "Peter Emberly" which follow are from a version sent to me by John A. Jamieson of East Bathurst, N.B., in 1957.

12. See William Main Doerflinger, *Shantymen and Shantyboys,* pp. 225-33, 348. Phillips Barry, Fannie Eckstorm, and Mary Smyth attribute it to Gorman in *British Ballads from Maine* (New Haven, Conn., 1929), p. 264. For further information about John Calhoun see below, p. 171 f.

13. See below, p. 133.

14. See above, p. 53.

15. See my article, "The Life and Work of Larry Gorman: a Preliminary Report," in *Western Folklore*, XIX (1960), pp. 17-18, for this interpretation. See also Doerflinger's description, p. 233.

16. The tune for this stanza has the following phrasal pattern: B,A,B,B,B,A.

17. See below, p. 132. See also Doerflinger, p. 258.

18. G. Malcom Laws, for example, lists seventeen different ballads that depend on this motif. See his *American Balladry from British Broadsides* (The American Folklore Society, Bibliographical and Special Series, Vol. VIII [Philadelphia, 1957], pp. 202-11.

19. Reprinted with the permission of the publisher from *Shantymen and Shantyboys* by William M. Doerflinger. Copyright 1951 by The Macmillan Company, pp. 259-60. Doerflinger changed the names; the real ones are Cain and Harrigan.

20. See Manny, "Larry Gorman," p. 10, and Doerflinger, p. 260. See also a rewriting of Dr. Manny's article in the Charlottetown (P.E.I.) *Guardian* (n.d.), where it is claimed that Larry wrote this piece after a dance in Bangor, Maine.

21. Doerflinger, p. 262.

22. Most of this line is supplied from another version, since van Horne's is not at all clear here. As near as I can come to it: "That worrum his losses so e'er he may be."

23. See below, pp. 175-76.

CHAPTER V: "Down on the Union River"

1. Herbert T. Silsby II, *A History of Aurora, Maine* (Ellsworth, Me., 1958), p. 4. Much of the material in these first few paragraphs is taken from this interesting little book. See also Samuel Wasson, *A Survey of Hancock County, Maine* (Augusta, Me., 1878).

2. Wasson, p. 77.

3. Letter to the author from G. R. Rowe, Brandon, Manitoba, 5/6/59.

4. I would like to thank Herb Silsby for digging out this bit of information for me.

5. It has been said that while Roderick McDonald got the credit, it was really George Tosh (McIntosh), his foreman, who did all the work. George was McDonald's right hand, it is true, and by the late eighties, McDonald himself was no longer driving, but he had done plenty in his day. According to George's brother Joe, Roderick would come to George often for advice, but George thought very highly of him and never belittled him at all.

6. Captain's Roll: a dangerous stretch of fast water on the West Branch some distance above Amherst.

7. Stavewood was wood cut in four foot bolts, rather than being left as long logs.

8. "On the rear": the tail end of the drive. As the drive went along, the men on the rear followed it down and made a clean sweep of the river by retrieving logs that were stuck in the bushes, in deadwaters, and on rocks.

9. Twynham's Dam was on the East Branch between the mouth of Middle Branch and Jordan's Bridge.

10. A drive was not measured by the number of logs it contained. If it was stavewood or other "short wood," the measure was the cord; if it was sawlogs, "long logs," the measure was the number of board feet of lumber the drive represented, and the normal unit was a thousand board feet.

11. He was in a deadwater, where the logs formed an almost solid floor — "a wooden river" — but he fell through a hole between two logs.

12. "And when the jam makes, he's always on deck." That is, he was always on hand when the logs jammed.

13. See above, pp. 14 ff.

14. See below, p. 103.

CHAPTER VI: The Henrys and the Lambs

1. Ola G. Veazie, *Manuscripts of the Federal Writers' Project of the Works Progress Administration for the State of New Hampshire.* Quoted in B. A. Botkin, *A Treasury of New England Folklore* (New York, 1947), p. 576. For convenience, page references are given to Botkin. Veazie gives the name of the recluse in the following anecdote as Pat McGuire.

2. Botkin, p. 579.

3. "One-to-a-thousand tree": A tree that will yield a thousand board feet of lumber. In other words, a big tree. Compare to "Joe Brook," below, p. 174 f., where, if we allow three or four logs to a tree, it would take eight or ten trees to make a thousand.

4. July 20, 1892. Quoted in C. Francis Belcher, "The Logging Railroads of the White Mountains," Part IV, *Appalachia,* XXXIII (June, 1961), 353. This whole article and its continuation, Part V, in the December, 1961, issue (pp. 501-25), are excellent sources of information on the Henrys.

5. For a good description (and twenty samples) of these famous forty-six rules, see ibid., Part V, pp. 514-15.

6. See ibid., Part IV, p. 365: "In the woods they depended on Frenchmen and polyglot imports from Bangor, the wharves of Boston, or the noted second-floor agencies of Scollay Square."

7. Reprinted with the permission of the publisher from *Shantymen and Shantyboys* by William M. Doerflinger. Copyright 1951 by The Macmillan Company, p. 215.

8. Ibid., pp. 215-16.

9. Skid the road: fill in the boggy places by laying down transverse logs.

CHAPTER VII: "Poor and Neglected"

1. Fannie Hardy Eckstorm and Mary Winslow Smyth, *Ministrelsy of Maine* (Boston and New York, 1927), p. 111.

2. *The Maine Woods,* in *The Writings of Henry David Thoreau* (Boston and New York, 1864), III, 91.

3. Eckstorm and Smyth, p. 145.

4. Ibid., p. 140.

5. Ibid., p. 144.

6. Ibid., pp. 140-44.

7. See below, p.132.

8. Horace P. Beck, *The Folklore of Maine* (Philadelphia and New York, 1957), p. 245.

9. *The Northern* was first published in April, 1921, and was discontinued in October, 1928.

10. Eckstorm and Smyth, p. 120.

11. Ibid., p. 119. There is no record of a Tim Carey on the police force at this time. Most of my versions give the name as Tim Leary, and Timothy O'Leary *was* a well-known Bangor policeman of the time.

12. William Main Doerflinger, *Shantymen and Shantyboys,* pp. 218-19.

13. See below, p. 151 f.

14. See, for example, the letter mentioned above, p. 84.

15. See below, p. 172, for essentially the same story told about John Calhoun. For the same story about a Southern folk poet, see Byron Arnold, *Folksongs of Alabama* (University, Ala., 1950), p. 24.

CHAPTER VIII: The Larry Gorman Legend

1. See Mody C. Boatright, *Gib Morgan: Minstrel of the Oil Fields* (Texas Folk-Lore Society, Publication No. XX [Austin, 1945]).

2. See Daniel G. Hoffman, *Paul Bunyan, Last of the Frontier Demigods* Philadelphia, 1952).

3. The Macmillan Co., (New York, 1939), p. 235.

4. Bacil F. Kirtley, "John Ellis — Hunter, Guide, Legend," *Northeast Folklore,* I (spring, 1958), 13.

5. See above, p. 20 ("Here's to you, Mr. Plestid"); p. 37 ("'Tis to the Virgin"); p. 40 ("Oh Lord above"); p. 40 ("A stranger to the pasture came"); p. 56 ("Here's young Hutch"); p. 57 ("Mr. Teazle died of late,"). All except the last of these, and most of the material on the *cante-fable,* was first published in my article, "Larry Gorman and the Cante-Fable," *New England Quarterly,* XXXII (June, 1959), pp. 226-37. See also the *cante-fable* told about Joe Smith below, p. 177.

6. See Herbert Halpert, "The Cante Fable in Decay," *Southern Folklore Quarterly,* V (1941), 194 (a version from Minnesota); B. A. Botkin, *A Treasury of New England Folklore,* p. 185; Newman Ivey White *et al.* (eds.), *The Frank C. Brown Collection of North Carolina Folklore* (Durham, N.C., 1952-60), I, 702; Fannie Hardy Eckstorm, "Local Rimes," *BFSSNE,* No. 3, 1931, p. 19; Kenneth Porter, "Some Examples of 'The Cante-Fable' in Decay,'" *Southern Folklore Quarterly,* XXI (June, 1957), 100-103; Sean O Suilleabhain, *A Handbook of Irish Folklore* (Dublin, 1942), p. 655; *Nebraska Folklore Pamphlets,* No. 26, (February, 1940), p. 9; Stith Thompson, *Motif-Index of Folk Literature,* J1341.12; see also Ernest Warren Baughman, "A Comparative Study of the Folktales of England and North America," (Diss., Indiana University).

7. *The Northern,* April, 1926, p. 5.

8. William Main Doerflinger, *Shantymen and Shantyboys,* p. 254.

9. For an interesting parallel from New York, see Norman Studer, "Yarns of a Catskill Woodsman," *New York Folklore Quarterly,* XI (1955), 188-89. See also George Korson, *Minstrels of the Mine Patch* (Philadelphia, 1938), p. 287. And in James Joyce's *Ulysses,* an almost identical verse appears (New York, 1934), p. 578.

10. Louise Manny, "Larry Gorman," p. 9.

11. Doerflinger, p. 258.

12. Letter to the author, July 15, 1960.

13. See Doerflinger, pp. 160, 351.

14. See above, p. 126.

CHAPTER IX: The Ghost of Larry Gorman

1. *The Northern,* May, 1925, p. 15.

2. See above, p. 103 ff.

3. "The Winter of Seventy-Three" was published under the title of "The Lumberman's Song" in the July, 1923, issue, p. 13.

4. Horace P. Beck, *The Folklore of Maine,* p. 245.

5. Fannie Hardy Eckstorm and Mary Winslow Smyth, *Minstrelsy of Maine,* p. 103.

6. See above, p. 133.

7. Eckstorm and Smyth, p. 106.

8. See my article, "'Ben Deane' and Joe Scott: a Ballad and its Probable Author,'" *JAF,* LXXII (1959), 53-66.

9. See Chapter XI below.

CHAPTER X: "That Sounds Like Gorman"

1. G. Malcom Laws, *British Broadsides,* p. 86.

2. See above, p. 97 f.

3. See above, pp. 103 ff.

4. New York, 1901.

5. See particularly Herbert Halpert, "Vitality of Tradition and Local Songs," *JIFMC*, III (1951), 40; Henri Davenson, *Le Livre des Chansons* (Boudry, Switzerland, 1946), p. 85. There are scattered references to this practice in many of the major American collections.

6. Halpert, "Vitality of Tradition," p. 40.

7. See Phillips Barry, "Notes on the Ways of Folk-Singers with Folk-Tunes," *BFSSNE*, No. 12, 1937, p. 4.

8. *British Broadsides*, p. 51.

9. For further examples, see Manus O'Conor, *Irish Com-all-Ye's* (New York, 1901), especially the following: "The Tipperary Christening," p. 15; "Mc-Fadden's Picnic," p. 39; "Mrs. McLaughlin's Party," p. 61; "The Wedding of Ballyporeen," p. 63.

10. Helen Hartness Flanders and Marguerite Olney, *Ballads Migrant in New England* (New York, 1953), p. 15.

11. The manuscript of this song was given her by Elsie Newton Howe, Newfane, Vermont. The song itself was written by a man named Greenleaf. Margaret MacArthur's singing of the song is delightfully available on her Folkways record, *Folksongs of Vermont* (FH 5314).

12. Carrie B. Grover, *A Heritage of Songs* (privately printed, n.p., n.d.), pp. 165-66.

13. John Holland, Glenwood, N.B., at the Fourth Miramichi Folksong Festival, August, 1961, sang "Champion of Court Hill" to the same tune Mr. Mace used for "Champion of Moose Hill."

14. I have made a rather careful search and have been unable to find a printed source for the poem. A letter from Joan M. Ellis, Assistant Curator of the West Virginia Collection, The Library, West Virginia University, Morgantown, West Virginia, did clear up the following point: "The hero of the Wheeling Fort incident was Samuel McCulloch, and while the event is described in all the history books, there was no verse." There is a marker at the spot where the leap was made. Mr. Mace's recitation is available in the Archives of Folk and Primitive Music (ATL 2145.1).

15. O'Conor, p. 32.

16. For a detailed discussion of the tradition of this much-parodied piece, see D. J. O'Sullivan (ed.), *The Bunting Collection of Irish Folk Music and Songs* (Dublin, 1930—), V, 13-21. The editor makes it clear that the well-known patriotic version is only a late eighteenth century re-working of a much older song and that there are both Gaelic and Anglo-Irish forms extant, some of the Gaelic ones being quite unprintable. The "Ballycohy" slipsheet I quote from above is eleven stanzas long. The italics indicate my corrections in this wretchedly printed sheet. It deals, by the way, with the mass evictions made by a well-known Tipperary landlord.

17. See above, p. 44 ff.

CHAPTER XI: The Satirical Song Tradition

1. *Means of Social Control* (New York and London, 1925), p. 238.

2. "The Origin of a Ballad," *Modern Language Notes*, L (1935), 465-68.

3. "Songs from Pittsburg, New Hampshire," *JAF*, XLVIII (1935), 341-42.

4. See Phillips Barry, *The Maine Woods Songster* (Cambridge, Mass., 1939), pp. 70-71.

5. Colm O Lochlainn, *Irish Street Ballads* (New York, 1960), p. 79. See also pp. 207-9, 124-25. For another Irish example, see "The Battle of Ballycohy," above, p. 165.

6. John Ord, *The Bothy Songs and Ballads* (Paisley, Scotland, 1930), p. 219. For a general description of these songs, see Gavin Greig, *Folk-Songs of the North-East* (Peterhead, Scotland, 1909), No. IV. For further examples, see Ord, pp. 225-26, 229-30, and Greig, Nos. LXXXIX, XCII, CXXXVIII, CXLII, CXLV, CXLVI, CLXXVIII, CLXXIX.

7. John C. Bruce and John Stokoe, *Northumbrian Minstrelsy* (Newcastle-upon-Tyne, 1882), p. 134.

8. Byron Arnold, *Folksongs of Alabama*, pp. 26-27.

9. Newman Ivey White *et al.* (eds.), *The Frank C. Brown Collection of North Carolina Folklore*, II, 645-55.

10. *Minstrels of the Mine Patch* (Philadelphia, 1938), p. 6.

11. *Black Rock* (Baltimore, 1960), p. 349. See also his short biographies of bards and minstrels in *Minstrels of the Mine Patch*, pp. 289-302.

12. Franz Rickaby, *Ballads and Songs of the Shanty-Boy* (Cambridge, Mass., 1926), p. xxxii.

13. *Ibid.*, p. xxv.

14. See E. C. Beck, *Songs of the Michigan Lumberjacks* (Ann Arbor, Mich., 1942), pp. 50, 52, 59, 74, 81, 83, 99, 183, 196; Harold W. Thompson, *Body, Boots, and Britches* (Philadelphia, 1940), p. 267; Helen Hartness Flanders *et al.*, *The New Green Mountain Songster* (New Haven, Conn., 1939), p. 177.

15. See above, pp. 93-95, 151-52.

16. "Canaday I O," *BFSSNE*, No. 6 (1933), 11.

17. For further material on Hanson, see *BFSSNE*, No. 4 (1932), 16, and No. 5 (1933), 15-16.

18. See particularly, pp. 62, 63, 65, 103, 107, 108, 113, 131, 328, 332-39.

19. Helen Creighton, *Songs and Ballads from Nova Scotia* (Toronto and Vancouver, 1933). See particularly pp. 230-34, 268-69, 288-90, 324-25.

20. Elizabeth Bristol Greenleaf and Grace Yarrow Mansfield, *Ballads and Sea Songs from Newfoundland* (Cambridge, Mass., 1933). See particularly pp. 240-43, 272, 303-5, 327-28.

21. See William Main Doerflinger, *Shantymen and Shantyboys*, especially Chapter Nine, pp. 253-69; James R. Wilson, "Ballad Tunes of the Miramichi," (Master's thesis, New York University, 1961). Professor Wilson is collaborating with Dr. Manny on a forthcoming book, *Folksongs of Miramichi*, which will contain over one hundred songs from the region. For material on the Miramichi Folksong Festivals, see *Northeast Folklore*, I (1958), 62-64; *The Atlantic Advocate*, LI (September, 1960), 92-94, and LII (September, 1961), 74-75. See also the record, *Folksongs of the Miramichi* (Folkways, FM 4053), for recordings made at the 1959 Festival.

22. See Manny, "The Ballad of Peter Amberley," p. 73, for a complete version. Doerflinger publishes a fragment of it, p. 266.

23. For two of George Calhoun's songs, see Doerflinger, pp. 220 and 225. Fannie Hardy Eckstorm and Mary Winslow Smyth print two of Munn's pieces, in *Minstrelsy of Maine*, pp. 166-69. For his "The Dungarvon Whooper" and Michael Whelan's song on which it is based, see Wilson, pp. 60-64.

24. As sung for me by J. Victor Norrad, Bloomfield Ridge, N.B., 7/31/61. James Cameron of Bloomfield Ridge also sang me a twelve-stanza version to the same tune, which is so close to the tune for "Morris Ellsworth" (see above, p. 58) that it seems pointless to repeat it here.

25. The mills paid for the logs by how many prospective board feet they contained. The scalers, who measured the cut, in this case said that it would take thirty or thirty-four of his logs to make a thousand board feet, which meant that he got less for his cut than he would have had they scaled the logs at twenty.

26. Sung for me and my son Stephen, 7/25/61, at his home in Glenwood, N.B. For another singing by Wilmot, see ATL 2173.1, as he sang it at the First

Miramichi Folksong Festival, 9/4/58. There are two typed copies of other versions in Louise Manny's files. Wilmot used the same tune for his singing of "The Winter of Seventy-Three."

27. See above, pp. 72-76.
28. Sung for me by Nick Underhill, at his home, Northwest Bridge, N.B., 7/8/61.
29. See Wilson, pp. 25, 74-75.
30. Collected by Louise Manny, for the Beaverbrook Collection. Sung by Jared MacLean. For a complete text, see Wilson, pp. 81-82.
31. Collected by Louise Manny for the Beaverbrook Collection. As sung by Oran Jardine.
32. Sent to Louise Manny by Mrs. Catherine MacDonald of Chatham, N.B.
33. Sung for me and my son Stephen at his home, Eel River Bridge, N.B., 8/14/61.

CHAPTER XII: Conclusion
1. Fannie Hardy Eckstorm and Mary Winslow Smyth, *Minstrelsy of Maine,* p. 113.
2. William Main Doerflinger, *Shantymen and Shantyboys,* p. 215.
3. Halpert, "Vitality of Tradition," p. 39.
4. *The Singing Englishman* (London, n.d.), p. 58.
5. See above, pp. 177-79.
6. Mrs. Kathleen Rowe Justice, in a letter to the author, May, 1959.
7. Eckstorm and Smyth, p. 340.
8. Manny, "Larry Gorman," p. 6.
9. See above, p. 135.
10. Doerflinger, p. 254.

EPILOGUE
1. What follows is based on a story a woman told me while I was up on Prince Edward Island in 1957. No important elements have been changed, but since some of the details are my own additions, I have altered the main character's name.

List of Works Cited

The following abbreviations have been used throughout:

BFSSNE: *Bulletin of the Folk-Song Society of the Northeast.*
JAF: *Journal of American Folklore.*
JIFMC: *Journal of the International Folk Music Council.*

Arnold, Byron. *Folksongs of Alabama.* University, Ala.: University of Alabama Press, 1950.
The Atlantic Advocate, incorporating the *Atlantic Guardian,* Fredericton, N.B.: University Press of New Brunswick, Ltd., 1956——.

Bangor Daily Commercial. Bangor, Me., 1872-1946.
Barry, Phillips. "A Trip to the Grand Banks," *BFSSNE,* No. 4 (1932), 16.
——. "The Schooner Fred Dunbar," *BFSSNE,* No. 5 (1933), 15-16.
——. "Notes on the Ways of Folk-Singers with Folk-Tunes," *BFSSNE,* No. 12 (1937), 2-6.
——. *The Maine Woods Songster.* Cambridge: The Powell Printing Co., 1939.
——, Fannie Hardy Eckstorm, and Mary Winslow Smyth. *British Ballads from Maine.* New Haven, Conn.: Yale University Press, 1929.
Baughman, Ernest Warren. "A Comparative Study of the Folktales of England and North America." Unpublished dissertation, Indiana University. Ann Arbor, Mich.: University Microfilm Service, 1954.
Baxter, James Phinney. *A Memoir of Jacques Cartier.* New York: Dodd Mead & Co., 1906.
Beaverbrook Collection. The Lord Beaverbrook Collection of New Brunswick Folksong is a collection of recordings made by Louise Manny under the sponsorship of Lord Beaverbrook. The original recordings are in Dr. Manny's home in Newcastle, N.B. Copies have been deposited in the Archives of the National Museum of Canada, Ottawa.
Beck, E. C. *Songs of the Michigan Lumberjacks.* Ann Arbor, Mich.: University of Michigan Press, 1942.
Beck, Horace P. *The Folklore of Maine.* Philadelphia and New York: Lippincott, 1957.
Belcher, C. Francis. "The Logging Railroads of the White Mountains," *Appalachia,* XXXIII (June, 1961), 353-74; XXXIII (December, 1961), 501-25.
Belden, Henry Marvin. *Ballads and Songs Collected by the Missouri Folk-Lore Society.* (University of Missouri Studies, XV) Columbia, Mo., 1940.
Boatright, Mody C. *Gib Morgan: Minstrel of the Oil Fields.* (Texas Folklore Society, Publication No. XX) Austin, Tex., 1945.

Botkin, B. A. *A Treasury of New England Folklore*. New York: Crown Publishers, 1947.

Broadwood, Lucy E. *English Traditional Songs and Carols*. London: Boosey and Co., 1908.

Bronson, Bertrand Harris. *The Traditional Tunes of the Child Ballads*. Vol. I. Princeton, N.J.: Princeton University Press, 1959.

Bruce, John Collingwood, and John Stokoe. *Northumbrian Minstrelsy*. Newcastle-upon-Tyne, 1882.

Bulletin of the Folk-Song Society of the Northeast (Cambridge, Mass.), Nos. 1-12, 1930-37.

Bunting Collection. See O'Sullivan, D. J.

Cazden, Norman (ed.). *The Abelard Folk Song Book*. New York: Abelard-Schuman, 1958.

Chickering, Geraldine J. "The Origin of a Ballad," *Modern Language Notes*, L(1935), 465-68.

Colby, George N. *Atlas of Hancock County, Maine*. Ellsworth, Me.: S. F. Colby Co., 1881.

Cooney, Robert. *A Compendious History of the Northern Part of the Province of New Brunswick and the District of Gaspé in Lower Canada*. Chatham, N.B.: D. G. Smith, 1896. (This book was first published in Halifax, N.S. in 1832.)

Creighton, Helen. *Songs and Ballads from Nova Scotia*. Toronto and Vancouver: J. M. Dent, 1933.

Davenson, Henri. *Le Livre des Chansons*. Boudry (Neuchâtel), Switzerland: Editions de la Baconnière, 1946.

Davis, Albert H. *History of Ellsworth, Maine*. Lewiston, Me.: Lewiston *Journal* Printshop, 1927.

Day, Holman. *King Spruce*. New York: Harper and Brothers, 1908.

Defebaugh, James E. *The History of the Lumber Industry in America*. 2 vols. Chicago: The American Lumberman, 1906.

Doerflinger, William Main. *Shantymen and Shantyboys*. New York: The Macmillan Company, 1951.

Doyle, Gerald S. *Old-Time Songs and Poetry from Newfoundland*. 2nd ed.; St. John's, Newfoundland. Privately printed, 1940.

Earle, Emily Mae. *Footprints in New Brunswick*. Perth, N.B.: Privately printed, 1959.

Eckstorm, Fannie Hardy. "Ballads, Texts, and Papers." A collection of manuscript material on deposit at the University of Maine Library, Orono, Me.

———. Chapter on the history of the lumber industry in Maine, in Hatch, Louis C., *Maine: A History*. New York: The American Historical Society, 1919, III, 689-95.

———. "Local Rimes and Quatrains of the Northeast," *BFSSNE*, No. 3 (1931), 17-20.

———. "Canaday I O," *BFSSNE*, No. 6 (1933), 11.

———, and Mary Winslow Smyth. *Minstrelsy of Maine*. Boston and New York: Houghton Mifflin Co., 1927.

Ellis, Preston. *History of the Ellis Family and the Descendants of William Ellis of Bideford, Prince Edward Island*. n.p., 1950.

The Ellsworth American. Ellsworth, Me., 1851——.

Flanders, Helen H. *A Garland of Green Mountain Song*. Northfield, Vt.: Green Mountain Pamphlet No. 1, 1934.

———, Elizabeth F. Ballard, George Brown, and Phillips Barry. *The New Green*

Mountain Songster: Traditional Folk Songs of Vermont. New Haven, Conn.: Yale University Press, 1939.

_____, and Marguerite Olney. *Ballads Migrant in New England.* New York: Henry Holt, 1953.

Ford, Ira W. *Traditional Music of America.* New York: E. P. Dutton, 1940.

Fuson, Henry H. *Ballads of the Kentucky Highlands.* London: The Mitre Press, 1931.

Ganong, W. F. "The Physiographic Characteristics of the Upper Main Southwest Miramichi River," *Bulletin of the Natural History Society of New Brunswick,* No. XXVII, Vol. VI, part II (1909), 85-103.

Gardner, Emelyn Elizabeth, and Geraldine Jencks Chickering. *Ballads and Songs of Southern Michigan.* Ann Arbor, Mich.: University of Michigan Press, 1939.

Gray, Roland Palmer. *Songs and Ballads of the Maine Lumberjacks.* Cambridge, Mass.: Harvard University Press, 1924.

Greenleaf, Elizabeth Bristol, and Grace Yarrow Mansfield. *Ballads and Sea Songs from Newfoundland.* Cambridge, Mass.: Harvard University Press, 1933.

Greig, Gavin. *Folk-Songs of the North-East,* articles contributed to *The Buchan Observer.* 2 series. Peterhead, Scotland: 1909 and 1914.

Grover, Carrie B. *A Heritage of Songs.* Privately printed, n.p., n.d.

The Guardian, Charlottetown, P.E.I., 1891——.

Halpert, Herbert. "The Cante Fable in Decay," *Southern Folklore Quarterly,* V(1941), 191-200.

_____. "Vitality of Tradition and Local Songs." *JIFMC,* III (1951), 35-40.

Hempstead, Alfred G. *The Penobscot Boom and The Development of the West Branch of the Penobscot River for Log Driving.* (University of Maine Studies, No. 18.) Orono, Me.: The University Press, 1931.

Hoffman, Daniel G. *Paul Bunyan, Last of the Frontier Demigods.* Philadelphia: University of Pennsylvania Press for Temple University Publications, 1952.

Illustrated Historical Atlas of the Province of Prince Edward Island. (From surveys made under the direction of C. R. Allen.) n.p.: J. H. Meacham & Co., 1880. (This book is familiarly known as "Meacham's Atlas.")

The Island Argus. Charlottetown, P.E.I., 1869-81.

Ives, Edward D. "'Ben Deane' and Joe Scott: A Ballad and its Probable Author," *JAF,* LXXII (January, 1959), 53-66.

_____. "Larry Gorman and the Cante Fable," *New England Quarterly,* XXXII (June, 1959), 226-37.

_____. "Larry Gorman and 'Old Henry,'" *Northeast Folklore,* II (fall, 1959), 40-45.

_____. "The Life and Work of Larry Gorman: a Preliminary Report," *Western Folklore,* XIX (1960), 17-23.

_____. "Satirical Songs in Maine and the Maritime Provinces of Canada," *JIFMC,* XIV (1962), 65-69.

Journal of American Folklore. (Published for the American Folklore Society.) Philadelphia, 1888——.

Journal of the International Folk Music Council. (Published for the International Folk Music Council.) London, 1949——.

Kaiser, Robert A. "Lumberman's Ballad, 'Shannel's Mill,'" *New York Folklore Quarterly,* XI (1955), 133-35.

Kirtley, Bacil F. "John Ellis — Hunter, Guide, Legend," *Northeast Folklore,* I(Spring, 1958), 13-17.

Korson, George. *Minstrels of the Mine Patch.* Philadelphia: University of Pennsylvania Press, 1938.

_____. *Black Rock.* Baltimore: The Johns Hopkins Press, 1960.

Laws, G. Malcom, Jr. *Native American Balladry.* (The American Folklore Society, Bibliographical and Special Series, Vol. I.) Philadelphia, 1950.

_____. *American Balladry from British Broadsides.* (The American Folklore Society, Bibliographical and Special Series, Vol. VIII.) Philadelphia, 1957.

Linscott, Eloise. *Folk Songs of Old New England.* New York: The Macmillan Co., 1939.

Lloyd, A. L. *The Singing Englishman.* London: Workers Music Association, n.d.

Lumley, Frederick. *Means of Social Control.* New York and London: The Century Company, 1925.

MacKinnon, D. A., and A. B. Warburton. *Past and Present of Prince Edward Island.* Charlottetown, P.E.I., Bowen, n.d.

Manny, Louise. "Larry Gorman — Miramichi Balladist," *The Maritime Advocate and Busy East,* XL, No. 3 (October, 1949), 5-15.

_____. *Ships of Miramichi.* (New Brunswick Museum, Historical Studies, No. 10.) St. John, N.B., 1960.

_____. "The Ballad of Peter Amberley," *The Atlantic Advocate,* LIII (July, 1963), 67-74.

_____, and James R. Wilson. *Folksongs of Miramichi.* Fredericton, N.B., University Press, 1964.

Nebraska Folklore Pamphlets. (Issued irregularly by the Federal Writers' Project in Nebraska.) Lincoln, Neb., 1937-40.

New England Quarterly. (Published by the Colonial Society of Massachusetts and The New England Quarterly.) Brunswick, Me., 1928——.

New York Folklore Quarterly. (Published for the New York Folklore Society.) Cooperstown, N.Y., 1944——.

Northeast Folklore. (Published by the Northeast Folklore Society.) Orono, Me., 1958——.

The Northern. (Company paper for the Great Northern Paper Co.) Augusta, Me., Vols. I-VIII(April, 1921-October, 1928).

O'Conor, Manus. *Irish Com-all-Ye's.* New York: L. Lipkind, 1901.

O Lochlainn, Colm. *Irish Street Ballads.* 2nd ed.; New York: The Citadel Press, 1960.

Ord, John. *The Bothy Songs and Ballads.* Paisley, Scotland: Alex. Gardner, 1930.

O Suilleabhain, Sean. *A Handbook of Irish Folklore.* Dublin, 1942.

O'Sullivan, D. J. (ed.). *The Bunting Collection of Irish Folk Music and Songs,* Dublin, *Journal of the Irish Folk Song Society,* 1930——.

Pike, Robert E. "Songs from Pittsburg, New Hampshire," *JAF,* XLVIII (1935), 337-51.

Porter, Kenneth. "Some Examples of 'The *Cante Fable* in Decay,'" *Southern Folklore Quarterly,* XXI (June, 1957), 100-103.

Randolph, Vance. *Ozark Folksongs.* 4 vols. Columbia, Mo.: State Historical Society of Missouri, 1946-50.

Rickaby, Franz. *Ballads and Songs of the Shanty-Boy.* Cambridge, Mass.: Harvard University Press, 1926.

Sandburg, Carl. *The American Songbag*. New York: Harcourt Brace, 1927.

Sharp, Cecil J. *English Folk-Songs from the Southern Appalachians*, ed. Maud Karpeles. 2 vols. London: Oxford University Press, 1932.

Silsby, Herbert T., II. *A History of Aurora, Maine*. Ellsworth, Me.: The Hancock County Publishers, 1958.

Southern Folklore Quarterly. (Published quarterly by the University of Florida in cooperation with the South Atlantic Modern Language Association.) Gainesville, Fla., 1937——.

Spaeth, Sigmund. *Weep Some More, My Lady*. New York: Doubleday Page, 1927.

Springer, John S. *Forest Life and Forest Trees*. New York: Harper and Brothers. 1851.

Stokoe, John. *Songs and Ballads of Northern England*. Newcastle-on-Tyne: Walter Scott, Ltd., n.d.

Studer, Norman. "Yarns of a Catskill Woodsman," *New York Folklore Quarterly*, XI (1955), 188-89.

Thompson, Harold W. *Body, Boots, and Britches*. Philadelphia: Lippincott, 1940.

Thompson, Stith. *Motif-Index of Folk Literature*. 6 vols. Bloomington, Ind.: Indiana University Press, 1955-58.

Thoreau, Henry David. *The Maine Woods*, in *The Writings of Henry David Thoreau*. Vol. III, Boston and New York: Houghton Mifflin Co., 1864.

Wasson, Samuel. *A Survey of Hancock County, Maine*. Augusta, Me.: Sprague, Owen, and Nash, 1878.

Western Folklore. (Published for the California Folklore Society.) Berkeley, Calif., 1942——.

White, Newman Ivey *et al.* (eds.). *The Frank C. Brown Collection of North Carolina Folklore*. 7 vols. Durham, N.C.: Duke University Press, 1952-60.

Wilgus, D. K. *Anglo-American Folksong Scholarship Since 1898*. New Brunswick, N.J.: Rutgers University Press, 1959.

Wilson, James Reginald. "Ballad Tunes of the Miramichi." Unpublished Master's thesis, New York University, 1961.

Wood, Richard G. *A History of Lumbering in Maine, 1820-1861*. (University of Maine Studies, No. 33.) Orono, Me.: The University Press, 1935.

Index

[(I) following the name of an individual means "informant."]

Adams, Clarence (I), 111, 112, 113, 122, 128, 189, 194, 199, 201, 202
Aitken, Traven, 59
Allaby, J. Spurgeon (I), 4, 30, 194, 197
Allen, W. N. "Billy" (folk poet), 170
Anderson, John, 129
Archer, Freeman (folk poet), 93-95, 170, 186
Archer, Harold N. (I), 94, 100, 192, 194, 199, 201
Avery, Del, 85, 100, 192
Ayer, Frederick W., 111, 130

Bangor, Me.: described, 110-11, 118-19; mentioned, 80, 81, 151, 185
"Bangor Fire, The," 158
"Banks of the Gaspereaux, The," 81
"Banks of the Little Eau Pleine, The," 170
Barry, George (I), 200, 203
"Battle of Ballycohy, The," 165
"Bathurst Murder, The," 4
"Bay du Vin Farmer, The": text, 177-79, 182
Beaverbrook Collection, 62, 64, 194, 196, 200, 202
Beck, Horace P., 122, 151
Beggar's Opera, The, 163
Bell, William (I), 3, 49, 113, 127, 128, 129-30, 133, 136-37, 189, 190, 191, 193, 194, 197, 198, 199
"Ben Deane," 153
Black, Col. John, 79
"Black-Eyed Susan," 2
"boom" (term defined), 53
Braley, Ephraim (folk poet), 170-71
Brewer, Col. Jonathan, 111

Brewer, Me.: described, 110-11. *See also* Gorman, Lawrence
"Bright Eyed Etta Lee," 168
Brown, Israel, 72-76, 78, 175, 176, 192
Brown, James (I), 193
Brown, Leon (I), 81, 198
Buchanan, Donald, 17
Bunyan, Paul, 138

Calhoun, George (folk poet), 172, 183
Calhoun, John (folk poet), 61, 158, 168, 171-72, 183, 186, 187
Calhoun, Sandy (I), 200
"Canada-I-O," 170, 181
Cannon, Susan (I), 192, 196, 204
cante-fable: special type defined, 143; about Joe Smith, 177. *See also* Gorman, Lawrence
Carr, Arthur (I), 186, 198
Carson, Leroy P. (I), 200
Carter, Mrs. Louisa (I), 190
Cartier, Jacques, 8
"Champion of Court Hill, The," 163
"Charming Laura Brown", 175-76 (text)
Chickering, Geraldine J., 168
"Clerks of Parch's Cove, The," 169
Cooney, Robert, 51, 52-53
Coughlan, Thomas W. (I), 64, 196
Coughlin, Mrs. John (I), 189, 190, 194, 195, 199, 202
Crawford, Hugh U., 4, 192
Creegan, Walter M. (I), 150
Creighton, Dr. Helen, 49, 122, 128, 193, 194, 199
Crosby, Fanny, 37

219

Crossman, Alexander (I), 190, 201
Curtis, Silas (I), 57, 75, 182, 198, 204
Cushman, James, 3, 81, 85
Cushman, Ralph (I), 3, 80, 81, 82, 83, 93, 142, 191, 192

Dalton, Arthur (I), 3, 29, 113, 123, 125, 158-59, 184, 190, 191, 195, 199, 200, 203, 204
Davidson, William, 52
Davy Crockett (folk hero), 142
Day, Holman F. (author of *King Spruce*), 2, 3, 139-42, 147, 158, 185
Dempsey, Jack, 152
DeRusha, George, 127
Doerflinger, William M. (author *Shantymen and Shantyboys*), 2, 13, 61, 68, 106, 123, 144, 146, 171, 181, 186, 190, 194, 195, 199, 200, 201, 202, 203, 204
Donahue, Ann. *See* Gorman, Ann
Donovan, Dan (folk poet), 93, 103
Doucette, Earle (I), 112, 194
Doucette, Edmund (I), 6, 13, 42, 123-25, 191, 194, 196, 200
Doyle, Mrs. Harold (I), 44, 192, 200
Doyle, Larry (folk poet), 49, 171
Doyle, Thomas (I), 203
"Drive Dull Care Away," 5
"Drive on Cooper Brook, The," 150-51
"Dungarvon Whooper, The," 172, 211 (n. 23)
Duplessis, George (I), 177-79, 180, 182
Dyment, David (I), 5-6, 16-17, 25, 134-35, 185, 193, 202

Eastern Manufacturing Corp., 3, 111-34 *passim*
Eckstorm, Fannie Hardy: folklorist, 171; author *Minstrelsy of Maine* (with Mary W. Smyth), 2, 110, 118, 119-21, 122, 123, 150, 152, 171, 181, 183, 185, 193, 195, 202
Ellis, Mrs. Ernest (I), 12, 190
Ellis, John (folk hero), 142
Ellis, William ("Grandfather" Ellis), 8-9
Ellsworth, Me.: description and history, 80-81, 108, 122, 123. *See also* Gorman, Lawrence
Estey, Mose (folk poet), 90, 95, 170

Flanders, Helen Hartness, 162-63, 191
Foley, John (I), 16
folk poet: definition, 2; status, 183.

See also individual folk poets by name
Friend, John J. (folk poet), 158
Frost, Irving G. (I), 3, 61, 87-89, 198, 199, 201

Gay, John, 2, 163
Gaynor, Mary (I), 82
Gib Morgan (folk hero), 138, 142
Gillies, J. A. (I), 46, 49, 199
Gillis, Ellsworth (I), 191, 195, 199
"God bless the sheep meat that we eat," 144
Goldsmith, Oliver, 2
Gorman, Ann (*née* Donahue; mother of L.G.), 9-10, 13, 16, 161, 185
Gorman, Bridget (sister of L.G.), 26
Gorman, Charles (brother of L.G.), 11
Gorman, Charles (I) (nephew of L.G.), 5, 26, 27, 29, 84, 161, 190, 192, 194, 196, 199, 204
Gorman, Ellen (sister of L.G.), 84, 136
Gorman, James (older brother of L.G.), 10-11, 24, 29, 50, 161
Gorman, John (brother of L.G.), 11
Gorman, Julia (sister of L.G.), 26
Gorman, Julia (*née* Lynch; L.G.'s second wife), 100, 109, 110, 112, 121, 126, 134, 137
Gorman, Lawrence: physical description, 12, 82, 112, 136; Trout River (P.E.I.), 12-28; Lot Seven (P.E.I.), 25, 26-28, 29-50, 56, 71, 143, 144, 146, 185, 186, 187; Miramichi, 13, 30, 50, 54-78, 122, 123, 145, 186, 187; Ellsworth (Me.), 81-100, 109-10, 181-82, 184, 185, 186; Brewer (Me.), 5, 25, 49, 61, 110-36, 147, 182, 185, 186; St. Croix (Me.) valley, 106-08; Maine (gen.), 13, 29, 50, 68-69, 78; New Hampshire, 101-06, 182, 187; first marriage (to Mary Mahoney), 84, 185; second marriage (to Julia Lynch), 109; death and funeral, 136; grave described, 137; as a character in *King Spruce,* 139-142; letter by, 132; song-making described, 42, 112-13, 129, 166; selling printed copies of his poems, 112-13, 122, 135; telling *cante-fables* about himself, 147; as writer of protest songs, 181-82; his unpopularity, 82, 184-85; his fame analyzed, 185-87. *See also* Gorman, Lawrence (songs and poems)

Gorman, Lawrence (songs and poems): prosody and diction discussed, 154-59; tunes discussed, 157, 159-60; analysis of subjects, 49, 160-61; models, 161; use of parody, 160, 163-66; individual songs by title:

"Ace Williams' Foolish Girl," 93, 189

"A.P.A., The," 189

"Arlington Maid, The," 22-24 (text), 157, 189

"Away to the States to Get Rich," 131-32 (text), 189

"Bachelor's Hall," 20-22 (text), 42, 155, 162, 185, 190

"Baptists, The," 37, 38-39 (text), 160, 163, 190

"Barren Town," 68-69, 69-71 (text), 156, 160, 161, 190

"Beaver Jack," 129-30 (text), 190

"Bill Watts," 91-92 (text), 161, 190-91

"Boys of the Island," 122-23, 123-25 (text), 151, 161, 181, 191

"Bully of Lot Eleven, The," 18 (text), 191

"Carrying Coal in a Basket," 114, 191

"Champion of Moose Hill, The," 95, 96-97 (text), 160, 163, 191, 196, 202

"Cruel Submarine, The," 136, 192

"Dame Bruin," 44-45 (text), 157, 162, 165, 184, 189, 192

"Del Avery," 100, 192

"Devil's Back, The," 57, 192

"Doctor O'Connell," 100, 192

"Donahue's Spree," 71-72, 72-74 (text), 78, 157, 192, 199

"Dyment's Auction," 16-17 (text), 193

"Ellsworth News of the Day," 99, 193

"Fight at Hall's Mill, The," 99-100 (text), 193

"Freeman Archer," 95 (text), 193

"Gaynor's Trained Pig," 127, 193

"Good Old State of Maine, The," 4, 103-105 (text), 136, 139, 151, 157, 181, 193

"Great John Mac and His Polack Brigade, The," 128, 194

"Great Pond Tramp, The," 93, 184, 194

"Gull Decoy, The," 30-34 (texts), 35, 49, 78, 112, 148, 155, 160, 177, 182, 183, 194

"Hail Fishermen Assemble," 40 (text), 160, 194

"Happytown Wedding, The," 194

"Head of Grand River, The," 28 (text), 194

"Hoboes of Maine, The," 108, 118-19, 119-21 (text), 121-22, 157, 160, 161, 181, 195

"Horse's Confession, The," 25-26 (text), 112, 135, 157, 189, 192, 195

"I'm a Poor and Blighted Old Maiden," 42 (text), 195

"I'm Poor Old Fan," 184, 195

"In Eighteen Hundred and Seventy-Nine," 76-77 (text), 78, 195

"It's a Wonder," 130-31 (text), 195

"Luke and His Rambles," 27 (text), 155, 195-96

"McElroy," 41, 196

"Man Who Wheels the Ashes, The," 127, 136, 196

"Mary Mahoney," 64, 65-66 (text), 161, 162, 191, 196, 202

"Michael McElroy," 41 (text), 156-57, 167, 181, 196

"Michael O'Brien," 42-44 (text), 185, 196

"Michael Riley," 35-36 (text), 196-97

"Mick Riley," 36-37 (text), 197

"Monaghan," 197

"Monaghan's Raffle," 197

"Morris Ellsworth," 57-60 (text), 155, 197

"Myles Everett More," 97-99 (text), 156, 157, 184, 197

"Nero and the Great John Mac," 128, 162, 197

"Newcombe's Goose," 127, 198

"Now I Lay Me," 198

"Old Barlow Was Blind," 99 (text), 198

"Old Mike Abrams' Five Saw Dam," 100, 198

"Old Pod Auger Days, The," 116-18 (text), 160, 161, 198

"Old Prowler, The," 74-76 (text), 198

"O'Leary Road, The," 198

"On Lead Mountain's Lofty Brow," 100, 199

"Pack of Hounds, The," 27-28 (text), 199

"Prince Edward Isle, Adieu," 46-49 (text), 181, 199

"Prize Was Not So Very Great, The," 113 (text), 199

"Roderick McDonald," 87-89 (text), 163-64, 170, 181, 199

"Sanitary Jane," 129, 199

"Scow on Cowden Shore, The," 61-64 (text), 78, 89, 156, 161, 186, 200

"Shan Van Vogh, The," 13-16 (text), 93, 162, 164-65, 185, 194, 200

"Song of All Songs, The," 135-36 (text), 196, 200

"Spree at Summer Hill, The," 19-20 (text), 200

"Steelshank," 200

"That Reptile McElroy," 40 (text), 201

"There's That Whistling Cody," 201

"Tomah Stream," 106 (text), 108, 161, 201

"Union River Drivers, The," 89-91 (text), 93, 95, 155, 161, 201

"Unfortunate Cook, The," 201

"Winter of Nineteen Five, The," 113 (text), 201

"Winter of Seventy-Three, The," 4, 54-56 (text), 64, 151, 156, 161, 162, 191, 196, 202

"Workman, The," 114-15 (text), 155, 160, 161, 185, 202

"Yeo's Party," 18-19 (text), 162, 202

"Yeo's Shipyard," 17, 161, 202

"You Can't Leave the Yard 'Til the Whistle Blows," 127, 202

"Young Billy Crane," 66-68 (text), 136, 161, 162, 202, 207 (n. 19)

Cante-fables: "Going Down to Mrs. Yeo's," 147, 203; "Davis' Camp," 203; "Eyes Stick Out Like Prongs," 145, 185, 192, 203; "Fish and Potatoes," 144, 203; "Here's To You, Mr. Plestid," 20, 203; "Here's Young Hutch," 56-57, 203; "How Sentners Got Their Riches," 146, 203; "Lord Be Praised," 139, 143, 203; "MacMillan's Wether," 144, 204; "Mr. Teazle Died of Late," 57, 204; "Oh Herring," 146, 204; "Robert Bell," 145, 204; "She Told Me That Her Bread Was Fine," 146, 204; "A Stranger Came," 40, 204; "This is Rotten," 40, 144, 204; "'Tis to the Virgin," 37, 204

Gorman, Mary (Mahoney; L.G.'s first wife), 82, 84

Gorman, Mike (folk poet), 143, 150-51, 153

Gorman, Thomas (father of L.G.), 9-10, 13

Gorman, Thomas (brother of L.G.), 11

Gorman, Thomas (I) (nephew of L.G.; son of James G.), 195

Gorman, Bishop Thomas K. (I) (nephew of L.G.), 11, 134, 136, 142, 191, 200

"Grace before meat," humorous, 143-45

Grant, Lorey "Pompey," (I), 191

Great Northern Paper Co., 122, 150, 151

Griffin, William (I), 4

Gross, "Uncle Bill," (folk poet), 169

Guthrie, Woody, 180

"Guy Reed," 153

"Hackler from Grouse Hall, The," 169

Halpert, Herbert, 159, 181

Hanson, Amos (folk poet), 171

Harris, Mrs. George (I), 194, 195, 202

Henry, J. E., 4, 101-06, 152, 181

"Here's To This Old Hat," 93

Hinchey, Herbert (I), 66, 194, 202

Hodgkins, E. N. (I), 81

Holland, John (I), 190

Holmes, Hazen (I), 132

Houghton, Lloyd (I), 150

"Howard Carey," 153

Howell, Rednap (folk poet), 170

Hughes, Luke (folk poet), 26-28, 171, 196, 199

Hunter, Davey (folk poet), 172-73, 183, 197

Huntington, E. G., 165

Hutchison, Richard, 56-57

"I'm Captain Jinks, a Man of Fame," 93

"Jack Haggerty," 168

Jackson, "Aunt Molly," 180

James, Prof. Thelma, 181

Jamieson, John A. (I), 4, 102, 103-05, 181, 193, 202, 206 (n. 11)

Jamieson, Peter (I), 102, 103, 105, 181, 202

"Jeremiah of Bartibogue," 177

"Joe Brook," 173-75 (text), 202

Jordan, Anton (I), 190, 191, 201

Keating, Al (I), 177

"kennebecker": defined, 206 (n. 5)

Kenniston, Harold (I), 201
Kingston, Paul (I), 190
Kirtley, Bacil F., 142
Korson, George, 170, 191

Lamb, H. E. (I), 108
Lamb, Natty, 106-08
"Larry Magee's Wedding," 162
Laws, G. Malcom, 161
Lecky, Kenneth (I), 189
Leeman, James (I), 149
Linscott, Eloise H., 142
"Little Barber, The," 152
"Little Bird of Little Wit," 177
"Little Brown Bulls, The," 183
"Lizzie's Canoe," 177
Lloyd, A. L., 181
Lumley, Frederick, 167
Lynch, Clarence (I), 192
Lynch, James (I), 61, 133, 151
Lynch, Jeremiah, 109, 137
Lynch, Julia. See Gorman, Julia
Lynch, Mrs. Sidonia, 192

MacArthur, Margaret, 163, 210 (n. 11)
MacArthur, Robert (I), 106-08
"McCauley's Leap," 164, 210 (n. 14)
McClellan, Mrs. Cyrene (I), 20-22, 190, 195, 203
McClellan, W. B. (I), 196, 201
McCulloch, Samuel, 164, 210 (n. 14)
MacDonald, Mrs. Alan (I), 74, 198-99
MacDonald, Edward (I), 192
MacDonald, Peter (I), 126, 143, 147, 152, 184, 196, 198, 203, 204
McDonald, Roderick, 3, 85-89, 101, 181-82, 184, 207 (n. 5)
MacDonald, Wilmot (I), 173-75, 202
MacDougall, Joseph (I), 49, 122, 128, 194, 199
Mace, A. Russel (I), 131, 193, 195, 199, 200
Mace, Alden F. (I), 3, 87, 91, 96-99, 164, 190, 191, 197, 199
Mace, Emery "Muck," 95-97, 163
Mace, Frank, 87, 184
McElroy, Michael, 39-42, 101
McGuiness, Jack, 152
MacInnis, "Beaver Jack" (folk poet), 123, 151-52, 153, 170
McInnis, George L. (I), 16
McIntosh, George, 207 (n. 5)
McIntosh, Joseph (I), 3, 82, 83, 84, 89, 99, 102, 184, 185, 194, 195, 198, 199, 207 (n. 5)

McKay, Howard (I), 192
McKay, William "Barlow Bill" (folk poet), 177
McKenzie, Colin, 83-84, 110
McLaughlin, Patrick, 56, 64, 78
MacLean, Jared (folk poet), 4, 69, 177, 190, 191
MacLeod, George (I), 127, 133-34, 198, 199
MacLeod, Thomas (I), 206 (n. 9)
McMahon, Fred (I), 62, 200
McNally, Lawrence (I), 25
McNally, Dr. William P., 109, 136
McNamara, John, 127-28, 184
"Making My Will," 163
Manny, Dr. Louise, 2, 4, 53, 56, 57, 59, 62, 64, 68, 123, 132, 144, 171, 184, 185, 190, 192, 196, 197, 200, 201, 202, 203, 204
"Marlboro Medley, The," 163
Marston, Mrs. Annie, 171
Mary Clare, Sister (I), 127, 134, 196
"Messenger Horse, The," 172
"Michael Dignam's Spree," 177
Mills, Alan, 27
Minstrelsy of Maine. See Eckstorm, Fannie Hardy
"Miramichi Fire, The," 53
Miramichi Folksong Festival, 171, 190, 193, 196, 202, 211 (n. 21), 212 (n. 26)
Miramichi River: description, 51-52; history, 52-54; the Great Fire, 9-10, 52-53. See also Gorman, Lawrence; satirical songs
Monaghan, Michael, 26, 44, 45, 197
Moore, William (I), 200
Morgan, Gilbert (folk hero), 138, 142
Mullin, E. A. (I), 197
Munn, Abraham (folk poet), 172, 183
Murphy, Mrs. John (I), 203
Murphy, Mrs. Lawrence (I), 13, 190, 196, 200
Murphy, Steve (I), 33, 194
"My Boy is of a Tedious Length," 94
"My Name's Billy Oakes," 171

"Napoleon Bonaparte," 4
"Near The Cross," 37
Northern, The, 150, 151, 208 (n. 9)
"Norway Bum, The," 153

O'Brien, Harry (I), 42, 196
O'Brien, James "Big Jim," 42, 184
O'Brien, Michael, 42, 184

O'Connor, John (I), 3, 11, 12, 61, 83, 114, 125-26, 198, 200, 202
O'Hara, Frank (folk poet), 173-75, 183
O'Holleran, Frank (I), 34, 190, 192, 194, 196, 197, 200, 204
"Old Bob Christie He Died Late," 206 (n. 9)
Olney, Marguerite, 162-63
"One Morning of Late," 170
"One Night Sad and Languid," 165-66
oral tradition, 168-69
Oregon Smith (folk hero), 142

Paul Bunyan (folk hero), 138
"Peelhead," 177
Pendergast, James (I), 5, 22, 25, 32, 190, 194, 195, 196, 201
Penobscot River (Me.), 102, 103, 110, 150, 153. *See also* Bangor; Brewer
"Peter Emberly," xi, 51-52, 59, 60, 61, 171, 197. *See also* Calhoun, John
Pike, Robert, 168
"Plain Golden Band, The," 4, 153
"portage team," defined, 206 (n. 6)
Price, Billy (I), 200
Price, Everett (I), 69, 76, 77, 78, 190, 195, 198, 200
Prince Edward Island: description, 4-5; history, 8-9, 46; mentioned, 111, 114, 122-23, 126, 136, 143-44, 171. *See also* Gorman, Lawrence

Richardson, Merle (I), 94-95, 193, 199, 201
Rice, Herbert (I), 142, 144, 146, 151, 181, 203, 204
Rickaby, Franz, 170, 191
Riley, Dan (folk poet), 171
river-driving, described, 53
"Robin Spraggon's Auld Grey Mare," 169
"Rocky Brook" ("Samuel Allen"), 168, 171
"Rose Ann Song, The," 172-73 (text), 182, 197
Ross, Mrs. Nina G., 6, 205 (n. 3)
Rowe, G. R. (I), 27, 198, 199
Rowe, Henry L., 84, 87, 88, 92

"Sailor's Grace, The," 146
"Samuel Allen" ("Rocky Brook"), 168, 171
satirical song: definition, 167-68; a traditional practice, 169, 180; function of, 180-83; in the British Isles, 169; in the South, 169-70; among coal miners, 170, 180; in the lumbercamps, 170, 180; in the Maritimes, 171; in the Miramichi valley, 171-179
Scott, Joseph W. (folk poet), 152-53, 158
Shantymen and Shantyboys. See Doerflinger, William M.
"Shan Van Vogh, The," 13-16, 164-65, 210 (n. 16)
"She Took the Kettles and the Pots," 94
Silsby, Herbert T. II, 79, 207 (n. 1)
Silsby, William (I), 193
Smith, Joe (folk poet), 74, 175-77, 182, 183, 186, 187
Smith, Seba, 2
Smyth, Mary Winslow. *See* Eckstorm, Fannie Hardy
Spurling, Andrew ("The General"), 81
Stevens, James, 138
Stuart, Donald (I), 198
Stymiest, John B. (I), 194
Sugden, Ernest (I), 171
Sullivan, Martin (folk poet), 177
"Swaggers," 169
Sweet, Frank (I), 17, 100
Sweet, Mrs. Frank (I), 19-20, 46, 199, 200

Thackeray, W. M., 2
"There's a Man Called Bob Mulligan," 181
Thompson, Harry (I), 11, 26, 190, 192, 194, 195, 196, 197, 203, 204
Thoreau, Henry David, 110
Tosh, Joe. *See* McIntosh, Joseph
Tradition. *See* oral tradition
Tremblay, Edward (I), 146, 204
Tremblay, Gerald (I), 146, 203
"two sled": defined, 53-54

Underhill, Nicholas (I), 54, 62, 172, 196, 202
Underwood, Hugh, 64, 78
Union River (Me.): description, 79; history, 79; lumbering and river-driving on, 80, 102, 103; mentioned, 3, 6, 186. *See also* Gorman, Lawrence

van Horne, Irvine (I), 72-74, 192
Vose, Thomas W., 120, 121

Waldron, William (I), 6, 83, 189
Wasson, Samuel, 81
Whelan, Thomas (I), 192
Wilbur, Mrs. Jasper (I), 193
Wilgus, D. K., xi, 206 (n. 3)
Wilson, James R., 71, 171, 191, 192, 194, 196, 202
woods poet: definition, 2. *See also* folk poet

Woodworth, Archie, 56, 64

Yeo, James Sr., 17
Yeo, James Jr. ("Little Jimmy"), 17-19, 101
Young, Mrs. Herbert (I), 193, 195
"Young Charlotte," 2
"Young Jimmy Folger," 4